Pat Schroeder:
A Woman of the House

WOMEN'S
BIOGRAPHY *series*

SERIES EDITOR
Kristie Miller

Pat Schroeder:
A Woman of the House

JOAN A. LOWY

University of New Mexico Press ▪ Albuquerque

Library of Congress Cataloging-In-Publication Data

Lowy, Joan, 1956–
    Pat Schroeder : A Woman of the House / Joan Lowy.— 1st ed.
      p. cm.— (Volume 1 of the women's biography series)
Includes bibliographical references and index.
    ISBN 0-8263-3098-3 (alk. paper)
  1. Schroeder, Pat.   2. Women legislators—United States—Biography.
3. Legislators—United States—Biography.   4. United States. Congress. House—
Biography.   5. United States—Politics and government—1945–1989.   6. United
States— Politics and government—1989–   I. Title.   II. Women's biography series ; v. 1.
    E840.8.S36 Z76 2003
    328.73′092—dc21

                        2003006262

Design: Melissa Tandysh

To my husband, Michael,

whose encouragement and countless hours of child care

made this project possible.

Contents

1

Pioneer Pat

Pat Schroeder had been a member of Congress for less than a year when she committed an unthinkable act for a freshman: she deliberately and publicly humiliated her committee chairman. Given the seemingly unassailable power chairmen wielded at the time, it would have been an audacious act for any lawmaker, but it was an especially breathtaking move for a relatively young woman new to the legislative arena and struggling to find her niche.

Ultimately, the episode set the tone for a remarkable twenty-four-year congressional career that would make Schroeder one of the best-known women in American politics, a hero to legions of liberals who admired her uncompromising championship of underdog causes and delighted in her ability to deflate conservative opponents with her stinging wit.

A thirty-two-year-old Harvard-trained lawyer and mother of two young children, Schroeder was a political neophyte when she was elected to the House from Colorado in 1972 in her first bid for public office. She was outspoken in her opposition to the Vietnam War and during her campaign had warmly embraced virtually every left-of-center social cause of the day, from the plight of migrant workers to school busing for desegregation to women's rights. All of which, plus the fact that she was a woman, made her an unlikely candidate for a seat on the House Armed Services Committee, which was controlled by defense hawks from both parties. It was no accident that the committee had never had a woman member.

But Schroeder successfully lobbied House leaders to get on the committee. At that time, the Armed Services Committee controlled more than a third of federal discretionary spending. Schroeder reasoned that if she wanted to redirect defense dollars to the social welfare programs that were her priorities, then she would be better off working from the inside. She was also anxious to expose Pentagon waste and what she saw as the folly of many defense policies.

There were also parochial reasons why a seat on Armed Services would be desirable to Schroeder. The economic importance to Denver of defense spending was modest compared with the districts represented by many of the other members of the committee, but it was not insignificant. Lowry Air Force Base in Denver was an important local employer. Fitzsimons Army Medical Center was just across the city's eastern boundary and many of the hospital's workers lived in Denver. The army's Rocky Mountain Arsenal, which had manufactured and stored chemical weapons, and the Rocky Flats nuclear weapons plant, which manufactured plutonium triggers for missile warheads, were also close by, presenting serious safety and environmental problems. Denver's suburbs were home to several large defense contractors, while the North American Aerospace Defense Command and the U.S. Air Force Academy in Colorado Springs, an hour's drive south of Denver, created a strong air force presence in the state.

Committee assignments are far more important in the House than in the Senate. They can make or break a lawmaker's career. With 435 members vying to place their imprint on legislation, lawmakers tend to specialize in issues that fall under the purview of their assigned committees. That is where they have their greatest chance for influence. There are opportunities to amend bills when they reach the House floor, but those opportunities are fewer and more circumscribed than in committee.

A House member's committee assignment often determines which political action committees will contribute most generously to his or her campaign. A member of the Armed Services Committee can reasonably expect a high volume of contributions from the defense industry. Members of the Interior committee (since renamed the Natural Resources Committee) are courted by the mining, timber, oil, and gas industries. House members generally tried to avoid committees that did not attract the attention of many well-heeled industries, such as International Relations or the former Post Office and Civil Service Committee. The panels with the broadest reach—Ways and Means, which sets tax policy; Appropriations, which allocates money for all federal agencies and programs; and Commerce, which handles more bills than any other committee—generate the most contributions.

Thus, trying to secure a seat on one of the House's more powerful and important committees is usually the first task of any freshman. The jockeying often begins on fund-raising trips to Washington before the candidates are even elected.

When Schroeder was sworn into office in January 1973, it was the Democrats—the majority party in the House for most of the past fifty years—who determined how many seats were available on each committee and how they were apportioned between the parties. The top Democratic and Republican leaders would then divvy up their respective seats among their party members. Most of the time, party leaders made an effort to give new lawmakers seats on committees that dealt with issues relevant to their districts. Thus, lawmakers from western states with vast public lands had a major presence on the Interior Committee. Seats on the now defunct Merchant Marine and Fisheries Committee went mostly to lawmakers from coastal states with shipping and fishing industries. Armed Services has always been made up largely of lawmakers with large military bases or defense industries in their districts.

As the Ninety-third Congress convened, reform was in the air. Democratic leaders were under increasing pressure to give female and African American lawmakers seats on the House's more powerful committees from which they had traditionally been shut out. Only four years earlier, Democratic leaders had drawn criticism for putting Rep. Shirley Chisholm, the first black woman elected to Congress, on the Agriculture Committee even though her congressional district in Brooklyn didn't contain a single farmer. Only after Chisholm protested publicly was the former teacher appointed to the Education and Labor Committee. In 1971, Democratic leaders had turned down feisty Rep. Bella Abzug of New York when she sought, for many of the same reasons as Schroeder, a seat on Armed Services.

It was in that context that House Speaker Carl Albert, an Oklahoma Democrat, granted Schroeder's request for a seat on Armed Services. Schroeder said she discovered years later that she had had an anonymous ally in Rep. Wilbur Mills of Arkansas, who was often called "the second most powerful man in Washington" because of his chairmanship of the tax-writing Ways and Means Committee. In those days, the Ways and Means chairmanship also entitled Mills to the chairmanship of the Democratic Committee on Committees, which assigned lawmakers to committees. It seems Mills's wife, Clarine, had read about Schroeder's unexpected election victory and had taken an interest in her career. Clarine Mills persuaded her husband to help Schroeder.

Republican leaders made a similar decision that year, awarding one of the GOP's slots on the committee to freshman Marjorie Seward Holt of Maryland. Twenty years Schroeder's senior, Holt was a lawyer and a native of Birmingham, Alabama, who sported a lacquered beehive hairdo, kept a low profile, and zealously supported increased defense spending.

What tilted the decision in Schroeder's favor—her own vigorous lobbying, Mills's assistance, or political pressure on House leaders to appoint a woman—is unclear. Nevertheless, Albert decided to appoint Schroeder to Armed Services over the vehement objections of the committee's septuagenarian chairman, F. Edward Hebert of Louisiana. Overriding Hebert's veto of Schroeder was a dramatic break with tradition and a clear insult to the chairman.

Hebert (pronounced "a-bear") had risen to chairman in 1970 after thirty years on the committee. A tough-talking former newspaper city editor from New Orleans who entered Congress the year Pearl Harbor was attacked, Hebert had a broad, blunt face, receding gray hair, and black-rimmed glasses. He ruled the Armed Services Committee like a feudal lord, enthroned on a dais in the committee's hearing room, military flags draped on either side of him, a carpet of stars spread out at his feet. He had no patience with the new breed of reform-minded House members. He would later address a roomful of freshmen House members as "boys and girls." And he did not mind being called a "male chauvinist," making no effort to disguise the fact that he did not want women on his committee, especially an unrepentant liberal like Schroeder. "I hope that you aren't going to be a skinny Bella Abzug," he told her in one of their first meetings.

Hebert didn't want an African American any more than he wanted a woman. Rep. Ron Dellums of California, then in his second term, was a self-described "commie pinko Afro-topped bell-bottomed dude from Berkeley." Dellums was also a psychiatric social worker, an ex-marine, and an antiwar activist who had been arrested.

Dellums would have preferred to be on a committee that dealt with social programs, but the Congressional Black Caucus wanted to gain entry to the white male bastion of the Armed Services Committee. They tapped Dellums for the job partly because he had military experience.

As he had with Schroeder, Hebert opposed giving Dellums a seat on the committee. He called every Democrat on the Committee on Committees trying to prevent the appointment of "the black male bomb-thrower from Berkeley" and "the white woman bomb-thrower from Denver," as he referred to them.

Dellums decided to take his case to Albert and Majority Leader Tip O'Neill. For support, he brought with him two other members of the black caucus, the fiery Bill Clay of Missouri and the lawyerly Carl Stokes of Ohio. "The idea was to have Stokes make the case, and Bill to sit there and look mean," Dellums told the *Washington Post*'s Megan Rosenfeld.

At first, Albert and O'Neill resisted Dellums' plea to override the chairman. They told him that Hebert thought Dellums would be a security risk. Stokes tried to softly press Dellums' case, while Clay denounced Hebert. Finally, Clay threatened to have the black caucus call a news conference and denounce the Congress as racist if Dellums weren't put on the committee. "The blood drained from Albert's face," Dellums recalled. "They said, 'Let us go back and reconsider.' Forty minutes later I got the call: 'You've been appointed.'"

Incensed that he had been saddled with Schroeder and Dellums, Hebert decided that if he couldn't control who the leadership put on his committee, he could at least control the number of chairs in the committee's hearing room. When Dellums and Schroeder arrived for their first committee meeting, they found only one chair for the two of them at their adjoining places on the dais, which were marked with nameplates. Hebert "said that women and blacks were worth only half of one 'regular' member, so he added only one seat to the committee and made Ron and me share it," Schroeder would later write. Rather than admit defeat and leave, the two lawmakers sat cheek to cheek as they dueled with the chairman.

"Everything in me wanted to rage against this indignity," Dellums told Rosenfeld. "But I thought, let's not give these folks the luxury of seeing that."

Three decades later it is hard to imagine such blatant sexism and racism's not provoking a national outcry. But, according to Schroeder, none of her colleagues on the committee who witnessed the pair's humiliation was willing to take a public stand on their behalf. "Nobody else objected, and nobody offered to scrounge up another chair," Schroeder wrote. "Armed Services was the most powerful committee in Congress during the Vietnam War. . . . Many of the 42 committee members had military bases in their districts and had a vested interest in pleasing the chairman, no matter how outrageous he was. They felt their political careers depended upon their being able to go home and tell their constituents, 'Look how much money I got for you this year for our base.'"

Holt, on the other hand, encountered far less hostility, partly because she was ideologically in tune with Hebert and the majority of committee members and partly because she was a Republican. If Hebert, a Democrat, had abused Holt, Republicans might have felt called upon to defend her, creating partisan strife within the committee. Holt was also by nature less inclined to make waves than Schroeder or Dellums.

"It was interesting to be a woman in that world," Holt told the *Baltimore Sun* in 1992, recalling her early days in Congress. "As long as you were quiet and moving slowly, nobody got upset. But as soon as you became pushy or strident, the men realized that you were threatening them. So you had to move carefully."

Not long after joining the committee, Schroeder sought a private meeting with Hebert to try to smooth things over. They met in Hebert's office, a seven-room suite with a patio—palatial by congressional standards. In his office, Hebert had one room which he called the "adult room," where he met with official guests, and another room, which he called the "adultery room," equipped with a bar, a couch, and nude paintings on the walls. He met with other guests there. And he boasted of all this to the idealistic young congresswoman.

"The Lord giveth and the Lord taketh away, and here I am the Lord. You'll do just fine on this committee if you remember that," Hebert advised her. Hebert also told Schroeder that if she used her female body parts—he reportedly used another word—more and her mouth less, she would go further on the committee.

Schroeder didn't heed his advice, but she remembered his words. Hebert had told her that women weren't fit to serve on the Armed Services Committee because they knew nothing of combat. Schroeder decided to check into the military histories of her male colleagues on the committee, discovering that many of them had no combat experience either. And she wasted no time in publicly pointing this fact out, both in committee hearings and elsewhere.

Embarrassing one's colleagues is not the way to win friends on a committee, and Schroeder made none with her remarks. But then most of her colleagues on the all-male committee weren't predisposed to welcome her anyway. And they learned quickly that she didn't play by the traditional go along–get along rules. When mistreated, she bit back.

Schroeder further inflamed the chairman and threatened the long-standing cordial relationship between the Pentagon and the committee when she insisted on filing a minority report to the military procurement budget authorization bill. Any committee member who disagrees with a bill can file a minority report that is published at the end of the committee majority's explanation of the bill and printed in the *Congressional Record*. In her seven-page report, Schroeder condemned the committee as "the Pentagon's lobby on the Hill" and ridiculed it for trying to stifle debate and dissension, for holding hearings that were closed to the press and the public, and for calling only witnesses who agreed with the Pentagon's proposals.

Filing minority reports that are at odds with the views of the chairman of the committee is not uncommon today, but it was less common in 1973. Schroeder was not the only member of the committee to file dissenting views, but her language was far more blunt and she was far more sweeping in her criticism. "Some members," she wrote, "gave the impression that doing the hard and tedious work of analysis and criticism of our complicated military program is somehow unseemly, unmilitary—indeed, unpatriotic." Her tone was a rare enough breech of decorum that it must have felt like a sharp poke in the eye to autocratic Hebert. Even Schroeder admits that she knew beforehand that the report would inflame the Louisiana lawmaker.

"Of course, I recognize her expertise after she has been here for six months," Hebert sarcastically told the *Denver Post.* He added angrily: "I was in the House of Representatives before she was born!"

Hebert retaliated by refusing to approve the payment of any expenses associated with Schroeder's appointment by Albert to the U.S. delegation to a Strategic Arms Limitation Talks (SALT II) conference in Geneva, Switzerland, that summer. The disarmament conference was one of a series of discussions between U.S. and Soviet officials aimed at placing caps on the number of nuclear missiles and bombers each side could have. "I wouldn't send you to represent this committee at a dogfight," Hebert told her bitterly.

Under House rules, Schroeder could not fly with the rest of the U.S. delegation aboard a military jet to Geneva without Hebert's approval. She was still able to participate in the conference thanks to intervention by the State Department, but she had to pay for a ticket on a commercial airline out of her own pocket.

It was shortly afterward that Schroeder committed her unthinkable act—she went public. In magazine and newspaper interviews, Schroeder laid out all of Hebert's boorish and insulting acts. She described being forced to share a single chair with Dellums. She described Hebert's attempt to prevent her from participating in the disarmament conference. And she described her meeting in Hebert's office, leaving nothing out—not his sexist views, not his self-aggrandizement, not even his "adultery room."

"He doesn't believe that anyone with a uterus can make a decision on military affairs," Schroeder told writer Judith Viorst for a cover story in the November 1973 issue of *Redbook* magazine.

"If you lived long enough to be chairman, wow, that was like being a demigod," Schroeder recalled. "They were the two-ton gorillas in the place and you didn't do anything to upset your chairman because you would pay so heavily. That was considered really quite obstreperous of me to do that. You were not to take on your chairman. You were to become a player. And if you wanted to look like a player as a freshman, that meant you courted them and you did whatever they asked you to do."

Shortly after going public, Schroeder joined an Armed Services delegation on a trip to the Middle East. As soon as she boarded the air force jet, Schroeder saw her face staring back at her everywhere she looked. Someone either with the air force or the committee had placed copies of *Redbook* with her picture on the cover in every seat. If the other committee members had somehow missed the full flavor of her rebellion before, there was no chance that they would remain ignorant now. Schroeder recalled the trip as long and lonely. None of her colleagues wanted to be associated with the woman who was foolish enough to feud openly with the chairman.

In the end, Schroeder won her point. In 1975, with the help of the reform-minded Watergate class of Democratic freshmen, Hebert and two other crusty Southern chairmen were toppled from their thrones by a vote of the Democratic caucus. It was a dramatic rebuke by his political peers. Hebert continued to serve as a member of the committee for another two years before retiring from the House, but his power base was gone.

The decision by Democrats to depose Hebert and the other two chairmen was a significant moment in the history of the House, marking the beginning of a new era in which chairmen were no longer nearly omnipotent in their spheres of legislative concern. From then on, in both their legislative agendas and their conduct, chairmen would have to pay greater heed to the desires of their fellow party members.

For Schroeder, the battle with Hebert was more than a brief, colorful episode in her life. By choosing to battle Hebert in such a fashion, Schroeder forever cast herself in the role of the outsider, the maverick. Whether she was right or wrong made no difference. Here, clearly, in the eyes of her congressional colleagues and the Washington political establishment, was an independent operator who could not be counted on to play according to the usual rules.

The traditional route to power, influence, and success on Capitol Hill has been for junior lawmakers to pay their dues by carrying water for their party leaders and chairmen while working their way up the seniority ladder and looking for acceptable opportunities to press their agenda.

The conventional political wisdom on outsiders who challenge the status quo, like Schroeder, is that if they are clever, they can gain a platform for their views, but at a price. They sacrifice much of their ability to directly affect legislation because they are not on the inside where the decisions are made and are not trusted by those who do make the decisions.

There is a long line of congressional mavericks whose histories both confirm and disprove conventional wisdom. In Schroeder's case, conventional wisdom was only partly true. Despite a career that outlasted those of most of her male colleagues, Schroeder never became a political insider. She never attained the chairmanship of a full committee or a post of power within her party. Democratic leaders, generally speaking, did not fully trust her. With Schroeder, they were never sure when she would turn her guns away from the opposition and toward them. While she was as partisan as the next House member—and more partisan than many—she was also quick to criticize members of her own party when they failed to live up to her expectations or compromised their ideals.

On the other hand, Schroeder's decision to play the maverick, to challenge the status quo—which she continued to do throughout her career—was empowering and, in some ways, made her more effective than she might have been had she followed a more traditional route. The members of Congress who are the most effective are not always the legislative virtuosos or the power brokers who cut deals behind closed doors. Occasionally they are the opinion makers, the ones who understand how to shape public sentiment in support of their cause. Once the public reaches a consensus, political action is often not far behind. Schroeder was at her best when she was communicating with the public, skewering her ideological foes and invigorating her supporters.

The hallmark of Schroeder's career was her championship of women's rights and concerns in the broadest sense, from funding breast cancer research to protecting abortion rights to more fully integrating women into the military. That championship helped bring Schroeder a national following and made her a political celebrity. There were other female lawmakers who could argue that they were equally as dedicated to the cause of women's rights—and maybe even more skillful at furthering that cause—but most remained relatively anonymous outside of their districts.

Partly that anonymity was because other women in Congress usually tried to win acceptance and power by playing by established rules, rules written and enforced by men, rules that paid homage to the status quo, rules that Schroeder felt free to disregard whenever they interfered with her agenda. And partly it was because few of her female colleagues articulated the feminist cause with Schroeder's clarity and wit. Her personality was a natural fit with the national media, and the media made her a star.

When a male House colleague asked, shortly after her arrival, how she could be both the mother of two young children and a member of Congress at the same time, Schroeder coolly replied: "I have a brain and a uterus, and I use them both." The press and the public ate it up.

It was Schroeder who, in 1983, came up with an analogy for President Reagan's political invulnerability to the scandals that had rocked his administration, a phrase that would be forever linked with his name. "Mr. Speaker, after carefully watching Ronald Reagan, I can see he's attempting a great breakthrough in political technology. He has been perfecting the Teflon-coated presidency. He sees to it that nothing sticks to him. He is responsible for nothing—civil rights, Central America, the Middle East, the economy, the environment. He is just the master of ceremonies at someone else's dinner," Schroeder said in a speech on the House floor on August 2, 1983.

Instantly, Reagan's critics had a two-word image, the "Teflon president," for their frustration that the president's popularity remained undimmed even while so many of his top appointees had been forced to quit or had been dismissed under fire. The phrase became so widely used that DuPont went to the extent of buying advertising to remind everyone that "Teflon" was a trademark not to be bandied about lightly. The company even had its lawyers send letters to newspaper and magazine editors.

That same year, reflecting her outrage at escalating Pentagon arms spending, Schroeder commented both to her hawkish colleagues on the Armed Services Committee and to a panel of military brass at a hearing on the Reagan defense budget: "If you guys were women, you'd all be pregnant. You just can't say no."

Of the Bush-Quayle ticket in 1992, Schroeder opined, "They have no qualifications except that they came from the lucky sperm club. They don't even know what a bar code is in a supermarket."

Schroeder's glibness struck some people as irreverent and shallow. It was the one thing about her that annoyed her critics more than anything else, particularly those on the political right. She was an itch they couldn't scratch, and she delighted in their discomfort, seeing it as a confirmation of her success.

Schroeder has said she was disappointed not to have been included in Nixon's infamous "White House enemies list" during Watergate, although she was probably too new to the Washington political scene at the time to have expected it. But she would boast two decades later of being chosen one of the "twenty-five most dangerous politicians in America" by Iran-Contra figure Oliver North.

"My theory has always been . . . that you don't have very long to get to people. You've got to break through the clutter and noise with something that tries to paint a word picture of what you think is going on," Schroeder told the National Press Club. "I wish we all had more time to sit around and read 'The Federalist Papers' and great documents and debate, but people are just too busy. So the quips were always to try and get to your heart."

It can be argued that because she was a woman, Schroeder never had a realistic chance of gaining power through the traditional route anyway. Women were not part of the congressional power structure in 1972. They generally did not chair committees. They did not hold important party leadership posts. When legislative deals were cut, both Democratic and Republican women usually were left out. Three decades later, less has changed than has remained the same.

"I think women still should never kid themselves that they're going to come here and be part of the team," Schroeder told Melissa Healy of the *Los Angeles Times* as she prepared to retire from office in 1996. "And you ought to come here with a very clear definition of what it is you want to do, and that you will not be deterred. There's a whole group of little harpies out there every day trying to talk you out of it. They really don't want you pushing the envelope because then it becomes choose-up-sides time for everybody."

When Schroeder entered Congress, there were no women senators and only 14 women, including herself, among the 435 members of the House. She would later laughingly tell how Carl Albert had thought it was her husband, Jim—who was standing next to her when they were introduced to the House leader—who had come to be sworn in on that first day of her congressional career. "It's her, it's her!" Jim Schroeder hissed repeatedly to Albert, discreetly jabbing his thumb sideways at his wife several times before the senior congressman caught on.

Ten years after the publication of Betty Friedan's *The Feminine Mystique* had helped to launch the feminist movement, Congress was still a tradition-bound professional men's club in 1973. Although the House had had seventy female members since feminist pioneer Jeannette Rankin's election in 1916, nearly half of the women had initially been appointed or elected to fill a vacancy created by the death or otherwise unavailability of their husbands. One early congresswoman served two terms in the House to preserve the seat her husband lost while serving a term in a federal penitentiary for bootlegging. With relatively few exceptions, the women who proceeded Schroeder in the House had served on the periphery of power, not at its center. They were tolerated, not consulted, by their male colleagues, and most served but a few terms and moved on.

Still, 1973 was a heady and exciting time for feminists such as Schroeder. The same month she was sworn in, the U.S. Supreme Court came down with its decision in *Roe v. Wade* legalizing abortion. The drive to ratify the Equal Rights Amendment (ERA) was still fresh and full of hope. Four months into her first year in Congress, Schroeder brought her two-year-old daughter, Jamie, with her to the House floor, joining thousands of other women around the country who brought their children to work that day to protest a lack of decent, affordable child care and Nixon's proposal to cut $1 billion from social services programs.

"Women were coming together in an explosive movement to challenge sexual discrimination in the schools, the workplace and at home," Schroeder recalled in her book *Champion of the Great American Family.*

Feminism came naturally to Schroeder. Born in Portland, Oregon, she had been raised to prize the independence and self-reliance so admired by Westerners. Her parents were prairie populists, the children of farm families who had settled Nebraska's plains. They encouraged Pat and her brother to emulate the can-do spirit of their pioneer forebears.

All her life, Schroeder had stretched the limits of what was acceptable or even permitted for a woman, most of it with her parents' encouragement. Her mother, a public school teacher, went back to work after Pat and her brother entered school. Her father, an aviation insurance adjuster, encouraged Pat's interest in flying. She became a pilot at sixteen, certainly not a pastime encouraged for most teenage girls in the 1950s. At the University of Minnesota, she disdained the sorority-girl party life and the "husband hunt," hitting the books and racking up a brilliant academic record. She won admission to Harvard Law School at a time when female students were still a tiny minority largely shunned by their male classmates and law professors.

After all, the Harvard men were quick to point out, it was quite selfish for women to take up slots that could go to men when the women were going to get married, have babies, and not put their law degrees to any good use.

Indeed, Schroeder lived the feminist revolution of the 1960s and 1970s. The concerns of the feminist leaders of her youth and early professional career were not abstractions, but real problems she had experienced first-hand. She was frustrated, as a newly married law student in 1962, when she had to leave the state of Massachusetts in order to fill a prescription for birth control pills. Upon graduation from law school in 1964, she watched as prestigious law firms courted her husband, whom she had met at Harvard, but not her. The firms that granted her interviews wanted to know if she also could type. She resented being forced to give up her job as a government labor relations lawyer when she gave birth to her first child because there was no maternity leave for working women. She struggled with the child care dilemma when she returned to work. And she knew that her experiences were not unusual. Only her determination to bring about change set her apart.

The women Schroeder joined in the House were divided on the feminist movement, both in style and in substance. On one end of the spectrum there was Bella Abzug, confrontational and uncompromising in her demands for change. Elected in 1970, Abzug was the first woman since Rankin to run for Congress on a women's rights platform.

On the other end was Leonor Sullivan, a conservative Democrat from Missouri who had won election in 1952 to her late husband's seat and had worked her way up the seniority ladder to chair the Merchant Marine and Fisheries Committee, considered a "B" committee by House standards, but nonetheless a seat of power in its own sphere. Sullivan, the only woman in Congress to vote against the Equal Rights Amendment in 1970, believed women gained respect and advanced their careers by minimizing gender differences, not by drawing attention to them. She saw her role as carrying on her husband's agenda and liked to be called "Mrs. John."

Sullivan was not alone. Having won political office, some of Schroeder's female colleagues felt they should play the game the same way as the men. They wanted their share of power, to exercise influence on the glamour issues of the day. They wanted a slice of the appropriations pie, the money for projects and programs at home that help get you reelected. And they were willing to follow the rules, to work their way up the seniority ladder, to carry water for the leadership, and to make friends, not waves. Within that philosophy, there was less room for a women's rights agenda.

In between the Abzugs and the Sullivans fell congresswomen such as Corinne "Lindy" Boggs, D-La., who joined the House a few months after Schroeder, filling the seat of her husband, Majority Leader Hale Boggs, who had been killed in a plane crash. Boggs was from a different generation that believed women accomplished more when they were pleasing than when they were confrontational.

Into that mix came Schroeder, breezy and irreverent at times, sharply opinionated and self-righteous at others. The substance of Schroeder's politics was really no different from Abzug's, but the young congresswoman often softened her rhetoric with humor and charm. Schroeder was also different from her female predecessors in that she was at the forefront of a new generation of women politicians in the 1970s who had professional careers and who would win office on the basis of their own credentials, not as substitutes for their husbands.

And, she was one of the first women elected to Congress who was the mother of young children. When she stepped into the magnificent federal-style House chamber to be sworn into office in 1973, she had a two-year-old by one hand, a six-year-old by the other, and a handbag stuffed with diapers slung over one shoulder. Her coat had apple juice dribbles on the shoulder. Slim and pretty with her long dark hair swept back into a loose ponytail, she looked, in the words of one of her colleagues, like "a mommy on her way to the PTA."

Today, when better than 70 percent of mothers of young children work, it doesn't seem like such a radical notion that Schroeder could believe that she could be both a good mother and a good member of Congress. Back then, however, even feminists such as Abzug had their doubts. She called Schroeder after her upset victory in 1972 to congratulate her, and then told her that it wasn't possible for her to be both a good mother and a good House member.

But Schroeder did do the job and raise her children. Along the way, she also shaped the issues of her day in important ways. She helped found the Congressional Women's Caucus in 1976 and struggled to wrest the "family values" label from the religious right in the 1980s and '90s. She led the effort for family and medical leave for working parents years before the issue became politically popular. For divorced wives of diplomatic and military personnel, she secured rights to a portion of their husbands' pensions. She led the effort for a moratorium on nuclear weapons testing and helped formulate a comprehensive alternative defense budget, suggesting the surplus money might be better spent on social welfare programs.

Schroeder was an early advocate of legislation aimed at tracking down deadbeat dads. She fought for federally subsidized day care for working mothers. And she helped shift the historic focus of federal health research away from largely male ailments and worked to place into law requirements that research include female as well as male test subjects. Ironically, some of the family issues championed by Schroeder in the 1980s, such as adoption reform and ending the so-called marriage penalty in the tax code, were later embraced by Republicans, who gave them their own spin. To these social conservatives, Schroeder was an anathema, the embodiment of the feminist movement and all they disliked and feared about it.

Schroeder also had her setbacks. She broke new ground for women with her exploratory campaign for the 1988 Democratic presidential nomination, but then saw whatever gains she had made dissolve with the tears she shed when she announced that she was giving up her quest for the nomination. Critics accused her of undermining the chances of electing a woman president by feeding fears that women are emotionally unsuited to the demands of high office.

After President Clinton took office 1993, Schroeder was one of the more insistent voices in Congress for doing away with the Defense Department's ban on gays and lesbians serving in the military services. Clinton's support for ending the ban turned out to be one of the most significant political defeats of his first term, undermining his clout on Capitol Hill just as his presidency was getting off the ground.

The 1992 election was "The Year of the Woman" in politics. Law professor Anita Hill's allegations in testimony before the Senate Judiciary Committee that U.S. Supreme Court nominee Clarence Thomas had sexually harassed her drew national attention not only to the issue of sexual harassment, but to the dearth of women in Congress. In the wake of the Thomas-Hill hearings, which changed the course of gender politics, fifty-five women were swept into Congress. The years 1993 and 1994 saw the passage of sixty-six bills benefiting women and families, compared to about ten bills of special interest to women in all of the 1960s. The One Hundred Third Congress was a significant moment for women in American political history, and Schroeder, as cochair of the Caucus on Women's Issues and the senior woman in Congress, was a key leader.

But then came Newt Gingrich's Republican revolution, reversing in a short time many of the measures Schroeder and other congresswomen had struggled so long to pass. Most Democrats were thoroughly demoralized by the GOP takeover of the House for the first time in forty years. But some Democrats were better able to adapt than others, and Schroeder was one of them. She quickly went on the offensive, relentlessly challenging Gingrich and his "Contract with America." She joined in filing ethics charges that led to Gingrich's becoming the first Speaker to be formally reprimanded by a vote of the House in the two-hundred-year history of the institution.

Most members of Congress arrive in Washington determined to make a difference. More than many of them, Pat Schroeder actually did. And all the while, Schroeder kept in mind the advice her father had given her as child whenever the going got rough: Just keep smiling at the enemy, it drives them crazy.

2

Forging a Feminist

Patricia Nell Scott was born in Portland, Oregon, on July 30, 1940, the first child of Lee Combs Scott and Bernice Lemoin Scott. Lee was a pilot who managed a small airport in Portland. Bernice was a first-grade teacher. The hospital bill for their daughter's delivery came to $53.35, and the Scotts paid it in two installments.

Lee and Bernice had grown up on farms in Nebraska during the Great Depression and were married in 1936 when economic times were still bleak. They were Democrats rooted in the independent populism of the Western prairies. Lee's family had immigrated to Nebraska from Ireland in the 1860s to take advantage of the Homestead Act, which granted 160 acres of public land to anyone who filed for it and was willing to live there. His grandfather had served in the Nebraska state legislature, where he sat at a desk next to three-time Democratic presidential candidate and populist William Jennings Bryan. Lee's mother had come west in a covered wagon after her father left the whaling industry in Nantucket. Bernice was born in Gibbon, Nebraska, and earned a degree from Kearney State Teacher's College. She was a doer, not a complainer. "There are people who wring their hands and people who roll up their sleeves," she used to tell Pat—it was always Pat, never Patricia—and her younger brother, Michael.

"My grandparents came from Ireland. The focus was go forward, get involved. I was unduly shaped by that," Pat told Marian Christy of the *Boston Globe.* "I get up every day and see things as a clean slate, as opportunity. I don't see each day as a continuation of yesterday's oppression. Who knows what's going to happen each day? If you see something, pounce on it. To the pouncer goes the mouse."

Bernice stayed home while her children were young, but she returned to teaching after Pat and Michael, who was three years younger, started school. Pat's early years were not always easy. She had crossed eyes, which required her to wear glasses from the age of eighteen months and an eye patch during her early school years. Her mother worked with her daily on eye exercises. She outgrew it, but her memories of that painful period are vivid. "I couldn't understand why kids were reacting to me as if I were some kind of freak," Pat wrote in her memoirs. "Fighting their attitude toward me became just as much a challenge as strengthening my eyes. I was unprepared for all the barbs, and they were keenly felt, but I compensated for them by concentrating more on my schoolwork and by developing a sense of humor. Whenever I was teased, I always smiled and dished it back with humor."

Harder still, the family moved often: Dallas, Texas; Sioux City, Iowa; North Platte, Nebraska; Hamilton, Ohio; Kansas City, Missouri; and Des Moines, Iowa. By the age of three, Pat figured out her own way to make friends. She would line up her toys in the driveway or sidewalk in front of her house to tempt other children into coming over to play with her. "This ought to get 'em," she would tell her mother.

"I was always the one that was trying to get in," Pat said. "But in a way, it's one of the things people struggle with all their lives—to define themselves. If you move a lot, then you define yourself."

Most of the moves occurred during World War II, when Pat was still young. Her father, an army air corps reservist, had been called up to teach flying at army air fields. They were living in Dallas when the war ended, and Lee went into the aviation insurance business. As better jobs came along, they moved to Hamilton, where Pat went to junior high, and then to Des Moines, where she graduated from Roosevelt High School in 1958.

The Scotts were known for taking their children everywhere, even places that today would not be termed "kid-friendly," and for instilling in them an adult sense of assuredness that people remembered.

"Anyplace my husband and I went in those years, we never saw a child. The children were sent off someplace," Bernice Scott told author Lauren Cowen. "I said, 'I'll never do that!'"

From the start, Pat was a gifted student. "I was always kind of bored because it (schoolwork) came easy," Schroeder said in an interview. "I was always the one who got in trouble because I had it done in thirty minutes and it was supposed to take an hour, and now what do we do, you know?"

The family owned a small plane in which they flew to Florida, Alaska, California, the East, the South, all over. Vacations were a time to see the world, to be on the go. Both children became licensed pilots, Pat by the age of sixteen.

"Des Moines in the fifties looked like a scene from *American Graffiti* or

Bye-Bye Birdie," Pat recalled. "Teenage girls wore poodle skirts and ate at drive-in restaurants with waiters roller-skating out to the cars, and the most exciting thing to hit town was Elvis Presley."

The Scotts lived in a turn-of-the-century brick house with a big front porch that Lee spent hours and hours renovating. The house, which was only two blocks from the high school, became a hangout for Pat and her friends. When she was old enough to drive, Pat had a battered 1948 Studebaker that she would tool around town in with classmates.

Lee and Bernice taught their children to be independent and responsible and to manage their allowance for clothes and trinkets. "Dad was a resourceful man who valued time so much that he would mow the grass in his suit because he didn't want to waste time changing clothes," Pat wrote in her memoirs. "He hated to see his children idle and encouraged us to take up various projects. I learned to fly and Mike rebuilt cars. When we had a spare moment we were expected to help Dad with his projects—rebuilding an airplane or remodeling a house. He even suggested to boys I was dating in high school that they come over and work on the house instead of going out to the movies with me."

Unlike many other young women who came of age in the 1950s, Pat was not raised with a vision of her role in life as limited primarily that of helpmate and mother. Her own mother worked, and neither of her parents ever suggested she shouldn't do something simply because she was a girl and not a boy. Her father's sister, Myrna Gainsforth—a renown tomboy in her youth who could outshoot and outhunt her brother's friends—was also a strong influence. Myrna was a member of the national board of the Girl Scouts of America when Pat was growing up, and her niece became extensively involved in scouting. There were trips to scouting camps, including a camp in the Black Hills of South Dakota. She became a "mariner scout" and sailed on a square-rigger out of Mystic, Connecticut.

"I guess I didn't have that much to rebel against because the women in my family were really quite active," Schroeder said.

She had a Wonder Woman watch that she cherished and saved well into adulthood. Her role models were Amelia Earhart, Eleanor Roosevelt, and Margaret Sanger. They were doers, women who broke new ground and challenged the status quo. "These were just amazing women that totally broke out of the grain," Pat told writer Lesley Gold in 1998. "Eleanor Roosevelt was one of the wealthiest women in America and yet she was out picketing with the maids and she never got into this beauty thing. . . . I do not think of women as geisha girls."

It was not until she was an adult that Pat would look back and question the sexism of the times in which she grew up. "My generation was constantly told, 'Women are not team players' . . . We could be divas, but not trusted team members," Pat recalled in an article she wrote for the *Baltimore Sun.* "When I was young, basketball rules for girls let us dribble only twice, and we couldn't cross the center line. I guess we were considered too frail and fragile to play by boys' rules."

The Scotts attended Congregational churches. "We're kind of generic Protestants, I guess," Pat told a religious broadcaster. "But having come out of the Congregational tradition where the congregants rule, I think learning all of that as a young child in Sunday school, that gave me a lot of feeling about how representative democracy was supposed to work." The Scotts were also die-hard Democrats, and there were frequently animated political discussions around the dinner table. Lee Scott sometimes lent his private plane to Democratic candidates for governor and other statewide offices so they could fly around Iowa to campaign.

After high school, Pat went on to the University of Minnesota. To help pay her way through college, she was able through her father's connections to get a job flying to air crash sites and assessing losses. The university owned a fleet of small planes it used for the ROTC program. Pat was allowed to rent planes for ten dollars an hour. The work paid so well that at the end of her first year she had enough money left over to buy a long, splashy, aqua-colored Lincoln that reminded her of "an Easter egg on wheels."

The University of Minnesota had nearly as many female as male students and was considered progressive for its day. But it was in college that Schroeder began to feel the sting of blatant sexism. Most of the women students planned to go into teaching, nursing, library science, or other fields traditionally open to women. When Schroeder broached the idea of studying aerodynamics she was told by her faculty advisers that it would be a waste of her parents' money to have that degree "hanging over the changing table."

That may sound extreme today, but it was not an unusual attitude for the time. One of Schroeder's best friends in college was Betty Endicott. They were roommates at the Chi Omega sorority house. Like Schroeder, Endicott had been raised to believe she could do or be anything she wanted, and she wanted a career. The two young women faced the same quandary: they weren't interested in traditional women's careers or homemaking, but they weren't sure what professions were open to them.

"I think the reason we bonded then," Pat told the *Washington Post* in 1987, "was that we joined this sorority where we really didn't fit: beautiful girls, blond hair, pageboys, blue eyes, doting daddies. And here were Betty and I: We held the grades up."

As a high school junior in St. Paul, Minnesota, Endicott had taken a journalism class and was chosen to co-edit the student newspaper. After much soul-searching in college, she finally decided to major in journalism. "My adviser was screaming at me to declare a major and I didn't know what I wanted to do. I knew that I didn't want to be a teacher because that wasn't me. And I couldn't stand the sight of blood so I couldn't be a nurse. And what else was there for a girl in 1959?" Endicott told the *Washington Post*. "When I declared the major, a journalism professor said to me that I was wasting my time . . . because women don't make it in the news business, and that all we came to college for was to get our MRS. He really just blasted me. There was one other girl in the entire J-school, and she was on an advertising track. One other came in while I was there."

Endicott proved her professor wrong. She did make it in the news business. At a 1980 champagne toast honoring her as the first woman news director for a television station in Washington, Endicott recalled her college years with Pat: "We never did follow the rules, and everybody had written us off for ruined. We weren't studying to be nurses or teachers and they were never sure we would use our ability to make a living. But look at us now."

Pat gravitated toward liberal political activism during her college years. Sen. Hubert Humphrey came to the campus to speak about civil rights, drawing large crowds. "He fired our imaginations with talk of racial and economic justice," she recalled.

While Pat's idealism and liberalism were reinforced during her college years, the forces that drew her to political activism and forged her feisty nature had influenced life from the beginning. "I was born and raised in the West," Pat told Marian Christy. "I have an independent streak. I'm not a go-along, get-along type. I'm a fighter. Maybe that's part of the West, too. People in the West still think change is possible. They still believe government can be ethical and pure."

While serving as a member of the student senate, she got to know and came to deeply admire civil rights activist Allard Lowenstein, who was passionate about ending colonialism in Africa. He drew her into the antiapartheid movement in the days before Nelson Mandela was jailed. "He had a knack for focusing in on issues that no one else was paying attention to and getting people to understand that these were vital struggles," Pat said.

(In 1968, Lowenstein was deeply involved in the antiwar movement and became famous for leading the "dump Johnson" campaign, which drew

Sen. Eugene McCarthy of Wisconsin into the Democratic presidential primaries against President Lyndon Johnson, who was ultimately forced out of the race. But with the assassination of Robert F. Kennedy and other setbacks for Democrats that year, it was Republican Richard Nixon who claimed the White House on election day. Later, after serving one term in the House, Lowenstein was killed in his New York office by a gunman in 1980.)

In 1961, Pat graduated magna cum laude and Phi Beta Kappa with a major in history and minors in philosophy and political science. She earned her degree in only three years instead of the usual four. She didn't bother to attend her commencement, paying an undergraduate thirty-five dollars to go through the line and pick up her diploma for her. "I was in a hurry to begin life with a capital 'L,'" she wrote.

The question was, now what? Neither Pat nor the other young women in her sorority had given much thought to how they would manage after graduation. They presumed they would work, get married, and keep working until their first child was born. Pat didn't have a burning desire to be a lawyer, but she had long wanted to go to law school. "I saw it as a way of going up against the status quo," she recalled. But some of the attraction that law school held may have been a daughter's desire to win her father's approval. As a young man, Lee Scott had planned to go to law school and had even set his sights on the most prestigious law school in the country, Harvard, before the Depression ended that dream. Now his daughter had applied to Harvard and had been accepted.

Harvard Law School in 1961 was a tough place for women. When Pat entered, she was one of nineteen women in a class of 554. There were fifteen women in her graduating class three years later. It is a given that the school is so selective that all of the students, male or female, must have been among the brightest and the most competitive the nation had to offer or they would not have made the cut. This degree of excellence was especially true of the women, who were deliberately discouraged from applying in the first place.

One of the women in the law class one year ahead of Pat was Janet Reno, the daughter of two newspaper reporters from Miami, Florida, who would go on to become the first woman U.S. attorney general. Among those admitted with Schroeder in 1961 was Elizabeth Dole of Salisbury, North Carolina, who would hold two Cabinet posts in successive Republican administrations, win election to the U.S. Senate, and become the only other woman in the past twenty years besides Pat to mount a presidential campaign. In the class one year behind Pat was Elizabeth

Holtzman, a Jewish intellectual from Brooklyn, who would win election to the U.S. House of Representatives the same year as Pat, becoming at thirty-one the youngest woman elected to Congress at that time. Holtzman would go on to make two unsuccessful bids for the U.S. Senate in New York.

Despite having encountered some sexism as an undergrad, Pat was shocked by the climate at Harvard Law. On the first day of classes, a male classmate refused to take his assigned seat when he saw he had been placed next to her, telling Pat that she ought to be ashamed of taking a man's place. Many of the students had attended all-male prep schools and all-male private colleges. Quite a few considered it insulting to be asked to share classrooms and libraries on an equal footing with women.

The first week of school, Dean Erwin Griswold invited all the freshmen women to his home for dinner. An aging, white-haired man the students called "Cambridge Fats" behind his back, Griswold made no effort to disguise the fact that he opposed admitting women to law school. Indeed, Griswold informed the women students that the Harvard admissions committee counted the number of women they admitted each year and then increased the number of men admitted by the same amount because everyone knew women wouldn't use their law degrees and the school didn't want to shortchange society of Harvard lawyers. After dinner, he sat the women down on folding chairs in a semicircle and demanded that one by one they justify their legal education.

"I had an absolutely miserable time at Harvard," Pat wrote. "The dorms had orange ceilings and brown walls and the people had a lot of attitude. . . . Many of the students were utterly humorless grinds, underlining their textbooks and making outlines of the underlining."

Lee Scott had encouraged his daughter to attend law school, but both he and Bernice were unsure if Harvard were the right place for Pat. They weren't sure she could cut it academically and they didn't like the fact that she would be one of only a handful of women students. They also worried that "no one would want to marry me if I had a law degree," Pat wrote. "'You're nobody until you are Mrs. Somebody' was believed even by my progressive parents."

As out of step as that might seem today, it was a common enough concern in 1961. In her book *Unlimited Partners: Our American Story*, Elizabeth Dole described her mother's reaction to the news that her daughter was going to Harvard Law School as "less one of opposition than of puzzlement."

"Don't you want to be a wife and a mother and a hostess for your husband?" Dole recalled her mother's asking. Dole lived across the street from Pat in Cambridge. They met one day during their first year at law school when Dole forgot to use the parking brake on her car and the unoccupied vehicle rolled down a hill and crashed into Pat's car. Despite the damage, they became friendly.

Dole recalled a male student filled with moral outrage telling her on her first day of classes at Harvard: "Elizabeth, what are you doing here? Don't you realize that there are men who would give their right arm to be in this law school, men who would use their legal education?"

At the time, the property law course was taught by Professor W. Barton Leach, who refused ever to call on the handful of women students in his class. But once a year Leach would hold "Ladies Day," where he required the women students to stand up in front of the class and read a poem they had composed. The professor, seated with the male students, would then pelt the women with questions. "Charles W. Kingsfield at his most perverse could not have devised a more public humiliation," Dole wrote, referring to the professor-antagonist in the movie *The Paper Chase*, which centered on the infamous grueling pressure that Harvard Law prided itself on.

Students would study all hours of the day and night, barely pausing for a meal, Dole wrote. The competition was so fierce that some students would tear pages out of library books or textbooks to deny them to rivals. Dole, who wound up dropping out for some months and then returning to graduate the year after Pat, recalled spending an afternoon with her roommate, Jean Eberhart, later a Colorado Supreme Court justice, sitting on their beds and fretting that no man would ever marry them once he found out they had been to Harvard Law.

Not all the male Harvard Law students were put off by their female classmates, however. "The women were fairly visible and it didn't take long to figure out who the few girls were in your class or in the school," Jim Schroeder recalled. "Coming back from the Navy I thought it was great to be in this co-educational institution." Pat and Jim met at a party in the fall of 1961 shortly after starting law school. He later decided to ask her out after a chance meeting at the university's library. "One night in the library, she came in and asked me to get a book off the shelf," Jim said. "I said, 'Okay, you want to go out for dinner next weekend?' We went out in November and hit it off." By April they were engaged and by August they were married.

A wedding photo outside the Plymouth Congregational Church in Des Moines reveals a tall (five-seven), slender bride in a traditional white gown and veil. The groom, in a black tuxedo and white boutonniere beside her, has his arm wrapped protectively around her back. They were an attractive couple. Pat had thick, dark hair that was cut stylishly short, and bangs. With her high cheekbones, straight nose, and big smile, she was very pretty and could almost be called beautiful if not for a chin that was a little too prominent and eyes that would squint nearly shut when she smiled or laughed. Several inches taller than Pat, Jim had broad shoulders, short straight brown hair, and a round, genial face. They lived together, studied together, quizzed each other, and backed each other up. They were under pressure like the other students, but they were also partners. Many of their friends were students who had been in the service like Jim. "I was a pilot, they were pilots," Pat recalled. "When you find the real people, it's ten times more fun."

Jim Schroeder grew up west of Chicago in Elmhurst, Illinois, which had exploded in the postwar years from little more than a village to an upscale suburb. His father, Paul, was a dentist. His mother, Thelma, had a masters degree, knew Latin, and had been a junior high school teacher, but she gave up working after her children were born. With Jim and his younger sister, Sandra, the Schroeders were the stereotypical American family. Jim lived in the same house all of his life until he went away to college. Most of his relatives lived within 40 miles of his home.

"Through the 1940s and 1950s, there was not a better place in the world to raise kids than Elmhurst," Bob Stemple, a classmate of Schroeder's at York High School, recalled. "The steam engines, the California Zephyr, and other streamliners raced through town. As kids, we could ride our bikes anywhere and leave them unlocked."

Jim described it as an idyllic period for teenagers. "It was a fairly Norman Rockwellian time," he reminisced to the *Elmhurst Press* as the forty-fifth anniversary of his graduation from York High School approached. "There was no such thing as drugs. Maybe by the time we were juniors or seniors people went out and snuck a beer once in a while. There was no hard liquor. The only people that smoked even cigarettes, as I can recall, were girls. . . . The guys generally didn't smoke because of athletics."

At York, Schroeder was an overachiever—a standout scholar and an athlete. He played football and basketball and was on the track team. "In my freshman year, I wanted to go out for football," he recalled, "[but] my father was a dentist and my mother thought I'd get my teeth knocked out. I was the manager for the freshman-sophomore team, but then in my sophomore year, I convinced them that I really should start playing."

Schroeder was also vice president of the student council, a member of the National Honors Society, an Eagle Scout, and a student member of the "court system," where students accused of breaking driving rules at the school pleaded their cases before their peers. He and his family were active in the First Congregational Church, through which he met students of different backgrounds and races from Chicago and other suburbs.

Elmhurst "was white, middle-class suburbia," Jim told the *Elmhurst Press.* "There were no blacks, Hispanics, or Asians, really."

The Schroeders were a musical family. Paul played the violin and Thelma the piano. There were piano lessons for Jim, and he stuck with it until his sophomore year in high school, when sports soaked up his time. "I grew up listening to symphonies and operas. I like jazz. I like all kinds of music," Jim said. For entertainment, he traveled to Chicago's Wabash Street to listen to Dixieland jazz or to the York Theatre to watch Elizabeth Taylor movies.

The summer of his junior year, Jim lived with a family in Hanover, Germany, for nearly two months on an American Field Service scholarship, which is a student exchange program. "The family I stayed with was definitely upper class," Jim said. "This was 1953 and this was still occupied Germany. Vast areas of the country looked like urban-renewal areas. They had occupation forces all over the places." The experience "broadened my horizons significantly," Jim said, "both in terms of what I was doing with the rest of my life and what was out there. I was fortunate."

Jim sailed to Germany on a ship with other American students participating in the exchange program. Many of them were from elite prep schools in the East. The experience influenced his decision upon graduation in 1954 to attend Princeton University in New Jersey with the help of an ROTC scholarship. "I was lucky and graced, if you will," Jim told the *Elmhurst Press.* "I was probably the first American Field Service student that came from York. I was probably the second student from York that ever went to Princeton. The experiences I had were extraordinary."

But there was also loss and grief. Thelma Schroeder died of cancer while still in her forties.

At Princeton, which accepted only male students at the time, Jim studied history, economics, and political science at the university's Woodrow Wilson School of Public and International Affairs. In the summers, he attended naval training as a midshipman. After graduating from Princeton, he was commissioned as an ensign and stationed for three years in Norfolk, Virginia. During those years, he sailed to South America and the Mediterranean, rising to the rank of lieutenant junior grade.

"In the 1950s and 1960s, if you asked any male what was the number one issue in his head after he turned eighteen, it was joining the military,"

Jim said. "Everybody was either going to get drafted or have to serve in some program."

After leaving the navy, Jim applied to and was accepted at Harvard Law School. "I didn't have this burning desire to practice law, but at least I thought a law degree was a good basic education and a good credential to have," he said.

Contraceptives were illegal in Massachusetts when the Schroeders were first married. Pat could get prescriptions at the student clinic, but she would have to wait to fill them until the couple were back in Illinois or Iowa visiting their families. Technically, if she had ever been prosecuted and convicted of bringing birth control pills into Massachusetts, she would not have been allowed to practice law in most states. It wasn't until three years after the Schroeders were wed that the U.S. Supreme Court ruled that married couples throughout the country had the right to obtain contraceptives. The situation didn't cause the Schroeders any serious inconvenience, but it angered Pat nonetheless. It was a story she would tell frequently after she became involved in campaigning for abortion rights and in the women's health movement.

After graduation from law school, Pat and Jim searched for a place to live. Pat didn't want to live in Chicago and Jim didn't want to live in Des Moines. Finally they settled on Denver, where Pat's father had business interests and the family had a second home. While Jim was courted by Denver law firms, Pat had trouble finding a job. The firms made it clear they thought she was a waste of their time because she would surely quit working as soon as she had a child. Some asked her if she could type. One firm offered to hire Pat, but only if Jim came too. "No one ever told Jim, after the same three grueling years of study, that since he was sure to be a father sometime in the future he should think about another kind of work," Pat complained. Again, Schroeder's experiences were not unique to that period. Janet Reno also had trouble finding a suitable job practicing law after graduating, despite having a Harvard law degree in hand. As a law student in 1962, Reno was denied a summer job by a prominent Miami law firm explicitly because she was a woman. Fourteen years later, the same firm would offer her a partnership. Washington attorney Judith Richards Hope, who was in Schroeder's law school class, told the Harvard Law School Alumni Bulletin that she received more than 100 rejections from law firms, "all of which asked, 'Why are you trying to take the place of a man?'"

"I think when I got out of law school was the first time it really hit me you were going to be treated differently," Pat said. "Getting through law school was no picnic, but you thought, 'I'll get out into the real world and people will value this.' Then you find out they didn't value it at all. They really could care less."

Jim eventually joined a politically connected law firm and Pat took a job as an attorney with the Denver office of the federal National Labor Relations Board, which handles disputes between labor and management. Within a few years, the Scotts had moved from Des Moines to Denver and Pat's younger brother, Michael, who had also gone to law school, had settled into a law practice in Denver, too. Pat was comfortably and happily surrounded by family.

In 1966, after four years of marriage, Pat became pregnant with their first child, Scott. It started off as a normal pregnancy, but Pat and Jim almost died one night after a freak furnace accident caused gas to back up into their house. They spent many agonizing months wondering if the accident would have any effect on the baby. (It didn't. Scott is a graduate of Georgetown University and works in the financial services industry.)

Two years later, Pat became pregnant again, but by the fourth month she was bleeding and convinced that something had gone terribly wrong. She brought her concerns to her obstetrician, who dismissed them, saying she was "high strung." The situation went on for weeks. It was only when she went into an early labor that the doctor discovered she had been pregnant with twins—a girl and a boy—and that the girl had died earlier in the pregnancy. The boy was alive, but had suffered brain damage during a difficult delivery. He died the next morning. Pat believed he might have been saved if a cesarean section had been performed.

"I was angry at myself for having put up with it all," Pat wrote. "Here I was, a trained lawyer, letting a doctor convince me I had no right to question his judgment about my pregnancy and my baby. He intimidated me and made me feel powerless."

Her third pregnancy in 1970 with daughter Jamie was normal, but two days after Pat had returned home from the hospital she began hemorrhaging. She was hospitalized again, but doctors seemed unable to stop the bleeding. For nearly six weeks no one knew whether she would live or die. She spent her thirtieth birthday floating in and out of consciousness, certain she was going to die. It was a Catholic hospital and she was given last rites. Afterward, her doctor warned her that she shouldn't become pregnant again because another baby might kill her. "These experiences certainly reinforced my belief that a woman has a right to decide what happens to her own body," Pat wrote.

After her first child was born, Pat quit her job with the labor board. There was no such thing as maternity leave. At first she stayed home, but after a while she began doing pro bono legal work for causes that appealed to her, such as Rocky Mountain Planned Parenthood and the Denver Fair Housing Group. She joined Planned Parenthood's board. Eventually, she began working part-time as a hearing officer for the Colorado State Personnel Board, which adjudicated grievances by state employees. She would listen to both sides and then write a legal opinion. She also began teaching politics and constitutional law part-time, first at the University of Colorado, then at Regis College. Between teaching and her legal work, Pat was really working full-time by 1972. Although there was flexibility in her schedule and they had more means than most young couples, the Schroeders struggled with the question of how to care for their children while they worked, in an era when it was presumed that most women with young children would simply stay home.

However, other than the strains that most parents of young children encounter, life was pretty good. Pat and Jim bought a large Victorian house built during Denver's silver boom. They spent hours and hours fixing it up, combing flea markets and antique stores for just the right furniture or knickknacks. They enjoyed skiing, they had lots of friends, and sometimes they would get away for the weekend to Santa Fe, New Mexico. Pat discovered she didn't care for housework, but Jim didn't seem to mind. Housekeepers could be hired.

"When I grew up, every woman was looking for a prince and every man was looking for a mommy," Schroeder said. "The dream wife would have the laundry done, the dinner fixed, the candles lit, and she'd have taken her bath by the time her husband got home. The dream husband was going to have the money to get his wife things. My problem was that I wanted wings. When my husband came home, the children were not settled. There wasn't a drink ready. Our home was not an island of tranquility.

"The images I've just recited get boring real fast. Men don't want to talk to women about how well they folded the linen. My husband is remarkable in that he has his ego under control. Sometimes his head is higher than mine. Sometimes my head is higher than his and it doesn't bother him. There is no goalpost in our home. We don't keep score on each other. A marriage has to be a partnership. Each partner gains when one does better than the other. My husband and I see ourselves as an organic whole as opposed to competitors."

3

Guess Who's Coming to Congress

When Pat Schroeder announced her candidacy for Congress in May 1972, she was such an unknown that the *Denver Post* didn't even mention her name in the headline of the short story: "Woman Attorney to Run for Congress." *United Press International's* photographer had a request. Would Mrs. Schroeder please pose for a picture holding her child, her younger child? The attractive, thirty-one-year-old mother of two hoisted daughter Jamie, a curly-haired toddler still in diapers, into her arms. So was born a legendary politician who from the start seemed to be defined foremost by her gender.

"My generation of women did not think you were meant to be a candidate," Schroeder said. "You voted, you worked on a campaign, but you weren't a candidate."

Pat and Jim Schroeder were part of a group of younger, upwardly mobile Denver Democrats—this was before the term *yuppie* was coined—who were buying and restoring homes built in the Capital Hill, Cheesman Park, and Park Hill neighborhoods during the 1890s silver boom in Colorado. They opposed the Vietnam War, favored environmental activism, and were not reluctant to challenge the status quo.

Two years earlier, these rabble-rousing young Democrats had helped unseat incumbent Congressman Byron Rogers in a bitterly contested primary with a liberal lawyer, Craig Barnes. Rogers had been in office twenty years and hailed from an older, more staid generation. Philosophically, Rogers was moderate to liberal, but he had been reluctant to criticize the Vietnam War or even the conduct of the war. After a hard-fought primary, Barnes wound up defeating Rogers by a mere twenty-seven votes.

Like a family feud, the Rogers-Barnes primary fight left Denver Democrats divided and bitter. That provided an opening in the general election for Republican James D. "Mike" McKevitt, a popular former law-and-order district attorney. As a prosecutor, McKevitt had made headlines for closing a movie theater playing the controversial Swedish film *I Am Curious (Yellow)* and for threatening to close restaurants that catered to hippies. The key issues in the race were the Vietnam War, which Barnes opposed, and school busing, which McKevitt opposed. Denver had been involved for some years in court-ordered busing to end segregation, a volatile issue that had torn apart the local school board. On election day, the heavily Democratic city of Denver elected its first Republican congressman in more than two decades.

In the two years that followed, Congressman McKevitt "was so likable that had his voting record not been so conservative, he would have been unbeatable," Schroeder told the *Denver Post*. "He was the best-liked, and at one point either the first- or second-best-known politician, in Colorado."

It was Jim Schroeder who was supposed to be the politician in the family. He was considerably more active in the Democratic party than his wife. He had made an unsuccessful bid for the state legislature in 1970, losing by only forty-two votes, and he would have run again, but in the intervening two years the legislature had redrawn district boundaries, and Jim found himself living in a district where a race for the state House was no longer plausible.

Democrats should have been lining up to challenge McKevitt in 1972, which was the first time he was up for reelection. Colorado's First Congressional District had a substantial Democratic voter registration edge and McKevitt had been in office only two years. Conventional political wisdom holds that congressional incumbents are at their most vulnerable when they are still freshmen, before they have had a chance to cement their public image and earn the widespread gratitude of voters through political favors and services to constituents.

Indeed, several of Denver's most promising young politicos had looked hard at the race, but in the end they had all taken a pass. One reason was that all the portents indicated 1972 was going to be a very good year for Republicans. At the top of the ticket was President Richard Nixon, who was poised to win reelection to a second term. Nixon had just scored a diplomatic and public relations triumph with his visit to China in February. He signed a major arms treaty with the Soviets that June, and he was promising to end the war. There was no region of the country where Nixon's support was stronger than in the Rocky Mountain West and he was expected to run up a big margin in Colorado. Nixon aside, there was also the feeling that McKevitt wasn't going to be a pushover. He was popular, he hadn't made any major mistakes, and he was expected to have plenty of money for his campaign.

And finally, any Democrat who got into the race would first have a tough primary fight. Veteran State Sen. Clarence D. "Arch" Decker had made it clear to everyone that he was determined to run for the seat. Decker was a moderate and out of touch with the Democratic party's mainstream, but the party establishment had agreed to back him in the belief that he had paid his dues and deserved a chance. Besides, he wasn't going to get elected anyway. Still, a goodly number of Democratic activists in Denver were unhappy with Decker. They opposed the Vietnam War, the number one issue of the day, and Decker supported it. He was also a bit fuddy-duddy, a bit behind the times. "I'm an Arch Supporter," his campaign buttons read. The question was, who could they get to run against him? That was the topic at a political meeting one night that spring, when a Democrat turned to Jim Schroeder, who was a district captain, and asked, "How about your wife?"

"How about your wife?" Jim recalled firing back. He came home that night and told Pat about it and they had a good laugh. But when they talked it over, they realized it wasn't so absurd. The next day, they set about creating a campaign organization and launching a candidacy. At least that is how Pat and Jim Schroeder have told the story on countless occasions over the past three decades. It was supposed to be an honorable but hopeless race by an accidental candidate. In her 1998 memoir, *24 Years of House Work . . . and the Place Is Still a Mess,* Schroeder called it a "kamikaze run."

"I was the only person [Jim] could talk into it," she wrote. "If it had looked like a good political year, I would never have gotten my foot in the door. They figured it was a good time, since we were going to lose anyway, to run a woman and get looking progressive."

There is probably a great deal of truth to the story, but it is also reasonable to consider that Pat Schroeder—a woman of immense drive and great intelligence who had a keen interest in politics and public policy—may have been looking for an opportunity to put herself forward instead of simply playing a supporting role on the sidelines. "I'm not the cheerleader type," Schroeder has frequently said of herself over the years. She and Jim were partners, and he had had his turn. Perhaps they both felt this was her turn.

Still, Schroeder insisted in an interview that she had not thought about entering politics up to that point and probably would never have run if she had known beforehand that she might actually win. "Feminists used to get very mad at me when I'd say that," Schroeder said, "but I kind of got double dog dared into doing it because everybody said you won't win, but somebody's got to go carry the flag and who better than you because it's short term, it's temporary, it's not going to hurt your career—they had a thousand different reasons. I really didn't even think I'd win the primary. I thought it was like a May to September thing."

Another motivating factor may have been the thought of McKevitt's winning a second term. Schroeder had tried to meet with the congressman about the war, but had been turned down. "One of the reasons I got mad enough to run was that I had a congressman who didn't have time to talk to me about the Vietnam War, but who had time to send me complimentary cookbooks and baby books," Schroeder told *McCall's* magazine. "He could tell me how to cook and how to raise babies, but he couldn't talk to me about issues."

Schroeder was entering the race very late. It was mid-April and the party caucuses were in May. She would have to scramble because the caucuses were where delegates to the congressional district convention are selected. Candidates had to line up delegates who would vote for them at the convention in order to get their names on the primary ballot. Jim had already committed himself to managing the U.S. Senate campaign of his law partner, Democrat Floyd Haskell. Incumbent Sen. Gordon Allott, a Republican who had supported the Vietnam War, was facing reelection. Haskell, who opposed the war, had been a Republican, but had quit his party over the issue. It promised to be a high-profile race. Jim immediately told Haskell he'd have to find another campaign manager. He was going to have his hands full assisting his wife's campaign.

"Frankly, I said at the time, having written my thesis on Adlai Stevenson, it would be a Stevensonian campaign: talk sense to the American people and lose. I never expected her to win," Jim later told the *Rocky Mountain News.*

Another of Jim's law partners was the Denver Democratic party chairman, Dick Young, who was backing Decker for the nomination. He tried unsuccessfully to convince Jim that his wife was making a mistake.

"She was truly a political unknown," recalled Denver attorney Mike Cheroutes, who was Schroeder's top aide her first two years in Washington. "She didn't have any constituency base in the city. I'm not sure she was even that well known in the Democratic party."

Schroeder ran a campaign based on opposition to the Vietnam War, support for the environment, and the premise that Colorado—which was then bidding to be host for the 1976 Winter Olympics—had more pressing uses for its tax money than sports. There was intense opposition in Denver to the plan put forward by local business leaders for the Olympics on environmental grounds since it would have involved defacing mountainsides close to the city to accommodate events and spectators. "The Winter Olympics: A $40 million snow job," read one political button Olympics opponents were wearing around town that year. In the same election, Coloradans approved by a three-to-two margin a public referendum cutting off all state funds for the games.

Schroeder also called for a reordering of national priorities to emphasize education, child care, and health services and to de-emphasize defense programs. At first, she was virtually ignored. Indeed, when attention was focused on her candidacy, it was often to question whether the mother of two young children had any business running for Congress. Some voters, women included, were openly hostile.

"In my first campaign, it seemed like all I was asked about was what was going to happen to my family, who would do the laundry if I was elected," Schroeder said. Even Bernice Scott had mixed feelings about her daughter's candidacy. "I was afraid she wouldn't have time enough for the children," Scott told *People* magazine after Schroeder was in Congress. Dee Dukehart, the campaign's scheduler, recalled some people calling the campaign incensed that Schroeder was running for office. Some callers even accused her of trying to pass herself off as a man by using "Pat" instead of "Patricia."

"You had to have a sense of humor throughout because people were hateful," Dukehart said. "People would call and make horrible comments about her and how could she even possibly think about running when she had two small babies . . . Pat has some of the best haters in the whole world to this day."

But Schroeder turned out to be an energetic and irrepressible campaigner. If her critics tried to make her out to be a wild-eyed radical, she would respond with an ironic humor that many voters found appealing. "Hi!" Schroeder would start off a speech, "I'm that nut you've been hearing about, the one who doesn't shave under her arms, the one who leaps over barricades uttering obscenities, the one who keeps her kids in the freezer."

The average contribution to Schroeder's primary campaign was seven dollars and fifty cents. Despite her background in labor law, she had very little union support because they were convinced she couldn't win. Nor was there any help from local women's organizations. She was a member of the National Women's Political Caucus and had helped found the

Colorado Women's Political Caucus, but the Colorado chapter declined to endorse her. "It's just too soon," they told her. "Why don't you think about running for city council?"

At the Democratic state convention, where thousands of delegates from across Colorado gather to formalize which candidates' names will appear on primary ballots, candidates get a certain number of minutes on the podium, depending on their importance, to address delegates. It was a measure of Schroeder's lack of importance, and the party hierarchy's lack of support for her candidacy, that she was told as she walked on stage that she had thirty seconds to speak. Not knowing what else to say, Schroeder announced simply: "I support the lettuce boycott." Then she walked off. Boycotting lettuce to protest the treatment of migrant workers was an important issue in Denver's Hispanic community. The delegates roared their approval.

Schroeder did have help from Craig Barnes, who had lost to McKevitt two years earlier. Barnes put her in touch with the volunteers who had helped his campaign. Students from Schroeder's classes at Regis College also volunteered.

Two young advertising executives, Arnie Grossman and Chuck Bartholomew, friends of the Schroeders, came up with the campaign's slogan: "She wins. We win." Dukehart recalled driving Schroeder around town in an old blue Volkswagen Beetle with campaign signs plastered on the sides, asking store owners if they would put in their windows "She wins. We win." posters with a picture of the profile of the pony-tailed candidate. Bartholomew and Grossman also came up with the idea for a less traditional series of campaign posters to get Schroeder's message across to voters. These were a far cry from the usual red, white, and blue feel-good political posters that featured the candidate in a homey setting with his family or engaged in some vigorous-looking activity. The Schroeder posters were an emotional poke in the gut that people who were involved in Denver politics at the time vividly recall to this day.

One showed a row of tombstones at Arlington National Cemetery and a quote from Nixon: "Many of our troops have already been withdrawn from Vietnam." Another poster, printed entirely in a sort of distressed pink, depicted a very old woman shuffling down a Denver street beside the caption, "Cheer up. The Olympics are coming." Another had a picture of a young Hispanic child sitting under a crucifix on the dirt floor of a migrant labor camp. Underneath, it read: "This radical troublemaker is out to get something from us. Hope." In those days, posters were enjoying great popularity as an art form. Thirty years later, Washington and Denver are sprinkled with former Democratic political activists who have kept and treasured their posters from Schroeder's first campaign.

Ultimately, Schroeder surprised everyone and defeated Decker in the primary by 4,000 votes. Having won the primary, Schroeder gained the nominal support of the party and labor unions. Several of Decker's key campaign aides, not wishing to repeat the division and bitterness of two years earlier, also joined the Schroeder campaign. But the consensus opinion still was that she didn't stand a chance against McKevitt.

"The one trip we made to Washington to raise money and support from the Democratic National Committee had been fruitless," Schroeder wrote in her memoirs. "I wanted to run a campaign on the issues—the Vietnam War, housing, the environment, children, the elderly. The DNC didn't think I would win that way—or any way—and they sent me home empty-handed."

One of the few national Democrats to help was Rep. Phil Burton of California, who wanted to become Speaker of the House and thus was anxious to do favors for other Democrats who might be in a position to support him. He sent her a contribution. Feminist leader Gloria Steinem flew to Denver to help raise money for her race. *Ms.* magazine had published its first issue that July. Folk singer Judy Collins, who sang in a Denver church choir with some of Schroeder's campaign workers, also agreed to help. Collins wrote a song for Schroeder and recorded snippets of it for radio ads for the campaign. At one Schroeder fund raiser, guests milled around a mansion belonging to a political supporter as Collins played the piano and sang in the foyer. Guests paid just twenty-five dollars each to attend the private performance, Dukehart recalled.

After the primary, Schroeder moved her campaign headquarters out of the basement of the couple's home and into a rundown former drugstore, where they used orange crates for chairs. Meanwhile, she kept her job as a hearing officer for the state personnel board, believing that she would need "something to come back to" after the campaign was over. Her friends pitched in and gave lectures to her political science students at Regis College so she could campaign and not lose her teaching position.

Ultimately, Schroeder's secret weapon turned out to be her opponent, who underestimated her and ignored her until it was too late. The forty-four-year-old McKevitt also irritated Schroeder and got her competitive juices flowing. He would condescendingly call her "little Patsy" even though she was taller than he. "She's a schemer, but she makes it more effective by being a hard worker," McKevitt would tell *People* magazine fifteen years later when Schroeder was weighing a bid for the Democratic presidential nomination. "If anyone has fire in her belly, it's Pat."

On November 8, Schroeder campaign workers watched the election returns from the home of antiwar activist Sam Brown. There was a big board with bellwether precincts marked off. As the evening wore on, the bellwether precincts one by one went for Schroeder, and it suddenly dawned on everyone that she could very well win. At home with their children, Pat and Jim watched the election returns in stunned disbelief. Nixon was racking up the biggest GOP landslide ever, including carrying Denver. Democratic incumbents were falling all around the country, but against the tide Schroeder was defeating McKevitt. She wound up capturing 51.6 percent of the vote.

"At 2 A.M., wondering if we had veered off into the Twilight Zone, Jim drove to the Denver Election Commission, sure that the press reports of my victory were wrong. They were right," Schroeder wrote. "Jim and I were awake all night contemplating the enormity of what lay ahead." The upset victory, the *New York Times* said, was "worthy of Frank Capra," the famous director who made *Mr. Smith Goes to Washington* and *It's A Wonderful Life* in which an ordinary man fights for his principles and wins against overwhelming odds.

Schroeder was not alone in her victory. Haskell wound up defeating Allott and serving six years in the Senate. For any Democrat to win statewide in Colorado, they must generate a strong Democratic turnout in Denver on election day. Haskell's efforts to bring out Denver Democrats no doubt helped Schroeder, just as Schroeder's strong race against McKevitt excited local Democrats, which no doubt helped Haskell.

It is a testament to the Democratic nature of the district that McKevitt remains the only Republican to win election to Colorado's First Congressional District since 1950. Over the two and a half decades that followed her election to the House, Republicans would field a variety of candidates against Schroeder—an antibusing leader, a veteran state legislator, a wealthy political newcomer, a woman school board member, a woman stockbroker, and a prominent ex-Democrat, among others. None of them came close to unseating her. The most successful was State Rep. Don Friedman, who put together a campaign treasury that exceeded Schroeder's and held her to 53 percent of the vote in 1976. Decker eventually switched to the Republican Party and ran against Schroeder in the general election in 1982, but he had no more luck that year than he'd had a decade earlier.

Redistricting in the 1980s and 1990s tilted the district even more toward the Democratic column, enabling Schroeder to rely on a coalition of liberals, young professionals, blacks, and Hispanics. Eventually, Republicans would come to consider her virtually unbeatable in her district. In the record-shattering GOP landslide of 1994, when Newt Gingrich's Republican Revolution vaulted into power, Schroeder's percentage of the vote plummeted all the way down to 59.98 percent—a robust margin that most candidates would feel good about in any year.

"I've never done a poll, and I realize to say that in this city, it's like you're taking bread and butter away from half of them, and they don't like it," Schroeder told the National Press Club in Washington, D.C., in 1991. "But I have found from day one there are three things that count for the average American, and that is their family, their jobs, and their country—in that order. And I think it's still true today. I don't think you need to pay anyone to tell you that." When Schroeder retired from Congress in 1996 after twenty-four years in the House, she still had never paid for an opinion poll or hired a political consultant.

Schroeder was the first woman elected to Congress from Colorado, a state that had granted voting rights to women in 1893, twenty-seven years before the adoption of the nineteenth amendment to the Constitution. Only a handful of states had acted earlier than Colorado to politically emancipate women. Wyoming and Utah had acted, respectively, in 1869 and 1870 while they were still territories, and both became states with women voting. Kansas enacted suffrage in 1885, and Idaho followed Colorado in 1896. It was 1910 before other states began to follow suit. Ironically, although Colorado was one of the first states to grant women the right to vote, it took seventy-nine years afterward for a woman to emerge as a serious candidate for Congress. To this day, there has never been a woman governor of Colorado, a woman senator from Colorado, or a woman mayor of Denver, which are the three most visible public offices in the state. For 30 years after Schroeder's first campaign, the liberal first congressional district remained the only congressional district in the state to elect a woman to Congress, with Democrat Diana DeGette succeeding Schroeder in 1997. In 2002, Republican Marilyn Musgrave—a social conservative who was known in the state Senate for her fierce opposition to abortion, same-sex marriage and adoption by same-sex parents—broke new ground, winning election to the fourth district in rural northeastern Colorado.

Denver "was like Marlboro country at that time," Schroeder recalled.

"I was the first woman to ever run and the first woman to ever win. I had a two-year-old and I had a six-year-old, and people were in shock."

Although arbitrary discrimination against women candidates for Congress was on the wane in 1972, and a record number of women were running for office, the national election results essentially confirmed the status quo: The male-female ratio in Congress remained substantially unchanged. Local personalities and issues turned out, as usual, to be more pivotal than the burgeoning women's movement or any general desire to see women increase their numbers in public office. In fact, the election contained a significant setback to women's political progress: for the first time in a quarter of a century not a single woman would be serving in the Senate. Republican Margaret Chase Smith of Maine, the only woman in the Senate, lost her bid for reelection after thirty-two years in office.

The diminutive Smith was one of the first lawmakers to oppose "McCarthyism." Her "declaration of conscience" on the Senate floor in 1950 had encouraged other members to later join in censuring fellow Republican Joseph McCarthy, whose anti-communist crusade had viciously ruined numerous government careers and lives. "The American people," she said, "are sick and tired of being afraid to speak their minds lest they be politically smeared as 'communists' or 'fascists' by their opponents. Freedom of speech is not what it used to be in America. It has been so abused by some that it is not exercised by others."

Following a pattern set by many of the women who preceded her in Congress, Smith was elected to the House in 1940 to fill the House seat that had been held by her husband, Clyde H. Smith. After serving eight years, Smith ran for the GOP Senate nomination, defying Maine Republican leaders who said she was out of her league. She won the nomination by defeating the handpicked candidate of the GOP establishment and went on to trounce the Democratic candidate in the general election, becoming the first woman elected to both houses of Congress. In the Senate, she pursued a mostly moderate course in keeping with the New England Republicanism of the era. However, she was also a maverick who was known for resisting pressure from powerful members of her own party, including presidents Eisenhower and Nixon, on matters of conscience.

In January 1964, Smith announced her candidacy for the Republican presidential nomination, becoming the first woman to seek the presidency on a major party ticket. She received twenty-seven delegate votes, more than any candidate except the GOP nominee, Senator Barry Goldwater of Arizona. Yet, for all her experience in breaking new ground for women,

Smith was not generally regarded as a champion of women's rights and did not identify with the new generation of women leaders who were demanding equal treatment for women in the courts and in the workplace. "I definitely resent being called a feminist," Smith wrote in her book *Declaration of Conscience*, published the same year as her last political campaign. The unexpected defeat of the seventy-four-year-old Smith in 1972 was due to a combination of factors, including her age and Maine's poor economy. But it was also one more sign that the early 1970s were a period of transition for women in politics generally and women in Congress in particular.

Schroeder was one of approximately two-dozen women making their first try for Congress on major party tickets in 1972. The National Women's Political Caucus and other women's groups never expected all of them to win, but they had forecast a net gain of ten women in the House. Instead, they got half that number. Besides Schroeder, other women elected to the House for the first time that year were Democrats Yvonne Brathwaite Burke of California, Elizabeth Holtzman of New York, and Barbara Jordan of Texas, and Republican Marjorie Holt of Maryland. All five were lawyers and, unlike many of their female predecessors, none of them was filling vacancies left by their husbands.

At thirty-two, Schroeder was the second youngest woman to have been elected to Congress. The youngest was her Harvard Law classmate, Holtzman, who was thirty-one. Of the ten women seeking reelection to the House that year, only Democrat Louise Day Hicks of Massachusetts lost, a victim primarily of redistricting. To put into perspective how rare successful women politicians were at all levels of government in 1972, no woman had ever been elected governor of any state except as her husband's successor and no woman had ever been elected mayor of a major American city.

In 1972, the history of women who preceded Schroeder in Congress was a mixed bag, encompassing both placeholders and professional politicians, one-term wonders and proven vote-getters. There were so many congresswomen who had succeeded their husbands in the House in the early 1930s that they were known as "widows' row." Political analysts are divided over the importance of the "matrimonial connection." Those who would minimize its significance point out that the majority of congressional seats left vacant by death have not been filled by wives. There is also a feeling among some analysts of women's political history that placing too much emphasis on the matrimonial connection can result in overlooking the substantial political talents and accomplishments of some of the widows.

However, by downplaying the matrimonial connection analysts run the risk of overlooking the larger issue, which is that succession to the seat of a deceased incumbent, particularly that of a spouse, was the method of access for the overwhelming majority of early women members of Congress. Of the first eight women in Congress, five came by their seats through the death of an incumbent, according to *Climbing the Hill: Gender Conflict in Congress* by Karen and Herbert Foerstel. Up to World War II, nineteen of the thirty-two women who had served in Congress came there by filling the remainder of the term of a deceased incumbent. Even after the war, women tended to gain entry to Congress only through exceptional circumstances. Up until 1970, only two years before Schroeder first sought office, women filling out the term of a deceased incumbent still represented the majority of all women who had served in Congress.

That doesn't mean that many of the early congresswomen didn't eventually become successful politicians in their own right. For example, Republican Edith Nourse Rogers of Massachusetts, who was elected in 1925 to fill a vacancy created by the death of her husband, went on to be reelected seventeen times. Rogers focused her work in the Congress on military and veterans issues, playing a key role in the drafting of the GI Bill of Rights in 1944. President Roosevelt gave her the pen by which he signed the bill into law in tribute to her efforts. Three years later, by dint of seniority, Rogers became chairman of the House Veterans Affairs Committee. She was a candidate for a nineteenth term when she died in 1960 at age seventy-nine, after serving thirty-five years in office.

Shortly after her election, Schroeder got a phone call from then Congresswoman Bella Abzug of New York, one of the most famous feminists in the nation. Abzug told her, "Well, congratulations . . . but I hear you have a husband and two children." Yes, the children are two and six years old, Schroeder acknowledged. "I don't think you can do the job," Abzug told her, and take care of her children, too. "I thought, 'AAAAUGH, if she doesn't think I can do it, what am I doing?'" Schroeder recalled.

While Schroeder's youthful motherhood may not have been completely unique, she was certainly perceived by the press, the public, and her colleagues in Congress as a pioneer for women in politics. The only other congresswoman in office at the time Schroeder entered the House who had young children when first elected was Republican Margaret Heckler of Massachusetts. Her children were nine, seven, and six years old when she won election in 1966. Heckler's husband, John, an investment banker, chose to remain in Boston with the children and the couple commuted between Washington and Boston on the weekends.

"Sometimes," Rep. Heckler told the *New York Times* in 1976, "we are 727s that pass in the night." Eventually, they divorced.

At least two other mothers of young children preceded Schroeder in the House: Ruth Hanna McCormick of Illinois, who had a seven-year-old when she was elected in 1928, and Katharine Byron of Maryland, who had five sons ranging in age from three to sixteen when she was elected in May 1941 to fill the remainder of her late husband's term. Despite the backing of local Democratic leaders, Byron was not a shoo-in to replace her husband, William Devereux Byron. She narrowly defeated Republican Charles Stewart in a contest that centered on the nation's response to war in Europe. In campaign appearances with nationally known Democrats such as Rep. Estes Kefauver of Tennessee and First Lady Eleanor Roosevelt, Byron endorsed American support for nations fighting against the Nazis and recommended greater military preparedness for this nation.

Byron served eighteen months in the House. She had filed for reelection and begun to mount a new campaign when she changed her mind, saying that she wanted to spend more time at home with her sons. Years later, Byron told writer Hope Chamberlin that her decision was predicated primarily on the difficulty in securing child care as the nation geared up for war:

> Citizen morale was low. The military picture was bleak. The country still reeled from the crippling blow dealt by the Japanese to . . . the Pacific fleet. A call had gone out for women to pitch in. The governess who cared for my boys was also a registered nurse and she wanted to volunteer for Army duty. I knew I couldn't replace her. But what could I say?

Yvonne Burke, elected the same year as Schroeder, became pregnant and gave birth to a daughter during her first term. Burke decided not to seek reelection in 1978, remaining for more than two decades as the only woman to have had a child while serving in Congress. The next incumbent congresswoman to give birth was Republican Susan Molinari of New York in 1996. Molinari resigned her House seat a year later, citing, in part, a desire to spend more time with her daughter, Susan Ruby.

Although he believed his wife was qualified for the office, Jim Schroeder said they had never sat down before election day to discuss the effect the election would have on their personal lives because "I never thought she would win." Victory left him with no choice, Jim felt, but to move to Washington, "because we had little kids—Jamie was just one or two at the time, and our eldest was five. Also, we didn't live on the East Coast, so we couldn't do a weekend thing."

The weeks in between election day and taking office in January were frantic. The Schroeders rented their large Victorian house in Denver's Capital Hill neighborhood and bought a condominium in the same building where Pat's parents lived. Jim flew east by himself to buy a house, a brick split-level on a quiet cul-de-sac in a leafy Virginia suburb. Pat bought two cars over the telephone, including one from an auto dealer who couldn't believe that she wasn't going to test drive it and didn't care about the color. Jim stayed home with the children until the live-in nanny/housekeeper they had hired could move to Washington. It fell to him to make the trips to pediatricians and to do most of the other chores involved in raising young children.

At that time, only 27 percent of mothers with a child under the age of three were in the work force. Even for families of means, like the Schroeders, good child care was often difficult to find. Schroeder would frequently say of those early years after her election to the House that her greatest fear "was losing my housekeeper."

For Jim, the move to Washington would mean hunting for a job with a law firm whose work didn't present any ethical conflicts for his wife and taking a cut in salary. He briefly considered giving up law and experimenting with writing or photography. Pat's $42,500 congressional salary was more than their combined income before she was elected. "I expected I would support the family," Jim Schroeder said in an interview in 1990 with *Fortune* magazine. "But when you get married there's no road map. Everyone has the expectations of his parents, but all of life is a learning experience. I knew I was marrying a lawyer who wanted to practice."

It was extremely unusual at the time for the husbands of the few women in Congress to uproot their professional careers and move to Washington. Most stayed where they were, and the congresswoman returned home for long weekends. Jim said he found no advantages granted him in the legal arena as a congresswoman's husband. "If anything, it was a disadvantage when I was looking for a job, since Pat's term only lasts two years at a time and the employers knew they could lose me if she wasn't voted back in." Not until the move's turmoil eased months after Schroeder was sworn into office did Jim find a job for himself, joining an international law firm, Kaplan, Russin and Vecchi, which primarily represented foreign companies and governments doing business in the United States.

Jim Schroeder has said he had very few self-doubts about the move. "People over the years have always said, 'Wasn't it wonderful what you did?'

The thing is, I had no choice. . . . What was I going to do? My daughter was in diapers." Denver, he said, was simply too far from Washington. "I encouraged her to run. I was proud of her and enthusiastic and willing to move back there."

Looking back, Pat concluded that the move to Washington resulted in a better, though sometimes comic, relationship between Jim and the children. "He clearly was a solo parent a lot more because I would be gone," Schroeder said. "As a consequence he had to get to know the kids a lot more than he would have otherwise. If I'm not there, he couldn't defer to me. And some of the funniest things used to be my young daughter's hair when I used to return from a weekend. . . . He will never be a hairdresser." She dedicated her 1989 memoir, *Champion of the Great American Family*, to her husband "for giving up home-cooked meals, darned socks, and a dust-free home."

In the winter of 1972, having achieved the unthinkable and about to become one of only fourteen women out of 535 members in the Congress, having uprooted her family and forced her husband to give up his job, it was time for Schroeder to turn her rhetoric into reality, to live up to the promise of her candidacy.

"From the moment I won my first congressional campaign I had a gnawing feeling that this might be one job I could not do," Schroeder recalled in her book. "I found, to my surprise, that my fears echoed the common mythology that a woman couldn't and shouldn't combine career and family. Despite my education and the changing times, I had to disprove these myths for myself."

4

Queen of the Quip

On the first day of Pat Schroeder's congressional career, her husband drove up to the front of the imposing Capitol building and dropped her off while he went to park the car. "I just sat down on those steps and thought, 'My gosh, what's a mother like me doing here? I'm about to be sworn into Congress and I haven't even potty-trained my daughter,'" Schroeder recalled.

The Ninety-third Congress that took the oath of office in January 1973 marked the beginning of a new era in American politics, although few of the lawmakers would have recognized it as such at the time. The capital was preparing for President Richard Nixon's second inaugural. There was a sense of anticipation, of events waiting to happen. Antiwar demonstrators seemed to be everywhere, clogging the city. The pedestrian and subway tunnels beneath the Capitol building were filled with National Guard troops who sheltered there, rolling out their sleeping bags in the evening.

Within months, the Watergate scandal would come to dominate politics, and Congress and the White House would be locked in a constitutional crisis. Within less than two years, Nixon would be gone, the first president in the history of the nation to resign in disgrace. And in the wake of that cathartic event, the major institutions of government would be fundamentally altered.

"For more than a decade the grumpy tenants of Capitol Hill had watched as power ran in a one-way stream down Pennsylvania Avenue to the White House, there to be exercised by imperious cold war presidents in the conduct of foreign wars and the service of the national security state," John A. Farrell wrote in *Tip O'Neill and the Democratic Century.* "The Ninety-Third Congress would reverse that flow. In the process, the House of Representatives would bring down a president and complete a metamorphosis from a sleepy feudal culture ruled by wizened southern hawks to a

'New Congress' that distributed its reclaimed powers among a host of youthful, more ideological, and determinedly independent representatives."

It was this "sleepy feudal culture" on the brink of change that the brash, energetic young congresswoman from Colorado entered in 1973. She was politically inexperienced, but she wasn't naïve. She knew what she wanted to accomplish, and she saw the traditional get-along, go-along route to power and influence as antithetical to her goals and unlikely to be successful even if she were to try it.

It was a conscious decision on her part to rock the boat, Schroeder has said. In a farewell speech to the National Press Club in 1996, she explained: "My view, when I came here, was that I was to be the burr under the saddle of the status quo. Whenever the status quo was cinching too tight around a certain group of people, I got to be the burr under the saddle to see if we couldn't get it loosened a little bit or changed. Now, a lot of people will call that being a liberal—if that's what you call it, fine, and I'm proud of that tradition—or a progressive, or whatever. I thought that's what it was all about. I thought we were here to try to correct courses to make things better and keep moving forward."

From her perch on the Armed Services Committee, Schroeder questioned expensive weapons systems from the MX missile to Reagan's Strategic Defense Initiative, also known as "Star Wars." She became a leader in the nuclear freeze movement of the 1970s and 1980s. She also became a champion for ordinary soldiers and their families, fighting for better pay, better housing, better medical care, moving expenses, and child care. Closer to home, Schroeder grappled with the future of the army's Rocky Mountain Arsenal, a former chemical weapons factory on Denver's eastern boundary. Ultimately, she would play a leading role in its conversion to a wildlife refuge.

Schroeder was also a member of the Post Office and Civil Service Committee, considered one of the "B" committees in the House, but one of significance to Denver, which is a federal center for many western states. On that committee, Schroeder quickly became a champion for federal workers, especially women.

From the start, Schroeder gave House Democratic leaders and many of her colleagues heartburn. It seemed as if every time they turned around, she was up to something. Early in her first term, a Denver television crew flew to Washington to spend a week with the freshman congresswoman. She gave the TV crew a tour, including taking them into the taxpayer-supported House stationery store in the basement of the Longworth office building, where she happily pointed out for the cameras all the luxury items for sale at very reasonable prices that had absolutely nothing to do with conducting congressional business. Smarting from the publicity generated by that incident, House leaders responded by placing the stationery store off-limits to the media. It has remained that way ever since.

On another occasion, Schroeder had a private meeting with Speaker Carl Albert. There were many issues Schroeder wanted to talk to Albert about—the Vietnam War, abortion, children's issues, defense—but she was disappointed and insulted to find that there was only one issue the speaker wanted to discuss with her: hideaway offices. Hideaways are private offices in the Capitol set aside for the personal use of individual lawmakers. Almost all the offices are confined to the upper passages of the Senate side of the building. Some are quite lavishly decorated. Theoretically, they are places for senators to get away from the pressures of office, places out of the reach of constituents, staff, wives, children, whatever. Sometimes they are used for meetings to plot political or legislative strategy in secret. Sometimes they are used for sexual assignations. Only the most powerful senators have hideaways, and consequently they are one of the most prized perks on Capitol Hill.

Influential House members, Democrats and Republicans alike, wanted their own hideaways, but there was no room available on the House side of the Capitol. At the time, the west front of the Capitol was in terrible disrepair and in danger of collapsing in some places. House leaders were holding up legislation to pay for repairs to the building in an effort to pry money out of the Senate for the construction of hideaways for House members. What Albert wanted to know from Schroeder was: Would she support the House position on hideaways? Schroeder was so incensed that she laid out the conversation with Albert in detail over lunch with *Denver Post* reporter Leonard Larsen, who duly wrote about it for his newspaper.

"I think it took a little guts for her to do that," Larsen said, noting that the last thing most freshmen want to do is publicly criticize their party leaders. "I think most of the criticisms she had about Congress as an institution were true, sometimes overstated, but basically true and needed to be said, but they couldn't have won her much admiration from other members of Congress."

Shortly after leaving office, Schroeder told Charles Lewis of the Center for Public Integrity: "You know, when I got there, there was no way in the world I was ever going to be part of the leadership. I had that figured out on day one. So it was just never a goal. So I never did those types of things."

Still, setting herself against ingrained institutional behavior was clearly difficult at times. Schroeder called Congress "the whale," writing in her memoirs: "I felt swallowed by Congress. Every day was a fight to survive and not sell out."

From almost the very moment Schroeder crossed the threshold of the Capitol, she was a media star. At first, reporters were drawn to her because of her uniqueness as a young mother and one of only fourteen women in the entire Congress. But they quickly began to seek her out on a wide range of matters. The ingredient, the spark, that set Schroeder apart from other lawmakers and made her a national celebrity was her sometimes irreverent, sometimes biting wit. She had a talent for finding the ironies in any situation and reducing them to a single, humorous observation using colorfully drawn images. This skill was something she worked at, writing down lines as she thought of them, testing them out on her staff or family, and keeping those that worked, jettisoning others, according to former aides. Over time, she developed a rich repository of killer one-liners. Lloyd Grove of the *Washington Post* once described a typical Schroeder quip as an "edgy sound bite" akin to a "bonbon with a razor inside."

For example, during Schroeder's first few months in Washington, her husband, Jim, was in her office almost every day, directing traffic and keeping things from falling apart while her chief of staff was delayed moving from Denver. One day an older House member who had stopped by Schroeder's office noticed Jim. "I see your husband is working for you. You know, you're not supposed to have him on the payroll," he advised thoughtfully. Imagine his surprise when the young congresswoman shot back: "Oh, he's not on the payroll. I just let him sleep with me."

The rich and the privileged invariably belonged to "the lucky sperm club," according to Schroeder. On the growing clout of the women's caucus, she said: "We have moved beyond the toddler stage and now we hope we are terrors." Until the 1980s, Congress was "the planet of the guys." On the attitude toward women at the 1980 GOP convention: "If they had met two more days we'd all be in veils." Referring to Democrats returning to Congress after the 1980 Reagan landslide, she sighed, "It's nice to be out of the Alamo and still alive."

Describing life as a female candidate for public office during the militaristic Reagan years, she said, "This Rambomania, the macho, feel-good, real-man, thumbs-up kind of mood makes it really hard for a woman candidate. The electorate seems to be looking for representatives that are half-Marine, half-legislator. That's tough for a woman to pull off."

On how foreign competition sounds campaigning in the rural West: "It's hard to stand on a wagon tongue and explain to people why we need a 600-ship Navy to keep the oceans open so that the Japanese can send Subarus to our national ski team." On U.S. recognition of Cuba, she said, "I'd put Cuba in the baseball league and I think that probably solves it."

When conservatives tried to cut funding for public broadcasting, she accused them of trying to "pull the feathers out of Big Bird." Complaining about the slow pace of appointments to the Clinton administration in 1993, Schroeder said Defense Secretary Les Aspin had "fewer people at the Pentagon than Custer had at Little Bighorn."

In the midst of the sexual harassment controversy involving Sen. Robert Packwood, Schroeder noted, "Women who sleep around in this city are called sluts. Men who do it are called senators." Upon retiring from the House, Schroeder quipped: "I have spent 24 years in a federal institution."

When debate on completion of a child care assistance bill stalled in the House in 1990 amid an emotional dispute over minor details of the legislation, Schroeder spoke of her colleagues as if they were the children: "I think we're going to give everyone cookies and milk, put them down for a nap and then try again."

Former GOP Rep. Mickey Edwards of Oklahoma, who was president of the American Conservative Union, once sent House members a warning note: Be aware that the ACU is revising its rating system in order to give double weight to an upcoming vote on a key Reagan budget proposal. Edwards' expectation was that colleagues would want to vote with Reagan so they could look good in the ACU rating. "I certainly appreciate the tip," Schroeder replied. "I try to keep my American Conservative Union rating down to an absolute minimum."

Those who worked most closely with Schroeder say her lines were primarily her own creation, with occasional help from her administrative assistant, Dan Buck, who started with her in Denver shortly after she was elected in 1973 and came to Washington a few years later, where he remained until her retirement in January 1996—an unusually long tenure for Capitol Hill. Bearded and bespectacled with longish hair, Buck shared Schroeder's sense of humor and delighted in poking fun at conservatives, the status quo, and anything that might be considered hypocritical or stuffy. One of his responsibilities was to write and review testimony and speeches.

"Often I found the press to be very helpful in educating people about the issues I was trying to move forward.," Schroeder explained once. "If you could get journalists to write about issues, then eventually people might read about them and begin to move the body politic."

It wasn't long before there was an undercurrent of jealously among her colleagues about the amount of attention Schroeder received. Their pictures weren't on the cover of women's magazines on supermarket checkout stands. They didn't get photos of themselves with their kids in *People* magazine. Very few of them were invited on television talks shows as often as the congresswoman from Colorado.

"She was stealing their oxygen," Buck recalled. "But if they were adult about it they would know she was just good at it. There were certain members who would run over their grandmother to get in front of a camera. That wasn't her, but she knew how to say things that made them come alive, i.e., the soundbite, and so the press sought her out. . . . She was also accessible. You could get through to her in one phone call often."

There is no question that Schroeder's ability to wield political ridicule like a whip helped make her a media celebrity, but there were times when Schroeder would go too far in the eyes of many of her colleagues. She frequently referred to the House as "a coin-operated legislative machine." When she told *Newsweek* in 1989 that "everyone here checks their spines in the cloakroom," fellow Democrats were insulted and they let her know how they felt. Schroeder made the comment as Democrats were struggling with the ethics scandal that had embroiled House Speaker Jim Wright of Texas and that would ultimately lead to Wright's becoming the first Speaker in the history of the House to resign from office. The remark brought a rebuke from Democratic Rep. Tom Downey of New York, a liberal who had been a close ally of Schroeder's on arms control. First, Downey challenged Schroeder at a weekly closed-door meeting of the Democratic whip organization. Then he stated publicly, "Life is tough enough [in Congress] without other members dragging it down."

While her outspokenness may have made her some enemies inside Congress, it made her a hero to many reformers on the outside. "Many of us are very frustrated with the Congress and see it as a sea of midgets," said Gary Ruskin of the Ralph Nader–founded Congresswatch, which for many years pressed ethics complaints against members of Congress and publicly protested lawmakers' use of their offices for self-serving ends at the expense of taxpayers. "Pat Schroeder stood tall in a sea of midgets. She was willing more than many members to just tell the truth and say what was obvious."

One of the issues on which Schroeder consistently bucked the party leadership was congressional pay raises. House members hated to vote on pay raise legislation because a vote in favor of a pay raise is easy for political opponents to demagogue at home. Schroeder always opposed pay raises, even when the raises were tied to some other worthy effort. One example was House Speaker Tip O'Neill's attempt in 1977 to pass a congressional ethics reform package. O'Neill was under pressure to clean up some of the most egregious ethics conflicts that had come to light in the post-Watergate era. A special commission had recommended the House rules be changed to restrict the sources of outside income that lawmakers could earn. There should be limits on speaking fees and gifts from lobbyists, the commission said. Members should not be able to pay for personal expenses with campaign funds. And members should be required to publicly report their personal finances in far greater detail.

House rules cannot be changed except by a majority vote, but all the proposals were very unpopular with rank-and-file lawmakers. Some members felt that congressional salaries were too low and that speaking fees and other outside income were necessary to maintain a family and two residences—one in Washington and one in the district—in a style commensurate with their position. Others were simply loathe to give up perks. O'Neill, however, worked out a deal with members. In exchange for passing the ethics package, he would allow the pay raise to become law without a vote and would work to defeat any attempt to repeal it. On February 20, 1977, the raise went into effect, increasing members' salaries to $57,500. Three days later, the House passed the ethics package. This was one of the early tests of O'Neill's leadership, and he leaned heavily on rank-and-file lawmakers to support the measure. The key vote was on the rule permitting the ethics package to be brought up for debate and a vote. The rule was approved 267 to 153. The bill itself passed 402 to 22.

O'Neill delayed a vote on repealing the pay raise as long as he possibly could, but in July renegade lawmakers succeeded in bringing the issue to the floor. Democratic leaders portrayed the vote as an act of solidarity. Lawmakers who supported the repeal were described as selfish grandstanders who cared more about scoring political points than the good of the team. "You were told you were weak and cowardly if you didn't vote for it," Schroeder told Farrell, referring to Democrats like herself who favored repealing the pay raise. "There were none of us who didn't get leaned on."

The pay raise survived, 241 to 181, but Schroeder was among a handful of Democrats who voted against it. It was a popular position with the public, but it was also one of the things other members resented most about her. There was a feeling that she didn't need the raise as much as her male colleagues because she had a husband who was a lawyer, while other members had wives who generally did not work and they had to get by on one income.

"I was not rich, but I thought voting for our pay raises when we hadn't balanced the budget and done all sorts of other things we promised was the wrong priority," Schroeder said in an interview. "I thought we should do it when we fulfilled some of our other perennial promises."

In 1981, when House leaders engineered the quiet passage of a bill granting members an automatic seventy-five-dollars-a-day tax deduction for living expenses in Washington, Schroeder led the fight to repeal it. The effort earned Schroeder points with congressional watchdog groups and editorial writers who railed against the "special interest tax break." The public outcry was so great that the Senate repealed the tax break and the House agreed to a Schroeder amendment accepting the Senate repeal by a vote of 356 to 43. A few months later, when Republican Sen. Ted Stevens of Alaska proposed a federal commission to make a recommendation on congressional pay, Schroeder fought that proposal too. "I haven't seen any of these guys on street corners selling apples," Schroeder said, dismissing complaints of hardship.

Schroeder was also one of the few members of Congress who would publicly stick up for the rights of congressional employees. Congress had exempted itself from the Civil Rights Act of 1964 and the amendments to it that were included in the Equal Opportunities Act of 1972, which barred discrimination in hiring, firing, and promotions on the basis of sex, race, or age.

The rationale given by members of Congress for exempting themselves from these laws was that if they were applied to Congress they would violate the "separation of powers" principle of the Constitution—the federal branch should not be in the position of enforcing laws on Congress, which was an equal branch of government. However, many critics complained that congressmen and senators simply didn't want to have to abide by the laws they had imposed on the rest of government and the private sector. The House did passed its own nondiscrimination rule, but House rules are enforced by the Committee on Standards of Official Conduct and it was almost impossible for anyone but another House member to bring a complaint before the committee.

In 1978, Rep. Otto Passman, a Texas Democrat, fired his top aide, Shirley Davis, telling her quite plainly in a dismissal letter that he didn't believe women were physically capable of putting in the long hours he required and that he'd rather have a man for the job. If Davis had worked in the private sector or for any agency of the federal government except Congress, the letter would have been prima facie evidence of employment discrimination. Schroeder was the only member of the House to stand up for Davis, attending a fund raiser to help her raise money for a lawsuit against the congressman. Davis's lawsuit went all the way to the U.S. Supreme Court, which in 1979 overturned by a five-to-four vote a Court of Appeals ruling that Davis had no standing to sue. However, the question of whether Passman had violated Davis's rights was never decided because the aide and the congressman eventually settled the case privately for an undisclosed amount of money.

"My raising money to help her with legal costs and supporting her case caused many colleagues to shun me forever," Schroeder wrote in her memoirs. Later, Schroeder, along with Democrats Morris Udall of Arizona and Robert Drinan of Massachusetts, introduced a resolution to establish a protection and grievance procedure for House employees subject to job discrimination.

But as thorny and irritating as Schroeder could be at times, there developed as well a strong sense of appreciation and gratitude toward her in the Democratic ranks of the House. Many Democrats privately agreed with her criticisms of the institution even if they were unwilling to say so publicly themselves. When Schroeder turned her biting wit on Republicans, fellow Democrats took partisan pleasure in the GOP's discomfort. They were delighted when she labeled Ronald Reagan the "Teflon president," or when she accused George Bush of not knowing the purpose of a bar code at the supermarket.

As Schroeder came to be perhaps the best-known woman in Congress and a nationally recognized advocate for women's rights and children, she also became an asset to Democratic colleagues who wanted to energize the women's vote at election time or raise money for their campaigns. She was a headliner, and she was more willing than most members to travel all over the country to raise money and to campaign for her colleagues, from freshmen to committee chairmen.

"I think she probably drove the Democratic leadership crazy—a can't live with her, can't live without her kind of thing," said Louis "Kip" Cheroutes, who was an aide to Schroeder in Washington and then her district director. "She ignited, motivated a huge democratic constituency base, namely women. She was very valuable in that. At campaign time they would ask if she could show up and more often than not she would."

By all accounts, Schroeder had a nearly inhuman amount of energy. From very early on in her congressional career until her retirement, she was on an airplane traveling somewhere almost every single week, sometimes more than once a week. In 1996, she accepted forty-five trips paid for by outside interests—more than any other House member, according to an examination of congressional travel records by the Center for Public Integrity. That was fairly typical for her career. A similar study by Public Citizen in 1991 also listed Schroeder as number one, accepting ninety-eight trips paid for by outside interests in the previous two years. Of those trips, thirty-nine were to colleges and universities and twenty-eight were paid for by ideological or single-interest groups, usually liberal groups whose pocketbooks can't compare to those of business and industry. Those lists don't include government-paid trips, both foreign and domestic, on congressional business, which she also frequently took. "I've been every place on the planet where there is trouble," she once said, including Beirut, the Soviet Union, China, Thailand, Central America, Greece, Turkey, Israel, and an aircraft carrier in the Persian Gulf.

Schroeder tried to get back to Colorado twice a month, even if it meant leaving Washington on a predawn flight and returning the same day on the last flight out of Denver. In her travels, Schroeder thought nothing of scheduling a stopover for a few hours in a Democratic colleague's district in another state to attend a fund raiser or to hold a joint press conference. She made a special effort to help women running for Congress for the first time. Cynthia McKinney, a former House member from Georgia and an African American, recalled that while campaigning for Congress for the first time in 1992, she wasn't getting any help from Democratic party leaders in her state, who didn't take her candidacy seriously. She decided to write to all the women members of Congress for advice, but only two responded. One was Rep. Maxine Waters, a California Democrat. The other was Schroeder, who not only replied, but sent a campaign contribution and traveled to Georgia to campaign for her. "I love her," McKinney told John Brinkley of the *Rocky Mountain News.* "She was a role model for me even before I thought about running for Congress."

Sometimes it is the small things that make the most lasting impressions. Schroeder was in the habit of signing her name with a large P and drawing a smiley face inside. It was a reflection of nothing other than her whimsical humor, but it irritated her critics, particularly at the Pentagon and on the Armed Services Committee. They seemed to see it as confirmation that Schroeder wasn't really a serious legislator, that she didn't have the gravitas or intellectual heft to weigh in on such lofty issues as war and peace.

The irritation with Schroeder's girlish ways, as symbolized by the smiley-face signature, wasn't limited to the military and its supporters.

Even feminists and fellow Democrats would privately express frustration with her sometimes cutesy mannerisms, believing they detracted from her effectiveness and, because of Schroeder's high profile, provided ammunition to political opponents, who would dismiss her and, by extension, all feminists or all Democrats as frivolous.

Schroeder was aware of the criticism. The smiley-face signature was mentioned in numerous newspaper and magazine stories. "If Colorado Congresswoman Pat Schroeder ever wonders why some House members have trouble taking her seriously, maybe she should think about not signing her letters by filling in the 'P' with two eyes, a nose and a smile. After all, Pat, there are still those around who remember the time you walked into that intense hearing on the West Point cheating scandal and nearly drowned out witnesses by chomping into your ice cream cone," observed *Washington Post* style writer Nancy Collins in 1977. Even her friend, former NOW Legal Defense Fund media director Kathy Bonk, mentioned the signature in a 1987 article she wrote for the *Los Angeles Times* on Schroeder's abortive presidential bid:

"She's always liked doing things her own way. That smiley face, for instance, has jarred a lot of people—especially women's leaders around Washington who think it's inappropriate—but there's nothing to do about it. It's just Pat, the real Pat."

"I can blame that on my first-grade teacher," Schroeder explained to *Washington Post* gossip columnist Rudy Maxa in 1982. "There were four Pats in the class." So to distinguish herself from the others, Schroeder decorated her "P" with the smiling face and it became a lifelong habit. "It's really a hard habit to break when you start in the first grade," she told Maxa. But she ran into a roadblock when she was elected to Congress—the automatic signature machines used to sign official franked mail would not make the happy face. "They said, 'You can't do this—it's crazy, this is very official,'" Schroeder said. But she kept using the smiley face on everything she signed personally.

And then there was Schroeder's penchant for costumes. On St. Patrick's Day in Denver, she'd march in the parade wearing a crazy hat. On the Fourth of July one year, there was an Uncle Sam outfit. In her memoir, she includes a picture of herself, Jim, Scott, and Jamie dressed in Wild West costumes. "The best thing you could ever do as a staff person was wear a costume," said Kip Cheroutes, who ran Schroeder's district office. "There were a couple of campaigns where I would put on a gorilla suit and go marching around downtown with a Schroeder sign. She just thought that was the best thing in the world. You knew that to keep her spirits up and to be effective and to carry on the Schroeder wackiness, that this was something to do. . . . There was always this little girl inside her."

But in at least one instance, Schroeder's fascination with costumes rebounded on her. On an April 1979 Armed Services Committee trip to China, Schroeder donned an Easter bunny suit and passed out jelly beans and other candy to children at the U.S. embassy in Beijing. She also wore at least the head of the bunny suit—it was never exactly clear from news reports whether it was just the head or the head and the rest of the suit—during a visit to the Great Wall with the rest of the members of the congressional delegation. This was no simple costume, either. The bunny head was rather large with tall ears and certainly attention-grabbing. Before Schroeder got back to Washington, someone on the trip had tipped off the press to her bunny suit caper. Her office was bombarded with media calls. In the press reports, Schroeder's whimsy appeared flaky and foolish in light of the serious nature of the congressional mission to China.

Clearly embarrassed, Schroeder told two Denver reporters who came to her office to ask about the incident that it didn't happen the way it had been reported, that she had worn the bunny suit at the embassy with the children, but not earlier at the Great Wall. A big fuss about nothing, she implied. Both reporters wrote news stories based on her version of events. But after the stories were published in Denver, a photo turned up in the national media of Schroeder wearing at least the bunny head aboard the bus that took the congressional delegation to the Great Wall. "That's the only thing she ever did that really turned me off," said *Rocky Mountain News* political columnist Charlie Roos, one of the Denver reporters. "It isn't so much that she lied about it, but that she didn't tell the whole truth."

Unnoticed in all the uproar was that Schroeder had donned the bunny suit earlier that month to escort a "princess" from Colorado to one of the formal events held in conjunction with Washington's annual Cherry Blossom Festival, a duty that usually falls to the princess's local member of Congress. The festival committee told Schroeder that even though she had selected the princess—the young woman was her children's babysitter—she had to find someone else to escort her. "They said, 'No, you can't escort her in. It has to be a male member of Congress,'" Schroeder said. "So I thought I'd go as the male Easter rabbit." The stunt didn't attract much attention, but festival organizers did not appreciate her humor. "Obviously they never gave me another turn," she said. "I was written out of the Cherry Blossom Festival, which was just fine with me."

Schroeder's rhetorical style could also have a odd, Valley Girl flavor at times. On one occasion she ended a forceful, reasoned demand for U.S. allies to pick up a greater share of the defense burden or face trade tariffs with the declaration: "And if they don't like it, then tough munchies." She suggested replacing the national anthem with singer Aretha Franklin's *Respect* because the anthem is too hard to sing and Franklin's pop hit is what it's all about anyway. Commenting on the failure of presidential candidates to address issues of importance to women, she said: "It's just guy-ville. Women don't see anyone who talks like them."

Occasionally, her attempts to be clever would boomerang. In 1981, for example, Schroeder offered an amendment on the House floor, in a mock assault on Reagan, to bar presidents from seeking congressional votes by handing out presidential cufflinks to lawmakers or inviting them to barbecues at the White House. Schroeder then tried to withdraw the amendment, but Republicans turned the tables and blocked her, shouting down the amendment on a voice vote.

Schroeder's critics would seize on comments or incidents like these, using them to suggest that the Harvard-trained lawyer was somehow an intellectual lightweight or just plain goofy. "Over the years it has really annoyed me that she is called scatterbrained or flip," Jim Schroeder defended his wife to writer Susan Ferraro in 1990. "She has a commendable ability to simplify."

Like many accomplished public speakers, Schroeder had a tendency to embroider or embellish stories in an effort to make them more dramatic. Usually she followed fairly closely to the truth, but not always. The most glaring example is the story she has told many times over the years about being forced to share a chair with Ron Dellums at the Armed Services Committee.

On numerous occasions, Schroeder has said she and Dellums shared one chair for two years. For example, Schroeder told the National Press Club in 1996: "So Ron and I literally sat cheek to cheek for that first two years. It was very hard to retain dignity, and they were a very long, long two years. And many a day I used to think, 'What am I doing?'" That version of the story was reported over the years in several newspapers. "For two years, she and Ron Dellums, a Democrat from California, literally shared a single chair in the committee room," Rhea Becker wrote in the *Harvard University Gazette* after interviewing Schroeder in 1998. Likewise, David Wood of *Newhouse News Service* wrote in a 1996 profile, for which he interviewed Schroeder, that "for two years they [Schroeder and Dellums] were forced to physically squeeze into the same seat." Similar accounts have also appeared in the *Baltimore Sun* and the *Rocky Mountain News.*

While the incident with the chairs did indeed occur as Schroeder has often described, it lasted only one day, according to Dellums. "At the next meeting of Armed Services, we both had chairs, but our lack of welcome at the committee had been made abundantly clear," Dellums wrote in his memoir, *Lying Down with the Lions.*

Asked about the discrepancy, Schroeder said that the committee never did supply two chairs during those two years under Chairman Hebert. Rather, after the first meeting, she or Dellums would simply pull up a second chair from a row set aside for staff members when they were both present.

"I heard her tell time after time how for months at committee meetings she and Ron had to share a single chair. I don't believe that. I never believed that," Larsen said. "It's a prevarication that she insists upon."

Schroeder's personality turned out to be especially well suited to the role of the opposition party guerrilla fighter during the Reagan years. From her position on the Armed Services Committee, she was among a growing number of Democrats to caution against the excesses involved in Reagan's military buildup and to question Pentagon waste, fraud, and abuse. On the Post Office and Civil Service Committee, where she chaired the personnel subcommittee, Schroeder and her staff kept a close watch on the Reagan effort to remake the federal bureaucracy to suit the conservative ideology of the Republican grassroots. She repeatedly skirmished with Interior secretary James Watt, Environmental Protection Agency (EPA) administrator Anne Burford, and Office of Personnel Management director Donald Devine, as well as with lower-level Reagan political appointees caught abusing their power.

In 1982, while Reagan was seeking cuts in student aid, subsidized housing, and programs to enforce mine safety regulations, Schroeder proposed freezing the budget for the Executive Office of the President. She also accused Reagan of exaggerating how many women had been appointed to high-level jobs in his administration and provided statistics to back up the charge. She publicly protested administration actions that she said intentionally undermined enforcement of laws designed to promote equality for women.

"You have said that you are for equal rights and opportunities for women. Your administration's interpretation of laws Congress passed to insure those equal opportunities leads me to believe your words ring hollow," Schroeder said in a 1982 letter to Reagan. "Your administration is undermining the well-being of women in America."

In 1983, Schroeder used her civil service subcommittee to investigate allegations that EPA Administrator Burford and her subordinates had developed a "hit list" that they used to target senior career employees and members of scientific advisory boards for their political views. She successfully fought Reagan's efforts to limit pay and benefits for new postal employees, calling the move an obvious ploy to bust the postal unions. She tried to block an Education Department plan to require detailed background investigations of civil rights lawyers and investigators in the agency, saying the security investigations were designed to "scare employees, especially when they are ordered on a selective basis for employees already on the government payroll."

Schroeder also tried, with limited success, to increase protection for "whistleblowers" in the federal bureaucracy. She twice succeeded in passing legislation through the House to overhaul the process by which whistleblower grievances are dealt with to give additional recourse to employees fearful of harassment. She described the Office of Special Counsel of the Merit Systems Protection Board, which was supposed to protect whistleblowers, as a "joke." The first bill died in the Senate; the second was vetoed by Reagan. Finally, in the One Hundred First Congress, a compromise version was passed and signed into law by President Bush.

At the height of the antiapartheid movement in the mid- to late 1980s, Schroeder joined other members of Congress in efforts to pressure first Reagan and then Bush to take more aggressive action against the South African government. She marched, signed petitions, and met with black South African church leaders, including Anglican bishop Desmond Tutu. In January 1985, Schroeder was arrested along with a mayor and a state senator from Michigan, both black, in a peaceful demonstration outside the South African embassy in Washington. After they finished singing "We Shall Overcome," Schroeder and the two men were frisked, loaded into a police wagon, taken to a police substation, charged with demonstrating within 500 feet of an embassy, and released. Dozens of members of Congress and civil rights leaders were also arrested that winter and spring in demonstrations that took place nearly every day outside the embassy.

Apartheid "isn't just a black cause. This is for everyone," Schroeder said as she was arrested. "If we in the United States intend to be the leader of the free world . . . we cannot shut our eyes when members of our own free world family are ignoring very critical issues." When White House chief of staff Donald Regan suggested in 1986 that American women might not support economic sanctions against South Africa because they would have to "give up their diamonds," Schroeder angrily responded that it was more likely that Regan didn't want to give up eating South African lobster tails.

Schroeder's subcommittee staff kept a compendium of news clips, memos, and other background on scandals and embarrassments involving administration officials during the Reagan years, which they frequently shared with the media and staffers at Democratic campaign committees working on what is politely known in politics as "opposition research," or digging for dirt. When Bush succeeded Reagan as president, the compendium was enlarged to include the Bush years.

There has been a tendency to dismiss Schroeder's role during those years as simply one of a political gadfly. Yet that does a disservice to the role opposition parties play as a check on the abuse of power. Schroeder was very effective at times in that role because she understood how to focus public attention on an issue, sometimes forcing the administration to backpedal. Although Reagan remained personally popular, the Reagan years eventually came to be identified in the minds of many Americans with greed and excess, not only on Wall Street, but in government. Schroeder's public sparring with the administration certainly contributed to that perception.

But even in her role as Reagan watchdog, Schroeder sometimes went too far in the view of some of her colleagues. For example, Republican members of Congress particularly resented her ridicule of Health and Human Services secretary Richard Schweiker, a former GOP senator from Pennsylvania who was considered one of the few ideological moderates in the Reagan cabinet. In 1981, Schweiker, the nation's top welfare official, had the poor judgment to pose with his wife for the cover of *Dossier* magazine, a glossy, Washington-based society journal. In the photo, Schweiker is sitting in an ornate high-backed chair wearing white tie and tux, while his wife, Claire, is resplendent in a red Victorian ball gown. Together, they were the image of opulence at a time when Schweiker's department was being criticized for imposing draconian new rules allowing welfare families to own no more than $1,000 worth of nonessential items.

Schroeder seized on the photo, faxing a letter titled "The Two Sides of Reagan's America" to House colleagues. On one side of the letter was a copy of the magazine photo, while on the other was a cartoon portraying a poor grandma trudging off to the coal mines because of threatened Social Security cuts. The media had a field day. One pundit said Schweiker looked like "a robber-baron in a Thomas Nast cartoon."

It turned out that Schweiker had posed for the photo in connection with a fund raiser for juvenile diabetes, a cause with which he and his wife had long been associated. The tux was twenty years old, and Claire Schweiker's dress was borrowed. The photo was taken in a local historical mansion and the china, silver, and flowers were donated. House Republican leader Bob Michel of Illinois angrily fired back a letter to Schroeder complaining that her "insinuations" had been unfair. Rep. Henry Hyde, an Illinois Republican, took to the House floor, saying, "I know it is great fun to criticize the Reagan administration, but I wish they would not use the juvenile diabetes foundation to do it."

Was Schroeder's letter unfair? That question can probably be argued either way. Certainly Schroeder had ample reason from a liberal perspective to criticize Schweiker's lack of sensitivity to the plight of the poor. Whether she crossed the line of fair conduct in criticizing him personally is open to debate. It is clear, however, that the incident added to a perception among her political opponents that she was willing to take a cheap shot to further her goals.

While Schroeder was making her presence felt in Congress, she and Jim were struggling on the home front to balance the demands of two careers, a marriage, and children. The juggling act was especially difficult during Schroeder's early years in the House when the children were younger and the rhythms of congressional life were still new to her. "What the two of us desperately need is a wife," Schroeder told the *Houston Chronicle* her first month in office during an interview for a story about how she and Jim were coping with her new political career and raising children.

They couldn't get themselves a "wife," but they did hire a full-time, live-in housekeeper. Instead of home-cooked meals, they opted for an extensive list of take-out restaurants and dinners in the members' dining room of the House or at Capitol Hill restaurants. Schroeder kept crayons in her desk for when her children would come to visit and taped their artwork to her wall. During her first term, she would tuck clean training pants for Jamie into her briefcase alongside her schedule and speeches. She toilet-trained her daughter in the restrooms of her congressional office building. One of Scott's birthday parties was hastily moved to the House dining room when an urgent hearing came up. The congresswoman served the children peanut butter sandwiches under crystal chandeliers as they watched a hired magician and a clown.

"Children don't really care how clean their bedroom is and whether you did their laundry and hand-folded it," Schroeder said. Instead of shopping trips to the mall, Schroeder would buy everything she could, except shoes, by telephone and through catalogues. On business trips, especially trips abroad, she would find time whenever possible to go shopping, hiding gifts throughout the year in a closet in her office to bring out at Christmas or for birthdays.

During an interview in March 1976 at a Detroit airport en route to Denver, reporter Judith Serrin noted that Schroeder was toting a white suitcase packed with chocolate bunnies, horns, and a Black Beauty record—gifts she was hiding from the children until Easter. Hardly professional, Schroeder acknowledged, but absolutely essential.

"It was always very hard," Schroeder told the *Chicago Tribune* in 1985. "I always wondered what the next day would bring." Fortunately, she said, her children were "terribly" healthy, and Jim was "very" flexible.

In a two-profession home, one partner has to "accept a subordinate role," Jim told *United Press International*'s Iris Krasnow. "In the early days, my career was the primary career. When my wife was elected to Congress, there was a shift and hers became the primary career, which meant I ended up making more accommodations. . . . It was tough, earlier in our marriage, when we first came to Washington and the children were two and six. We had to scramble a lot."

Part of Schroeder's strategy for keeping her family together was to include them in her work, especially when she was traveling. She took them to peace conferences in Europe and refugee camps in Thailand. There were Christmas parties and summer barbecues at the White House. On one White House visit, Jamie complained to First Lady Rosalynn Carter: "This is the third time you've served brownies with nuts in them and we've told you we don't like nuts in our brownies."

Schroeder had only been in the House a year when Jim and the children accompanied her to a SALT (Strategic Arms Limitation Treaty) disarmament conference in Geneva, Switzerland. By the time Schroeder had been in the House a decade, twelve-year-old Jamie and sixteen-year-old Scott had been on many trips through Europe and the Far East. At the height of the cold war, years before the fall of the Berlin Wall, the family took a car trip through East Germany, stopping at Goslar, a fairy tale town of cobbled streets and gothic churches that was spared Allied bombing during World War II because it had been declared a hospital zone and pilots could see red crosses on every roof. "We treated my job as a seminar," Schroeder said. "My children were encouraged to be part of my political life, but only if they wanted to."

Over the years, Scott and Jamie accompanied their mother to dozens of receptions, picnics, committee hearings, press conferences, and other events. In 1983, Schroeder took Scott with her when the Motion Picture

Association of American invited members of Congress to preview the motion picture *Wargames* about a teenage computer whiz who accidentally accesses the Pentagon's master nuclear weapons computer, nearly setting off World War III. At age eight, Jamie hobnobbed with members of Congress and the Carter administration at a reception for the women's caucus in the spectacular reception room of the Organization for American States. That same year, Jamie testified before the White House Conference on Families about a survey she had taken of her fellow third-graders on the topic of work and family.

Jim managed his "spouse of" role with humor and self-deprecation, claiming to feel only pride when he was introduced as "Pat Schroeder's husband." His usual response when asked how he handled the role of obscure spouse was: "We say that Pat has gone a long way on my name." Indeed, it was Jim who urged his wife to get into politics in the first place, Jim who urged her to reach for the presidency and the vice presidency, and Jim who sought to discourage her from leaving Congress when she was leaning toward retiring. Given that he was fascinated with politics long before his wife's first election, some of Jim Schroeder's support is no doubt attributable to a vicarious enjoyment of the national political scene. He never appeared nettled by his wife's success and sometimes seemed even to revel in it.

During the 1980s, Jim became a founding member of the so-called "Denis Thatcher Society," which was a fraternity only in jest dreamt up by Charles Horner for the husbands of powerful women. Horner's wife, Constance, held several high-profile positions in the Reagan and Bush administrations, including director of the Office of Personnel Management and undersecretary of the Department of Health and Human Services. The society was named for the endearingly obscure husband of British prime minister Margaret Thatcher, and its password was "Yes, dear." Its members met a few times for lunch at private clubs to which their wives belonged. On at least one occasion, Jim joined fellow society members at Washington's elite Cosmos Club, where they signed the check in Mrs. Horner's name.

Although satirical, the society became the subject of several news stories. *People* magazine even photographed Jim sitting outside the British embassy with cutouts of the Thatchers. As a result of the media attention, Jim Schroeder and Charles Horner received an invitation from the embassy to meet the real Denis Thatcher during a visit to Washington. After shaking hands with Thatcher on a receiving line at a reception, the two men quickly explained their society to its namesake. Thatcher's only response was a characteristically reserved "Indeed?"

5

In the Trenches

Not long after joining the House Armed Services Committee, Schroeder and navy captain Jim Bush flew from Washington to Norfolk, Virginia, for a series of special background briefings by the navy on how its ships and manpower were deployed and what its future needs would be. Schroeder had recently hired Bush to handle defense issues for her. The other committee members had gone to Norfolk for the same briefings a few weeks earlier, but because of a conflict in her schedule, Schroeder had arranged to receive the briefings separately.

After a full day of meetings, Schroeder and Bush returned to Washington late that night. Shortly after he arrived home, Bush got a call at home from the admiral in charge of the Norfolk naval shipyard, whom he knew well. The admiral just wanted Bush to know that Armed Services chairman F. Edward Hebert had called him before Schroeder's visit and had essentially ordered him "not to tell her anything" in the briefings. In other words, navy officials were to be polite and to go through the motions, but not to impart anything of significance. The admiral, who was a friend of Bush's, decided to ignore Hebert's command and give Schroeder the full briefing, but he wanted Bush to know of the chairman's order.

Hebert's blatant attempt to thwart a committee member's seeking information would normally be outside the bounds of accepted congressional behavior, but it was in keeping with the hostile reception Schroeder received after she lobbied her way onto the committee in 1973. That animosity extended beyond Hebert to some of her more conservative colleagues on the committee and to many quarters of the Pentagon as well. Years after Hebert was no longer chairman, Schroeder still had to push harder than most other committee members to get the same basic information and cooperation from the Pentagon. "They just wanted to push Pat aside in the beginning, and she wasn't willing to be pushed," Bush said.

It was clear to Schroeder that her more hawkish colleagues would try to undermine her effectiveness by portraying her as ignorant of defense issues because she was a woman, because she had never served in the military, and because she was new to Congress. Schroeder fought back by using her office budget to hire her own defense expert rather than relying on the committee's staff or the Pentagon for information as did most committee members. Bush's background was in nuclear submarines and strategic forces. Like future president Jimmy Carter, he was one of "Rickover's boys," the brainy subordinates of Adm. Hyman G. Rickover, the father of the nuclear navy. He was also an unabashed liberal who felt passionately about reforming the Pentagon. At the time he joined Schroeder's staff, he had recently separated from the navy after a bout with cancer.

There were forty-three members of the House Armed Services Committee in 1973, few of whom questioned the status quo. For the most part, they were seasoned conservatives who had joined the committee so they could rattle their sabers, bring home defense contracts, and protect military bases in their districts. For generations the committee had been run by southern reactionaries like Hebert of Louisiana, L. Mendel Rivers of South Carolina, and Carl Vinson of Georgia. Slurs about "pinko-commie kooks" were commonplace. On one occasion, when Schroeder was pressing for answers about U.S. bombing raids in Cambodia, Hebert told her: "I wish that you'd support our boys like you support the enemy."

There was a cultural as well as an ideological gulf between the old guard and new upstarts on the committee. "You had to look at the 1973 makeup of that committee," Schroeder said. "They were all basically from the South. On Memorial Day they would start wearing little white suits. They looked like a bunch of ice cream salesmen. Ron [Dellums] and I used to laugh that you needed simultaneous translation to even understand what they were saying."

The only other women members of the committee in the 1970s were Republican Marjorie Sewell Holt and Democrat Beverly Barton Butcher Byron, both of Maryland. Holt, who joined the Armed Services Committee the same year as Schroeder and Dellums, received a much warmer welcome from its hawkish members because of her zealous support for greater military spending and because she was seen as a counter to feminists like Schroeder.

Holt was best known when she entered Congress as a hard-right crusader on social issues like abortion and school busing. In her first term in the House, she won passage of an amendment prohibiting the federal government from withholding funds from school districts that refused to meet desegregation standards. She called the Justice Department's desegregation policies "the new racism." On Armed Services, Holt was a strong supporter of the MX missile, the B-1 bomber, and Reagan's "Star Wars" space-based missile defense plan, and an opponent of a nuclear weapons freeze—almost the mirror opposite of Schroeder.

Holt set her sights on becoming a member of Congress when she was in junior high school. She was one of only five women in her graduating class at the University of Florida College of Law in 1949. After practicing law in Florida, she moved to Anne Arundel County, Maryland, with her husband, an electrical engineer with Westinghouse. She arrived in Congress at age fifty-two after long years of paying party dues as a precinct leader, local campaign organizer, elections supervisor, and circuit court clerk.

Unlike Holt and Schroeder, Beverly Byron stepped into the House as if by right. The daughter of Gen. Dwight Eisenhower's aide-de-camp during World War II, she grew up in Washington, attended prestigious private schools, and met her future husband, Goodloe Byron, while in high school. After briefly attending Hood College, she devoted herself to advancing her husband's political career and to civic activities.

Goodloe Byron was the scion of two socially prominent and politically connected Maryland families. His maternal great-grandfather, Louis Emory McComas, was a Republican congressman and senator from Maryland in the 1880s and early 1900s. His father, Congressman William Devereux Byron, a Democrat, was killed in a plane crash in 1941, and his mother, Katharine Edgar Byron, was elected with the support of local party leaders to complete her husband's term.

After a career in the Maryland legislature, Goodloe Byron was elected to the House in 1970 and easily reelected three times. In a case of history's repeating itself, Goodloe Byron dropped dead of a heart attack while jogging in October 1978, a month before election day, when he certainly would have won another term. His wife, Beverly, was the unanimous choice of Democratic leaders to take his place, and she was elected virtually without opposition.

Beverly Byron joined the Armed Services Committee six years after Schroeder and Holt. Although she was a Democrat, Byron was a conservative and an ardent supporter of increased defense spending, closer ideologically to Holt than to Schroeder. Byron went on to win reelection six times, serving fourteen years in the House before she was defeated by a primary opponent in 1992.

Schroeder, Holt, and Byron were outnumbered better than twelve to one by their male colleagues during their early years on the Armed Services Committee. Three more congresswomen join the committee in the 1980s: Democrat Marilyn Lloyd of Tennessee in 1983, and Republican Lynn Martin of Illinois and Democrat Barbara Boxer of California in 1985.

When Schroeder was elected to the House, defense spending accounted for about 40 percent of the national budget. "I wanted to see more money for daycare centers, more money for bilingual education, more money for food stamps," she wrote. "I realized I would be criticized as a big spender. I would be asked where I'd get the money. Well, the money is in Armed Services, so I went there."

While hawkish Southerners dominated the committee, there were also a handful of critics of wasteful defense spending, including Democrat Les Aspin of Wisconsin. Before his election to the House in 1970, Aspin had worked as an economist at the Pentagon and as an aide to Sen. William Proxmire of Wisconsin, who was famous for his zeal for cutting government waste. Aspin would eventually chair the Armed Services Committee and go on to become President Clinton's first secretary of defense.

In a scathing article she wrote for *The Nation* her first year in office, Schroeder said the committee treated Pentagon witnesses with "a deference bordering on adulation." The Defense Department and the committee were obsessed with building bigger and more powerful weaponry, she said, never stopping to ask whether it should be built at all. "What comes into play is the military equivalent of the Peter Principle: the capacity of American technology to produce a particular system governs the nature of the Pentagon's request."

"My constituents elected me to work for sensible changes now, not 20 years from now," Schroeder wrote. "I did not keep my views on runaway military budgets secret in Denver. There is no reason why I should keep them secret in Washington."

The committee was heavily dependent on the Defense Department for any analysis. In her memoirs, Schroeder recalled: "I thought the Constitution's system of checks and balances meant that Congress was to oversee other branches of government and act if they were out of control, but Armed Services under Hebert was just a mouthpiece for the military. . . . We had the fewest number of staffers of any congressional committee. The attitude was, 'What would we use them for?' The Pentagon justified its most extravagant costs with 'the Russians are coming' logic: Either the Russians were doing it, so we had to keep up, or the

Russians were not doing it, so we had to stay ahead. Oversight and analysis were not the committee's mission."

Obviously such dissident views were not warmly received. Hebert wasn't above manipulating the committee's rules of procedure to silence liberals like Schroeder and Dellums. In response, Dellums began bringing a copy of the House rules to committee meetings with him. "Pat Schroeder and I were waging a lonely battle against the insanity of the nuclear arms race, unneeded weapons systems, wasteful procurement practices, and a bloated military budget that was helping to bleed our cities of vitally needed sustenance," Dellums wrote.

But the balance of power in the House shifted sharply in the wake of the post-Watergate Democratic landslide of the 1974 election, and Hebert was one of the casualties of the new order. The election swept sixty-nine Democratic freshmen into the House—more than a third of the caucus. "The Watergate class," as they were called, were far more skeptical of the congressional seniority system and far more impatient with the old ways of doing business than their more senior colleagues. The freshmen banded together, opening an office and hiring a staff before they were even sworn in. They were ready to shake up the House.

The militant freshmen of the Ninety-fourth Congress caught Democratic leaders by surprise by forging an alliance with rank-and-file liberals in the House, giving them the votes necessary to dominate the caucus. At the top of the freshmen's agenda was breaking the grip of the old South on power as wielded by the committee chairmen. Ways and Means Committee Chairman Wilbur Mills of Arkansas had already sealed his fate by getting caught a month before the election carousing with Argentine stripper Fanne Foxe, whom U.S. Park Police fished from the Tidal Basin on the Mall in Washington after she had jumped from the congressman's Lincoln Continental.

In January 1975, the freshmen-liberal alliance, which included Schroeder, turned their attention to the other chairmen. Their top targets were Hebert; Agriculture Chairman Bob Poage of Texas, who favored farm subsidies over food stamps; Banking Chairman Wright Patman of Texas, an aging populist; and Appropriations Chairman George Mahon of Texas, who had opposed civil rights legislation and Lyndon Johnson's Great Society programs.

Under House rules, chairmen are elected at the start of each two-year congress by a vote of either the Democratic caucus or the Republican conference, depending on which party was in the majority. Before 1975, the choice of chairmen was almost always based on seniority and challenges were rare. The Watergate freshmen, however, had the audacity to call the current chairmen in one at a time for interviews with the class and to ask the legislative potentates to justify being allowed to keep their seats of power.

Hebert, who had declined to hold hearings on the bombing of Cambodia and had voiced his belief that the United States should have prosecuted the war in Vietnam more aggressively, was clearly out of step with the new majority. During his interview, the septuagenarian called the freshmen "boys and girls." His treatment of Schroeder and Dellums, particularly the chair incident and his refusal to approve Schroeder's inclusion in a U.S. delegation to SALT talks in Europe, was cited as evidence of his lack of fitness to continue to serve as chairman.

Mahon was more respectful and congenial when he met with the freshmen and he survived, although he retired at the end of the Ninety-fourth Congress. Three chairman—Poage, Patman, and Hebert—were defeated. Hebert's losing margin was the widest, 152 to 133.

Hebert was replaced with a more malleable chairman, Democrat Melvin Price of Illinois, who was next in seniority. First elected to the House during World War II, Price was a former baseball writer from East St. Louis who was more comfortable talking about the St. Louis Cardinals than about the defense budget. He bent over backwards to be fair to committee members, even at the risk of diluting his power as chairman. He created temporary subcommittees and handed them over to those lowest in seniority. Not long after he took over, Price invited Dellums to his office. "I feel badly about the way you've been treated," Price told him. "I want to assure you that I will deal with you with respect and will respect your rights and prerogatives as a member." To Dellums, it was a dramatic and much appreciated change.

However, it was a change in style, not in substance. Although not an autocrat, Price was nearly as conservative and tradition-bound as Hebert on defense issues. He believed strongly in the use of nuclear power both for military and civilian purposes. He was the coauthor of the Price-Anderson Act, which protected the nuclear power industry by limiting its financial liability in the event of an accident. For the next decade, the committee would continue under Price's leadership to reflexively support the Pentagon's view, to reward defense contractors who contributed generously to their political committees, and to protect military bases at home from cost-cutting measures.

The change in chairmen didn't affect Schroeder's style. Just as she had openly challenged Democratic House leaders and Hebert, Schroeder didn't hesitate to publicly confront her committee colleagues when she disagreed with them and to lay bare their secrets before the news media. No congressional vice, no matter how long-standing or widely accepted, was immune to criticism from the gentlewoman from Colorado. In 1976, for example, Schroeder and Democratic Rep. Bob Carr of Michigan went so far as to stage a sit-in during a closed-door House-Senate conference committee meeting on the annual military procurement bill. The rebels were upset by the time-honored practice of earmarking pork barrel projects for political contributors and other favored interests during conferences of the House and Senate defense committees, away from the scrutiny of the public and the press. (Conferences are held to iron out differences after the House and Senate have passed separate bills. It is the last step in the legislative process before final votes of the House and Senate.)

"Bob and I knew what they were doing," Schroeder said. "They would tell everybody that they were deciding what should be in the budget based upon the [military] threat and yet we had sat there and listened to them talk about how many tickets did [defense contractors] buy to fund raisers. 'All right, then we're going to give Boeing their planes.' It was really corrupt and we were really appalled."

Defense bill conference committees are usually made up of only the senior members of the House and Senate armed services committees plus a few other lawmakers selected by the respective chairmen. Neither Schroeder nor Carr had been given a seat on the military procurement conference committee that year, but they decided to attend its meetings anyway. The congressmen and senators on the committee were aware that the pair's purpose was to expose lucrative political favors hidden in the bill's fine print. Despite pleas from then Majority Leader Tip O'Neill not to provoke a confrontation, Hebert—who was no longer chairman, but was still a senior member of the committee—and Rep. Samuel Stratton, a hawkish Democrat from New York, tried to have the Senate sergeant of arms physically evict the pair from the meeting, which was being held on the Senate side of the Capitol. When that didn't work, the conference members canceled the meeting.

"I remember old [South Carolina senator] Strom Thurmond, I thought he was going to have a heart attack. 'Get them out of here. Get them out of here.' His temples were pounding," Schroeder said. "Of course we also talked to the press about it, which made them even crazier because they kept thinking we would be so ashamed that we didn't look professional that we wouldn't talk to the press. We thought, 'Oh, bullshit!

You guys are just awful.' So it was a little game that went on all year long. Wherever they went, we tried to find them."

Schroeder and other doves on the committee could rail against the system, but their victories were rare. For example, the same year they staged the sit-in, Schroeder, Carr, and Democratic Rep. Tom Downey of New York collaborated on a harshly worded minority report to the military authorization bill accusing the Ford administration of trying to "spook" the American people into approving higher military spending by telling "goblin stories" about the Soviet military threat. The report accused the Pentagon of staging a campaign using misleading statistics designed to magnify Soviet capability and minimize that of the United States. They urged the Congress to reject military spending "for the sake of military spending." Their report drew media attention and may have even changed some opinions, but there was no reordering of priorities either in Congress or at the Pentagon.

Year after year, Schroeder unsuccessfully offered amendments to cut money from the annual defense authorization and defense appropriations bills. Opposed to the draft, she offered an amendment on the House floor in 1979 to take out a provision in a bill approved by the Armed Services Committee that would have established a registration system for eighteen-year-olds. She won, but the victory was short-lived. The following year President Carter endorsed a registration system similar to the proposal killed by Schroeder's amendment, and it became law. In 1980, she was one of just three dissenters on a massive weapons procurement bill that she said had "become the tool of vested economic interests." In 1982, she offered an amendment to cut U.S. troop commitments abroad in half over the next four years, but drew only eighty-seven votes.

The early Reagan years were particularly lonely for liberals like Schroeder. A majority of the Congress shared Ronald Reagan's concern that U.S. military strength had deteriorated to a dangerous point and needed rebuilding. Pentagon supporters argued that in the years following the Vietnam War, the Soviets had increased their conventional and strategic forces to a point that put the United States at grave risk. Schroeder stood unwavering against the pro-defense spending tide. "If it's designed to shoot or fly or go boom," she once said, "we'll buy it." In 1981, the House defeated a Schroeder amendment that would have directed the Pentagon to identify $8 billion in wasteful spending and then cut it. "It is $8 billion," she told the House, "out of a projected $1.5 trillion that we are moving to spend over the next five years. I think that is a very small amount."

Columnist Colman McCarthy described her effort in the *Washington Post:*

Schroeder, in the style of generals and admirals who storm congressional committees with their arsenals of charts and graphs, had her own visual display: forty-four General Accounting Office reports that documented $16 billion worth of defense waste in one recent eighteen-month period. . . . She told of a 1980 Republican Study Committee report that found $16 billion of Pentagon waste. (She) called attention to the April *U.S. News and World Report* article, "Billions Down the Pentagon Drain," that spoke of the military's "apparent penchant for squandering money on a staggering scale." During the debate, Schroeder, as if to emphasize that she had not gone half-mad against American militarism, said that she wanted the administration only to look for the fat. If it is discovered, she said, that "there is not enough waste to total $8 billion, then let's stop looking."

Speaking in support of Schroeder's amendment, Dellums told the House that in his eight years on the Armed Services Committee, "We have never held a hearing on the general subject of waste, fraud and abuse." The amendment was trounced 276 to 142. That afternoon Congress approved by 354 to 63 a $136 billion weapons procurement bill that was a 32 percent increase, the highest defense spending increase in U.S. history up till that time. The sentiment carrying the day, according to McCarthy, was best summed up by Stratton, who told the House: "Instead of telling the secretary of defense that we ought to try to find some way of cutting the defense budget by $8 billion, we ought to be backing him up in this great effort to give us a defense bill that will overcome some of our obvious vulnerabilities. We are $240 billion behind the Soviet Union, and if we want any kind of balance with the Soviets we have got to catch up and catch up fast."

Schroeder was back the following year with more proposals to cut defense spending. She delivered copies of her alternative defense budget to reporters while standing in front of a battery of TV cameras outside the Pentagon within eyeshot of Defense Secretary Caspar Weinberger's office. Her budget, she told them, would save $13.4 billion and still build "a strong America" by improving the readiness of existing forces while making major cuts in costly new weapons systems like the MX mobile missile. Among other things, her plan would have eliminated all funds for the B-1 bomber, which was a centerpiece of the Reagan administration's long-term plan for strengthening U.S. strategic weaponry. "The fault of my party was not going after waste and abuse in social programs," Schroeder said. "The Reagan administration is doing the same thing in the military."

There were some victories. Schroeder led the successful effort in the House to pass a proposal by Democratic Sen. Sam Nunn of Georgia to force the Pentagon to report weapons cost overruns to Congress on a regular basis. She said it was time to tell the Defense Department that Congress would not tolerate deliberately low estimates of costs. "We want an explanation so we can explain to the taxpayer what is happening to their very precious tax dollar," Schroeder said.

Unlike some Democrats, Schroeder was never troubled about being viewed as soft on defense. She called defense contractors "the welfare queens of the '80s" and said the Reagan administration thought "arms control" meant "deodorant."

"We have all become afraid of being called a wimp," Schroeder said, arguing against the MX missile in 1985. "Our constituents are going to think we are the weak ones if we cannot possibly stand on our two legs and talk back."

By the mid-1980s, however, support for bigger and bigger defense budgets was weakening. The federal budget deficit was soaring and tales of Pentagon waste, fraud, and abuse had become legend—$300 hammers and $700 toilet seats. Critics, including a growing number of Republicans, were demanding that the military bear its share of budget cuts.

The time was also ripe for another coup on the Armed Services Committee, this time led by Aspin, who was recognized as a leading authority on defense policy. With the help of moderates and liberals, including Schroeder, Aspin leapfrogged over five more senior members to replace the ailing, eighty-year-old Price despite Price's support from the Democratic leadership. Tip O'Neill, now Speaker of the House, made an impassioned speech urging the caucus to reelect Price. He ultimately lost by three votes. The ouster of the aging Price was awkward and embarrassing compared to the revolt that toppled Hebert. There was none of the animosity toward Price that there had been toward Hebert, but there was a sense among Democrats that the committee was drifting toward the right under his leadership, while the caucus was leaning increasingly to the left.

Despite his history as a critic of Pentagon waste, Aspin was the candidate of the middle ground. He tried to reach out to liberals while preserving the panel's pro-military stance. Aspin and Nunn believed that the

Democratic party needed to change its anti-defense image, to become advocates for a leaner, smarter, more effective military. But only a few months after his election as chairman in January 1985, Aspin came to the aid of the multiwarhead MX missile, one of the Reagan administration's top priorities. Many liberals who had backed Aspin for chairman thought the MX was too expensive and disruptive of the relationship between the United States and the Soviet Union. His brokering of a compromise to save the MX was a deep disappointment to them.

Even though military contractors in suburban Denver would have benefited from the program, Schroeder opposed the MX on the grounds that it was wasteful and that the fixed silos were sitting targets for enemy attacks. Supporters contended fear of the MX missile would make the Soviets more willing to make concessions in arms control negotiations.

Schroeder's support for Aspin's bid to become chairman wound up costing her the chairmanship of the Armed Services personnel subcommittee. Aspin had been chairman of that subcommittee, but tradition obliged him to give up the post when he became chairman of the full committee. Schroeder was the next most senior member of the subcommittee, but when she tried to claim the chairmanship on the basis of her seniority, many members of the committee found the argument ironic and somewhat hypocritical given her support of Aspin's leap to the top over more senior members. Subcommittee chairmanships are determined by a majority vote of the majority party's members of the committee, as opposed to full committee chairmanships, which are voted upon by all the majority party's members in the House. In the smaller group, conservatives had control, throwing their support behind Beverly Byron of Maryland, who had six years less seniority than Schroeder but was staunchly conservative on defense issues. Ultimately, neither Schroeder nor Byron won the post. Aspin decided to end the fight by breaking tradition and keeping the personnel chairmanship himself.

In 1987, an unusual coalition of liberal Democrats and Pentagon loyalists tried to strip Aspin of the chairmanship. The liberals felt betrayed by Aspin's rescue of the MX missile and his support for U.S. aid to the Contras, who were trying to overthrow the communist government of Nicaragua. He temporarily lost the chairmanship by a vote of the Democratic caucus, but he came back a few weeks later, winning a second vote. Again, Schroeder backed Aspin.

It wasn't until 1989 that Schroeder was able to claim an Armed Services subcommittee chairmanship: military installations. By this time, power on the committee had shifted to the new breed of Pentagon critics. Dellums, who was opposed to every aspect of President Bush's strategic weapons modernization program, headed the important research and development subcommittee. Rep. Nicholas Mavroules of Massachusetts, an unabashed military reformer, was in charge of the investigations subcommittee, where he used his new position to probe army aviation fatalities and to prod the military into greater efforts to combat drug smuggling.

That same year, reflecting the breakup of the Soviet Union, Schroeder was part of a move by reformers to redirect defense spending away from weapons systems based on a U.S.-Soviet cold war. The House's 1990 defense authorization bill—which slashed money for two ICBMs, the B-2 stealth bomber, and the "Star Wars" missile defense system—was derisively labeled a "Michael Dukakis defense bill" by Aspin, referring to the liberal 1988 Democratic presidential candidate and former Massachusetts governor. Still, it was not surprising that after winning the presidency in 1992, Bill Clinton tapped Aspin to be secretary of defense. Clinton was a "new Democrat" who favored the moderate Nunn-Aspin approach.

That left Dellums, who twenty years earlier had had to fight his way onto the committee, the senior Democrat on the committee. In January 1993, he was elected the Armed Services chairman. "Eddie Hebert must be spinning in his grave," Schroeder said wryly.

Meanwhile, Schroeder moved over to the chairmanship of the more desirable research and technology subcommittee, where she supported programs to help defense contractors convert military technology to domestic use, such as night-vision goggles for police. "You will find our average law enforcement officer kind of still looks like Wyatt Earp, only he's got a car instead of a horse," Schroeder said. "There is any number of things that we have in the defense inventory that can be applied to much better law enforcement."

Shortly after Bill Clinton's election in 1992, Schroeder's was one of the loudest voices urging the president to move quickly to lift the ban on gays and lesbians serving in the military. With more gays coming out of the closet, the issue of gays in the military had been drawing increasing public attention. Horrific stories of violence against gay servicemen, including the beating death of navy seaman Allen Schindler by fellow sailors in Sasebo, Japan, had become a cause célèbre for gay Americans. The media highlighted cases of model servicemen and servicewomen, like navy petty officer Keith Meinhold, who were drummed out of the military for no other reason than their sexual orientation. Clinton had staked out his position on gays in uniform during an appearance at Harvard's Kennedy School of Government in October 1991, promising to do for gays what Harry Truman had done for blacks in 1948—eliminate the military's discrimination policies by executive order. His position drew relatively modest attention at the time.

In the first weeks of his administration, under pressure from gay and lesbian rights activists and their supporters in Congress, Clinton publicly stated his intention to fulfill his promise. Schroeder and Democrat Gerry Studds of Massachusetts, one of two openly gay members of the House, collected the signatures of fifty House members in support of Clinton's stand. But the Joint Chiefs of Staff, led by Chairman Colin Powell, threatened to resign as a group if Clinton chose an unacceptable plan for legitimizing the military status of gays. Schroeder had questioned Powell about his position at an Armed Services Committee hearing the year before. Powell had replied that he considered homosexual behavior to be inconsistent with maintaining good order and discipline. Wouldn't such thinking have kept Powell, a black man, out of the mess hall not so many years earlier in the name of good order and discipline? Schroeder asked. "Skin color is a benign, non-behavioral characteristic," Powell replied. "Sexual orientation is perhaps the most profound of human behavioral characteristics. The comparison of the two is a convenient but invalid argument."

Nunn publicly warned Clinton that Republicans would attempt to repeal any executive order and that they had enough support from conservative and moderate Democrats to override a presidential veto. Eventually, Clinton settled for a compromise proposed by Nunn that became known as "don't ask, don't tell." It was supposed to eliminate anti-gay regulations and witch hunts, allowing gays and lesbians to continue to serve, but only if they kept their sexual identity secret. In fact, the new policy was a sham, a face-saving gesture for a president who had been forced to back down. It did not change the section of the Uniform Code of Military Justice that makes sodomy a crime. Forcible discharges of gay personnel soared after the new policy went into effect. The president appeared to both supporters and opponents alike to be backpedaling on a matter of principle. It was a major setback, stealing the new president's momentum.

Republicans used the issue to portray Clinton as a liberal out of step with mainstream American values, and it served two years later as ammunition for Newt Gingrich's Republican revolution when the GOP took control of both the House and the Senate for the first time in forty years. The new GOP House majority was committed to increasing defense spending. Once again, the committee was dominated by defense hawks.

Throughout her political career, Schroeder was closely identified with the U.S. peace movement, first as an opponent of the Vietnam War in the early 1970s, then as a supporter of a nuclear weapons freeze in the late '70s and early '80s, and again in the late 1980s as a leading proponent of a moratorium on nuclear weapons testing.

The concept of a mutual U.S.-Soviet freeze on the production and deployment of nuclear weapons and their delivery systems had been floated during the Johnson administration and was reintroduced by antinuclear activists and antimilitarists in 1979. The movement took off first in Europe in the summer of 1980, when hundreds of thousands of Germans, French, Britons, and others joined antinuclear demonstrations triggered by the U.S. government's desire to locate short-range nuclear missiles in Western Europe. Alarmed by Reagan's militaristic rhetoric, the movement quickly spread to the United States and mushroomed seemingly overnight. On July 12, 1982, over half a million people joined a demonstration in New York City in favor of a freeze. Eight states, forty-three towns, cities, and counties, and the District of Columbia passed referenda in support of a freeze in the 1982 election.

The nuclear freeze movement was particularly strong in Denver and nearby Boulder. One of the lead organizers of the movement was Pamela Solo, a former nun in the order of the Sisters of Loretto, a Catholic religious community founded on the Kentucky frontier in 1812 that has embraced liberal causes ranging from improving the conditions of migrant workers to support for the victims of torture by oppressive Latin American regimes. Solo also managed Schroeder's 1980 and 1982 reelection campaigns.

The nuclear freeze movement helped nudge the Reagan administration and the Soviets away from their strategy of mutual nuclear deterrence. On March 23, 1983, Reagan abandoned nuclear deterrence as a legitimate public policy in an address to the nation in which he condemned deterrence as immoral and committed himself to making nuclear weapons obsolete. However, the plan he announced was the Strategic Defense Initiative, a proposal for space-based defensive weapons capable of shooting down incoming missiles. Extending the arms race into space wasn't what the freeze movement had in mind.

After Reagan's reelection in 1984, the focus of the peace movement shifted to a moratorium on nuclear weapons testing. A moratorium had long been a goal of the movement, but it gained momentum in late 1984 when two retired U.S. admirals, Eugene R. La Rocque and Eugene Carroll, pitched the proposal to the Reagan administration and the Kremlin. The administration immediately rejected the idea, but after several exchanges of letters, Soviet leader Mikhail Gorbachev went public with a moratorium proposal of his own. The Soviet Union, he announced, would unilaterally suspend all testing, beginning on August 6, 1985, the fortieth anniversary of the nuclear destruction of Hiroshima, and continue the suspension for one year. If the United States joined in, Gorbachev said, he was prepared to continue the moratorium indefinitely. A complete test ban, something both sides had paid lip service to since the 1940s, could become reality.

Publicly, the Reagan administration dismissed the test ban and other unilateral arms control moves by Gorbachev as mere propaganda. Critics saw Gorbachev's move not only as a cleverly tailored public relations gambit, but a kind of unilateral disarmament for the United States since they didn't trust the Soviets to abide by the agreement. The Pentagon was dead set against the moratorium on the grounds that testing was necessary to developing and maintaining weaponry. But moratorium proponents like Schroeder saw the test ban as a back door to a freeze—have your weapons and disarm too because neither side can be sure they will work without being able to test them.

"After several years of being in effect, [it] would cause both sides to question whether the weapons they still had left were working efficiently, and, therefore, they would be less and less apt to use them," Schroeder said in 1985.

When the Soviets announced they would stop testing, arms control advocates coalesced around a plan to pass a non-binding congressional resolution calling for a moratorium on U.S. nuclear weapons testing. The proposal was largely a public relations move since it wouldn't have the force of law, but advocates hoped it would put pressure on the Reagan administration to soften its hard-line stance. However, La Rocque proposed to Schroeder in a meeting on Capitol Hill that she go a step further and simply cut off funding for future testing. Schroeder immediately and enthusiastically agreed, according to Jim Bush, who was at the meeting.

Shortly afterward, Schroeder, along with liberal Democrats Ed Markey of Massachusetts and Tom Downey of New York, introduced a bill to block funds for any nuclear testing, above ground or below, greater than one kiloton. Weapons experts generally agreed that tests below the one-kiloton level were militarily insignificant. The timing was fortuitous. After more than five years in office, the Reagan administration had achieved little in arms control, and many lawmakers had decided that the administration didn't want to make or keep agreements that might stymie a U.S. arms buildup.

The proposal gathered momentum with astonishing speed. In a pragmatic move, and at the expense of her personal visibility, Schroeder deferred to two moderate Democrats—Aspin and Richard Gephardt of Missouri—to offer the amendment on the House floor, agreeing that it would give the measure a greater chance of passing. "This is an opportunity that hasn't come up before, and who knows if it will ever come again," Aspin told *Boston Globe* columnist Ellen Goodman. "There's willingness on the part of the Soviets to move toward arms control. We just can't let this one go." On August 7, 1986, it was adopted by a surprisingly wide margin, 234 to 155. "We were astounded," Jim Bush recalled.

White House officials, however, pressured House and Senate conferees to drop the ban in a show of unity with Reagan in advance of his upcoming summit with Gorbachev. The Soviet moratorium lasted until early 1987, when continued U.S. testing led Gorbachev to end it. Schroeder and other test ban supporters vowed to continue to reintroduce the measure until it became law, but the test ban effort lost some of its steam once Reagan began arms control talks with the Soviets. By 1988, the vote for a test ban was a much closer 214 to 186. To Schroeder's dismay, the ban provision was repeatedly scrapped by House and Senate negotiators under pressure from the White House.

Congress finally approved a test ban in 1992, and it was reluctantly signed into law by President Bush, although by this time the fight on Capitol Hill was being led by Republican Mark Hatfield of Oregon in the Senate, and Democrat Jerry Kopetski of Illinois in the House.

While the "evil empire," as Reagan described the Soviet Union, has disintegrated, the debate over the wisdom of a test ban continues to this day. Proponents contend a "comprehensive" multination test ban would discourage new countries from entering the club of nuclear nations because they would not know if their weapons worked. Opponents argue that testing is critical to nuclear deterrence.

"We rejected the nuclear freeze concept," Republican Sen. Jim Bunning of Kentucky said, arguing against ratification of a comprehensive test ban in 1999. "We put national security first. We won the Cold War, not through unilateral disarmament and symbolic gestures, but through strength, and we defeated the evil empire. The world is safer and we have been able to substantially reduce the number of nuclear warheads and the threat of nuclear conflict."

It was in the most prosaic area of defense work that Schroeder left perhaps her greatest mark. Early in her years on the Armed Services Committee, she began carving out for herself a niche as a champion of ordinary servicemen and women and their families. The role appealed to Schroeder as a way to extend her family and women's issues agenda to her defense work. But it was also a useful way for her to counter critics who accused her of being "anti-military." Look, she would argue, I care about the average soldier, it's just the policies of the muckety-mucks that I have a problem with.

Over the years, Schroeder tried to improve the lot of military families, pushing to spend more defense dollars on such things as moving allowances and schools. She would press the Pentagon on whether troops were being trained enough, whether they got enough basic pay, and whether they got enough combat or hazardous duty pay when the times demanded it. She wanted to know the condition of their housing and the quality of their health care. Was there twenty-four-hour day care to accommodate parents' work shifts? Was there any day care at all?

"I'd visit bases, and I'd have commanders tell me their biggest problem was day care, or their biggest problem was housing," Schroeder told *Frontline* in 1996. "They'd appear in front of the committee, and you'd say, 'What's your biggest problem?' And they'd say, 'Oh, ships or ammunition.' You'd say, 'Are you the same person?' They'd say, 'I know, but if I say that publicly, they'll think I have lace on my boxer shorts. You don't understand. That's a career ender.'"

As chairwoman of the military installations and facilities subcommittee of the Armed Services Committee, Schroeder insisted that no new chapels be built on army bases unless they included space for multipurpose family use. Army chaplains were furious. "I had members come to me and say, 'How can you be against the chaplains!'" Schroeder told the *Washington Post.* But she held her ground and won the point.

Alarmed by the low test scores of recruits, Schroeder urged better educational and career opportunities, saying they were necessary for a truly professional force. "After a while there was a grudging acceptance [in the Pentagon and on the Armed Services Committee] that she was never going to leave," said Kip Cheroutes, who handled defense issues for her in Washington for several years. "Once she started figuring out stuff that she could support rather than being just a complete critic . . . she got some support out of the Pentagon and out of the committee. That was sort of an evolutionary change."

"Two out of every ten colonels in the Pentagon would recognize and appreciate what she was doing," Cheroutes estimated. "It was sort of that locker room mentality. Of course you aren't going to go into the men's locker room and say, 'Hey, that Pat Schroeder she's really on the ball.' You just don't say that in the Pentagon locker rooms. You just sort of go along with what everyone else says. After a while, however, I think there did evolve in the Pentagon little pockets of admiration, support, and well-wishes."

Schroeder was also involved in two key defense issues affecting Denver, the closure of Lowry Air Force Base and the cleanup of the Rocky Mountain Arsenal. She had backed the creation of the Base Closure and Realignment Commission, made up of unbiased experts who were to choose which military facilities to close, taking politics out of the politically sensitive base closure issue. In 1989, she supported a base closure list drawn up by the commission as responsible and fair. However, in 1991, when the commission came up with its next list for additional closures, one of the facilities on the list was Lowery Air Force Base in Denver.

Schroeder fought to keep the base open, questioning whether it had been unfairly singled out. At the time, Schroeder was chair of the subcommittee on military installations, which had jurisdiction over base closures. "I will be scouring the Defense Department's submission to the commission to see if the decision to close Lowery is sound," Schroeder warned. "If I find anything wrong or questionable with what DOD did, and I expect to, I will raise it with the commission in the strongest way." The base closure system was one that pitted political and economic interests around the country against each other as communities tried to show why their base was more valuable than the bases in other communities. Ultimately, however, it appeared that Lowery was as deserving a candidate for closure—and arguably more deserving—than other bases that had been spared from inclusion on the list, and it was shut down.

The question regarding the Rocky Mountain Arsenal was not whether to close it down, but who was going to pay to clean it up. It was one of the most contaminated and dangerous pieces of ground in America. From 1942 to 1969, the army manufactured chemical weapons at the twenty-seven-square-mile arsenal just north of Denver. From 1952 to 1982, a subsidiary of Shell Oil Company leased a portion of the arsenal for the manufacture of pesticides. Thanks to massive amounts of chemical pollution emitted by the army and Shell, the soil and groundwater beneath were deadly.

The army, Shell, the Environmental Protection Agency, and the State of Colorado fought for years in court over what to do about the mess. One of the key issues was the arsenal's future use. Given the property's proximity to downtown Denver, the land had tremendous potential value if it could be made fit for human habitation. But how clean did that have to be? If it were going to be zoned for industrial use, that might be one level. If you were going to put a daycare center or a school there, that was another matter. If it were left as "open space," the standard would be lower and less expensive.

One day Kip Cheroutes was opening his mail in Schroeder's Denver office. In the stack was a letter from the National Wildlife Federation proposing that the arsenal be converted to a wildlife refuge. Included in the envelope was a model bill to do just that. Cheroutes immediately saw the proposal as the solution to the question of future use. Excitedly, he called Schroeder in Washington, faxed the bill to her Capitol Hill office. She introduced it that day. It became law in 1992. Separately, Congress also approved a measure authored by Schroeder requiring that all the monies paid by Shell go directly into a cleanup fund for the arsenal rather than to the federal treasury, an issue that had been a sticking point in the cleanup negotiations. It became known as the "Schroeder account." A $2 billion cleanup agreement was signed by the parties in 1996. After retiring from Congress, Schroeder would pose on the arsenal grounds for a photograph for the back cover of her 1998 memoir with one of the bald eagles that makes its home there perched on her upraised arm.

During Schroeder's time on the Armed Services Committee, the antiwar movement gave way to the peace movement. She saw the end of the Vietnam War and the end of the cold war. The membership of the committee moderated over time, but Schroeder's staunchly liberal views did not. She remained firmly in the committee's left wing, reviled by conservatives for her dovish views and beloved by antinuclear activists and military reformers for her stalwart refusal to accept the status quo. She acknowledges that her efforts to redirect defense spending to social programs were largely unsuccessful, although not for lack of trying.

"Hopefully we took some of the sacred cow status away from it," Schroeder said. "I think people realize that a lot of these decisions that were made were not because they [members of Congress] had some secret threat briefing and this is really going to fit the threat briefing. It had to do with campaign finance. It had to do with their district and jobs. It had to do with covering their backsides."

Schroeder served twenty-four years on the committee, but no one is likely to name a battleship after her or even a commissary. However, dozens and perhaps hundreds of defense-related laws and policies reflect her influence to some degree. It can be argued that Schroeder reduced her own effectiveness by cleaving so persistently to her left-of-the-mainstream views rather than moderating her positions on some issues in an effort to further her goals on others. On the other hand, it is doubtful whether she could have received greater acceptance from her committee colleagues or the defense establishment without fundamentally abandoning her beliefs. Looking back, Schroeder said she believes she proved that a woman in Congress could be a forceful voice on defense issues. When it came to articulating and defending the liberal viewpoint—a role as valid as that of legislative mechanic—she had few equals.

6

Women and Children First

Schroeder entered Congress determined to make government the ally of women and children just as the women's rights movement was beginning to hit its stride. Feminists were attacking ingrained attitudes and entrenched practices that seem anachronistic today, but which were commonplace at the time, often with detrimental and far-reaching consequences for women.

In the 1970s, during Schroeder's early years in the House, it was not unusual for prospective employers to ask female job applicants questions such as: Do you plan to be married? Will you have children? If you are married, what does your husband think of your taking this job?

Women were earning on average 40 percent less than men, confined primarily to jobs in pink-collar ghettos. Credit card companies routinely declined to grant married women credit in their own names, issuing them cards in their husbands' names instead. The "feminization of poverty," "comparable worth," and the "glass ceiling" were all buzz words that came into vogue during Schroeder's era in politics to describe the economic injustices faced by women. Women made up a disproportionate share of the poor, the kinds of jobs they filled paid less than comparable jobs held primarily by men, and even when women rose to mid-level management positions they seemed to face an invisible barrier that prevented them from reaching the top echelons of business and industry.

Until the mid-1960s, it was illegal in many states to prescribe, sell, or use contraceptives. In 1970, there was no such thing as a shelter for battered women. Until the early 1980s, a Louisiana statute gave husbands exclusive control over the disposition of jointly owned community property. It wasn't until 1984 that Georgia changed its domestic relations code so that the law would no longer begin: "The husband is the head of the family and the wife is subject to him." It wasn't until 1972 that Congress officially recognized that sex discrimination existed in schools and passed a law designed to remedy deep-seated practices. The month that Schroeder was sworn into the House was the same month that the Supreme Court legalized abortion. Congress had just passed the Equal Rights Amendment—a constitutional amendment guaranteeing women the same rights as men—and the drive for ratification in the states was under way. Female representation in federal, state, county, and local elective offices would double during the 1970s, from less than 5 percent in the beginning of the decade to 10 percent by 1980.

The revolutionary changes that were reshaping the roles of women and men in American society were slow to penetrate the tradition-bound corridors of the Capitol. As one of only fourteen women in the House in 1973 (sixteen after Lindy Boggs of Louisiana and Cardiss Collins of Illinois were elected to fill vacancies created by the deaths of their husbands in plane crashes), the life of a congresswoman felt "like being the only girl in a boy's school, and the boys won't let you play paddle ball in the gym," Schroeder said.

She was impatient with the rampant sexism on Capitol Hill. The only restroom near the House floor was a men's room. Even the high school–aged pages who ran errands on the floor were all boys—no girls allowed. "The day I wore a pants suit onto the floor you'd have thought I'd asked for a land base for China," Schroeder told the *Colorado Democrat* after she had been in the House six months. "I just want to do my job. Does it make any difference if I have a bow in my hair or not?"

There was a camaraderie among the small group of women in the House, but it had limits. The congresswomen would regularly reserve a table in the elegant members' dining room on the first floor of the Capitol and exchange legislative information over lunch, a kind of political coffeeklatsch. However, their personalities, backgrounds, political styles, and ideology were so vastly different that actually working together on issues was impractical.

On one extreme was truculent New York feminist Bella Abzug, a civil rights and labor lawyer known for her floppy hats and booming voice. In 1969, New York mayor John V. Lindsay told Abzug that if she thought male politicians were doing such a lousy job, she ought to get into politics herself. "Then and there, I decided to run for Congress," Abzug wrote in her 1984 book *Gender Gap: Bella Abzug's Guide to Political Power for American Women.* "It was like a light switch being turned on in my brain, that 'click' which my friends at *Ms.* magazine call the moment of recognition of a feminist truth. I had been working hard all those years to elect men who weren't any more qualified or able than I, and in some cases they were less so. . . .

"In talking to other women who have gone into politics, I found that many experienced similar clicks. . . . All it required was a closing of the perception gap, with the woman focusing on herself as a legislator and leader, not as the usual behind-the-scenes worker and supplicant. In the 1970s those individual clicks were becoming a chorus—small one, but with the promise of more to come."

On the other extreme was Democrat Leonor Sullivan of Missouri, the only female member of the House to vote against the Equal Rights Amendment. Sullivan had worked first as a volunteer and later as a paid aide in the congressional office of her husband, Rep. John Berchmans Sullivan. When he died in 1951, the St. Louis Democratic Central Committee refused to nominate her to fill the vacancy. She waited until the next election and then beat seven men in the Democratic primary by promising to adhere to the political course set by her husband. Her victory was aided by a special ruling she obtained from the state attorney general that allowed her to be listed on the ballot as "Mrs. John B. Sullivan."

One of nine children of a second-generation German-American tailor and a staunch Catholic, Sullivan believed that a woman's most important role was in the home. She feared the ERA would "accelerate the breakup of home life."

"There are differences between male and female roles in our society and I hope there always are," was the way Sullivan explained her vote against the ERA.

If the group had a den mother, it was Democrat Martha Griffiths of Michigan, the prototype of the modern woman legislator. Elected in 1954, Griffiths was one of the first women to have a professional political career on her résumé before coming to Congress. She had practiced law, served as a judge, and won two terms in the Michigan state legislature, where she had helped craft legislation regulating public utilities.

Griffiths is the person most responsible for the inclusion of women in the landmark Civil Rights Act of 1964, which outlawed discrimination in voting, access to public education, employment, public accommodations, and federally assisted programs. When the bill came to the House floor, it addressed discrimination based on race, ethnicity, and religion, but not sex discrimination. Since the main purpose the bill was to remedy racial discrimination, some of its key supporters didn't want to risk its defeat by bringing the volatile issue of sex into the debate. Griffiths, however, was determined to offer an amendment to add sex discrimination to the bill. But when she learned that Rep. Howard W. Smith, a conservative Democrat from Virginia who was opposed to the civil rights bill, was willing to offer the same amendment, she wisely stepped back, knowing that he could bring the amendment the votes of dozens of conservatives. Smith had been persuaded to introduce the sex amendment by the National Women's Party, which was spearheading a lobbying campaign for its inclusion.

The inclusion of women in the civil rights bill was seen as frivolous by many male lawmakers. When Smith offered his amendment on the House floor on February 8, 1964, some lawmakers openly mocked the concept of sex discrimination during a ribald debate. The laughter died when Griffiths stepped to the podium, telling her colleagues that their behavior only confirmed the second-class status of women. She ended her speech by warning that a man's vote against the amendment was a vote against his wife, his widow, his sister, and his daughter.

The sex discrimination amendment passed 168 to 133, thanks in part to the support of conservative southern congressmen who hoped its inclusion would kill the civil rights bill. Their strategy backfired. The entire bill, with the sex provision still in it, passed the House two days later. It was signed into law on July 2, 1964, but only after surviving the longest filibuster—eighty-three days—in Senate history.

When the Equal Employment Opportunity Commission, created to enforce the work-related aspects of the Civil Rights Act, refused to take the new law's provisions against sex discrimination seriously, Griffiths attacked the commission on the floor of the House, labeling its attitude toward sex discrimination "specious, negative and arrogant." Her office became a clearinghouse for women across the country who believed they had been victims of job discrimination.

Griffiths also pushed the ERA—the amendment had been a goal of the National Women's Party since it was first introduced in Congress in 1923—through the House almost single-handedly. She was also the first woman to serve on the powerful Ways and Means Committee and probably would have become the chairman of the committee if she had not decided to retire from the House in 1974. She later served two terms as lieutenant governor of Michigan.

It wasn't until 1977, after Sullivan had retired and Abzug had left the House, that the women in the House formed the Congressional Caucus for Women's Issues. In its early form, the caucus—cochaired by Democrat

Liz Holtzman and Republican Peggy Heckler—"was more an ongoing tea party than a convincing legislative caucus," Schroeder wrote in her memoir *Champion of the Great American Family*. The traditionalists were afraid of being called feminists and the feminists worried that they would be muzzled. There was a consensus in the group in favor of the ERA, but the abortion issue was set aside because some of the members were Catholic and would have quit the caucus as a matter of religious conviction if it had endorsed legalized abortion.

"It broke my heart," Schroeder wrote. "Since there were so few women in Congress, I felt it was better to hang together on other issues where we had consensus rather than break apart." A separate bipartisan group was put together to work abortion-related issues. It wasn't until 1993 that the caucus officially became pro-choice.

In 1981, Schroeder became the Democratic cochair of the caucus, a position she would hold for fourteen years. Over that time, the caucus gradually increased its numbers and its influence. Through the work of Schroeder and moderate Olympia Snowe of Maine, the Republican cochair for ten years, the caucus's support became a kind of Good Housekeeping seal of approval for legislation: If the women's caucus supported it, then it must be good for women and children. By the 1990s, the caucus had opened its membership to men who supported key women's issues and had over 150 members. Through her position as cochair, Schroeder was able to play a role, even if it were sometimes a small one, in virtually every piece of legislation of importance to women that passed the House.

Schroeder's high-profile support for women's rights, the fact there were so few women in Congress, and a sense that she was approachable all combined to make her everywoman's congresswoman. Throughout her career, Schroeder would receive letters and phone calls from women across the country far in excess of what was typical for most members of Congress. Women who came to the Capitol to visit their own representative would often drop by Schroeder's office as well. Many of these women came seeking help for problems ranging from inadequate day care to breast cancer to sexual harassment.

"Women all over the country would see her name in the paper and think, 'She's a champion, so she must be my champion, too,'" said former aide Louis "Kip" Cheroutes. "We could have opened a national casework office just for daycare problems."

In the mid-1970s, Schroeder began hearing in increasing numbers from distraught ex-wives of federal workers, military personnel, foreign service officers, and CIA employees. The former wives, most of whom had stayed home to raise families and support their husbands' careers, said that after decades of marriage they found themselves with no pension, no Social Security, and no health insurance. The women often mailed to Schroeder reams of documents—divorce records, marriage certificates, death certificates of their former husbands, and so forth—with their desperate pleas for help.

Although courts were increasingly dividing private pensions in divorce cases, the Supreme Court had placed federal pensions off limits, ruling they were salary and not property. (Federal employees do not participate in the Social Security system.) The plight of military and State Department wives was especially tragic. Many of the former wives had followed their husbands from assignment to assignment across the country and around the world, never in one place long enough to have a career of their own. The wives argued that marriage was an economic partnership in which they shouldered the family responsibilities and made social contributions that benefited their husbands' careers, and that therefore they deserved a share of the reward.

Indeed, for years a foreign service wife was expected to help her husband in his diplomatic work by entertaining at their home and performing charitable work in the host country. The wife and family were seen as such an important part of the husband's work that they were rated on his efficiency report. Officially, the ratings stopped in 1972 when the State Department issued an order terminating the grading system and telling spouses that they were no longer obligated to entertain. Unofficially, the subtle pressure on wives to devote their energies to advancing their husbands' careers remained. After all, it wasn't as though the State Department had hired anyone else to do the functions the wives had been performing.

In congressional hearings, ex-military wives told of being evicted from their homes, applying for food stamps, and turning to welfare. "If you were a wife in the military for thirty years or twenty years, you were in for the full duration," Schroeder said. "The concept is that you earned half that pension because you could never have a job and you had no independent life. You couldn't own a home because you were moving all the time. Those are the only assets in a marriage usually—somebody's pension and somebody's home. What we were finding was ambassadors' wives and generals' wives cleaning toilets in Washington because these guys would leave and they would have these pensions, which were generally quite handsome."

Schroeder was moved by the ex-wives' plight, understanding that most women are only a man away from poverty. In 1977, she introduced separate pension-sharing bills for former spouses—one each for the State Department, the military, the civil service, and the CIA. Separate bills were necessary for technical reasons having to do with the different pension systems involved and because each area of government fell under the jurisdiction of a different congressional committee. Schroeder proposed that state courts automatically provide a pro rata share of annuity and survivors benefits to former wives. The ex-wife's share would be based on a formula using the number of years of marriage during a husband's career at the time of the divorce. "All we can do under the present law is tell them to apply for food stamps," Schroeder said, introducing the bills.

The first bill to be dealt with was the civil service bill. The House civil services committee rejected the notion that ex-wives should automatically share in their husbands' pensions, but accepted a compromise that gave authority to state courts to decide case by case how to divide civil service pensions. That bill set precedents for the other bills. Over the next seven years, Congress would pass legislation permitting courts to divide federal pensions in divorce cases for each of the categories of government employees and to extend medical and survivors benefits to ex-wives who met certain criteria.

"Credit has to rest right in the lap of Pat Schroeder," Patricia Reuss, legislative director of the Women's Equity Action League, told *Washington Post* columnist Judy Mann when the military pension bill was enacted in 1982. "Six years ago, she talked about pensions for military, foreign service, and civil service wives and people thought: That's a nice, feminist thing to do, but don't expect anything to happen."

The issue brought together an unusual coalition of feminists, organizations for former spouses, and "pro-family" social conservatives who saw the bills as supporting the role of the traditional homemaker. Yet the opposition to the measures, particularly the military pension-sharing bill, was fierce and the debate often emotionally charged. Retired officers testifying before congressional committees repeatedly rejected the notion that ex-wives had earned a share of retirement benefits, saying they had taken none of the risks and endured none of the true hardships inherent in military service. The influential retirement associations of the military services weighed in heavily against the legislation.

As the law's chief sponsor, Schroeder became the target of disgruntled retired servicemen who blamed her for taking away at least part of their pensions. At the height of the controversy in the early 1980s, Schroeder and her mother, Bernice, and daughter, Jamie, flew to San Diego to attend a convention of women members of the Congregational church. Schroeder was the keynote speaker. When they arrived at their hotel, they were surprised to find about 150 retired navy officers with anti-Schroeder signs picketing outside.

When she flew to Pensacola, Florida, another community with a large contingent of retired navy personnel, to give a speech, the local sheriff picked her up at the airport and escorted her to her hotel, telling her it was necessary for her safety that he stick by her side, Schroeder said. On another occasion, a brick was thrown through the window of the congresswoman's car while it was parked outside her home in suburban Virginia. Schroeder can't be certain, but she has always suspected that whoever was behind the incident was upset about pension-sharing.

To this day, the law remains wildly unpopular with retired and active-duty service members. Groups ranging from the Air Force Association to the Fleet Reserve Association to the Veterans of Foreign Wars of the United States (VFW) continue to lobby Congress to either reverse the law or change it to prohibit benefits to former spouses if they remarry. (Courts already have the power to do that in divorce agreements.) Several bills along those lines have been introduced in recent years by sympathetic House members.

Even though she has left Congress, Schroeder continues to be accosted in public places by retired officers anxious to convey their displeasure with her efforts on behalf of ex-spouses. "I was on one of those little buses out at Dulles Airport six months ago with my husband and this guy comes running across the bus to us and Jim says, 'I bet it's about a pension,'" Schroeder said in an interview in October 2001. "We're at the point now where the two of us can spot them."

Schroeder was involved in literally hundreds of controversial and emotion-laden issues during her twenty-four years in the House, from abortion to nuclear weapons to gun control. Yet no other issue provoked as great an outpouring of tears and hostility, distress, and anger as the pension issue. "From day one to end of career we were always getting calls," Cheroutes said. "We had ex-wives crying on the phone because the husband had dumped them," and angry husbands complaining that Schroeder had robbed them of their pensions. "So we got it from both sides," he said. "Even in the district office we'd be getting calls from who knows where—Georgia, everywhere in the country. The interns were fascinated by it."

As women surged into the workforce in the '60s, '70s and '80s, conflicts were inevitable. One of the most troublesome was the treatment of pregnant women who took time off for childbirth, intending to return to work afterwards. While other employees were customarily given time off to recover from temporary disabilities, many companies expected women who became pregnant to simply leave their jobs.

It wasn't until 1972 that the Equal Employment Opportunity Commission ruled that companies had to treat pregnancy the same way they treated any other temporary disability. If employees were allowed leave time with pay, health insurance, and other benefits to recover from other conditions, then they had to be allowed the same leave time and benefits for childbirth. Four years later, however, the Supreme Court ruled that companies did not, in fact, discriminate against women by denying temporary disability benefits for pregnancy and childbirth.

The upshot was that in 1978 Congress passed the Pregnancy Discrimination Act, which overrode the court decision. Schroeder was one of the leading sponsors of the measure in the House. Pregnancy once again had to be treated the same as other temporary disabilities. However, the law did not require employers to provide pregnancy leave unless it was their practice to provide leave for other disabilities. Nor did the law guarantee that women who wanted to return to work would receive their old jobs back. Indeed, each year thousands of women who tried to return to work were told their old jobs had been filled while they were home with their infants.

That's what happened to Lillian Garland in 1981. A receptionist at the California Federal Savings and Loan headquarters in Los Angeles, Garland tried to return to work two months after the birth of her daughter by Caesarean section, only to be told her job had been given to the woman she had trained as her temporary replacement. But California had its own law guaranteeing pregnant women up to four months of temporary disability leave and their old jobs back. Garland complained to the state Department of Fair Employment, which ruled that California Federal had violated the state law. The savings and loan, backed up by the California Chamber of Commerce and other business groups, filed a lawsuit in federal court challenging the state law. The business groups argued that it was the company's right to set its own personnel policies and benefits.

In 1984, a federal judge sided with California Federal, declaring that the state law violated federal statutes, including the Civil Rights Act of 1964, that required equal treatment of men and women in the workplace. Since men could not avail themselves of maternity leave, the state law was discriminatory.

The case sent shock waves through the women's movement. Women's rights supporters in Congress wanted to introduce legislation to rectify the situation, but there were deep divisions over strategy. Several House members from California wanted to simply reverse the Cal Fed decision. But the Women's Legal Defense Fund and other feminist groups believed that laws written narrowly to protect women could have the opposite effect, codifying a double standard that served to discourage employers from hiring women or that permitted them to treat women differently in the name of "protecting" them. For example, some companies might limit women's working hours or bar them from strenuous or hazardous work.

Instead of focusing exclusively on maternity leave, feminists argued, Congress ought to broadly address the need for all employees, women and men, to take leave time from work for a range of temporary non-work-related disabilities and family situations. It was a radical idea, guaranteed to provoke the collective wrath of the mighty business lobbying community in Washington.

The schism over special protection versus equal treatment dated back to the early years of the women's movement. The legendary Alice Paul, chief strategist for the militant wing of the suffrage movement, wrote the first Equal Rights Amendment, which was premised on creating a level playing field for women and men. But when the amendment was introduced in Congress in 1923, it was denounced by the leaders of seven major women's rights organizations, including the League of Women Voters and the settlement-house movement of Jane Addams. These early reformers feared the amendment would undo protective labor laws for women in some states that they had fought so hard to win. At the time, Paul's notion of gender neutrality seemed utopian and possibly hazardous.

Agreeing with feminists that a broad approach was needed, Schroeder introduced the first parental and medical leave bill on April 4, 1985. The honor fell to Schroeder partly because she was the cochair of the women's caucus and partly because no one else was clamoring for it. For six months hers was the lone name on the bill. The measure would have required employers to provide up to eighteen weeks of unpaid leave to mothers and fathers of newborn or newly adopted children. It would have mandated up to twenty-six weeks of unpaid leave for non-work-related disabilities. Employers would be required to continue the health insurance and other benefits of leave-takers while they were home and to give them their old jobs back when they returned to work. It applied to all businesses with more than five employees.

It was a modest proposal compared to the leave policies of most industrialized nations. At that time, more than one hundred nations were offering new mothers paid pregnancy leave. The United States and South Africa were the only industrialized nations without national maternity leave protections. Surely if business and industry in Germany, France, and Great Britain could cope, so could their American counterparts, Schroeder argued. Even though most European countries required employers to offer parents paid leave, Schroeder sought only unpaid. "I figured if I proposed pay, then they [business lobbyists and their supporters in Congress] would get even crazier trying to defeat it," she told the *Chicago Tribune*.

Business and industry—including the U.S. Chamber of Commerce, the National Association of Manufacturers, and the National Federation of Independent Businesses—denounced the proposal as an intrusion into private-sector management decisions and predicted disastrous consequences for small businesses, which they said had less flexibility to cope with extended leaves. The groups predicted widespread business failures. The powerful business lobbies made defeat of family leave a top priority. "To hear the Chamber of Commerce talk about it, you'd think we were communists," Dan Buck, Schroeder's chief of staff, told the *New York Times*.

Schroeder, however, argued that family leave was something that ordinary Americans desperately needed. "We do not have a family-friendly workplace," she argued. "Everyone will tell you that in the workplace, they do much better off—if their child care breaks down or they have a sick spouse and it takes them longer to get out in the morning—to tell their employer that the car had problems. . . . We will tolerate technology problems. We will not tolerate human problems. That puts a lot of stress on the family."

Over the next eight years, Schroeder was repeatedly forced to whittle down the bill's benefits in an attempt to dampen business opposition. First, she altered the bill to exempt businesses with fewer than fifteen employees and then reluctantly upped that to fifty employees in order to win the support of moderate Republicans. That effectively excluded all but the largest 5 percent of the businesses in the country. However, that 5 percent of companies employed 57 percent of the nation's workforce. A requirement was added that an employee would have to work one year before becoming eligible. The leave itself was reduced from eighteen weeks to twelve weeks over a two-year period. Employers were allowed to exempt the top 10 percent of their highest paid employees if they could show that their services could not be replaced.

However, the bill's benefits were also expanded in two important ways that drew more support for the measure: provisions were added to allow employees to take time off to care for an elderly parent or a sick child or spouse. Lawmakers had become increasingly aware of the burdens carried by millions of women as they tried to raise families, hold down jobs, and care for ailing parents all at the same time. The Public Health Service's National Center for Health Service Research estimated that in 1982 2.2 million caregivers were providing care for 1.6 million seriously impaired individuals over the age of sixty-five. As the baby boomers and their parents aged, that number rapidly expanded.

"This has become the secret agenda of the superwoman," Myrna Lewis, an instructor in community medicine at the Mount Sinai School of Medicine and a gerontologist who specialized in issues of midlife and older women, told the *New York Times* in 1986. "Everybody knows about her babies, her housework, her career, but the secret job she bears as well is the care of the elderly."

"It is no longer 'leave it to Beaver' time," Schroeder said, referring to the classic TV family model of the working father and mother at home as she introduced a new version of the bill in 1986. "The superwoman has collapsed of exhaustion. The workforce has changed. It's time the workplace changed."

Armed with dire forecasts of the economic costs of the measure, business lobbies leaned hard on lawmakers to oppose the bill. The chamber of commerce first said family leave would cost business $16.2 billion a year in lost productivity, health insurance continuation, and temporary replacement costs. Its estimate assumed all workers would take the maximum leave and would be temporarily replaced. The chamber later amended its estimate to $2.6 billion.

The General Accounting Office, Congress's investigative arm, figured the cost at more like $500 million, or five dollars and sixty cents per employee per year. A nationwide study commissioned by the Small Business Administration estimated the cost of the policy would be six dollars and seventy cents per employee per year. Although the bill applied only to larger companies, the National Federation of Independent Businesses complained that the new mandate would prevent smaller companies with forty-five employees or so from growing because they would curtail hiring new employees rather than cross the fifty-employee threshold and have to follow additional labor regulations.

The cause of family leave received an important boost in 1986 when a study by the prestigious Bush Center in Child Development and Social Policy at Yale University recommended paid maternity leave for either parent for up to six months after the birth or adoption of a child, emphasizing the critical importance of the first months of life in child development. Meanwhile, the Labor Department was reporting that nearly 50 percent of the nation's married women with children one year old or younger were in the labor force—more than double the rate in 1970. "I sense a new grassroots movement of parents that no one can resist, and I think that parents themselves are going to demand these services," Harvard professor T. Berry Brazelton, a celebrated authority on child development, predicted in November 1985.

Nationally, an estimated 88 percent of employers allowed women some unpaid maternity leave, but far fewer employers guaranteed their jobs and seniority. A study of two hundred Fortune 500 companies revealed that only seven organizations, or 3.5 percent, had any formalized paternity leave. Only 40 percent of American working women received a paid six-to-eight-week disability leave, the birth recovery time recommended by most obstetricians. Five states had enacted pregnancy leave laws that protected workers' jobs: California, Hawaii, New Jersey, New York, and Rhode Island.

Because of the lack of employment policies to accommodate working parents, many women were forced to choose between job security and parenting, Schroeder argued. "I'm always hearing from young women who want to know what's a good time to have a baby," she would tell audiences. "Young people today are in a position of wondering if they can afford families. We should be doing everything we can to take stress out of family life, rather than adding to it."

While Schroeder was clearly the mother of family leave, passage of one of the most important workers' rights in recent decades was not the product of one member of Congress. Supporters of family leave legislation included groups as diverse as the Children's Defense Fund, the American Civil Liberties Union, the Pension Rights Center, the United Auto Workers, the Women's Legal Defense Fund and other feminist groups, and such traditional women's organizations as the Association of Junior Leagues. In the Senate, Democrat Chris Dodd of Connecticut was an early and ardent family leave advocate. After the bill was changed to exempt most small businesses, GOP Rep. Marge Roukema of New Jersey played a critical role in winning the support of moderate Republicans for the bill.

Even some social conservatives such as antiabortion foe Henry Hyde, a Republican congressman from Illinois, came around to supporting the measure as a way to strengthen families. The most militant social conservatives, however, saw the bill as a feminist plot to encourage more women to work, rather than to stay home with their children where they belonged. Conservatives argued that working women were selfishly putting their careers ahead of the needs of their children and society. To legislate benefits for them, conservatives said, was an affront to women making the noble sacrifice of staying at home. The drive to pass family leave was carried on against the backdrop of the Reagan years, an era of backlash against feminism, and the later "mommy wars," when feminists and social conservatives battled over women, work, and what defines a good mother.

"In a healthy society, heroes are the women and men who hold the world together, one home at a time: the parents and grandparents who forgo pleasures, delay purchases, foreclose options," conservative activist Gary Bauer, who served in Reagan's second term as domestic policy advisor, argued in a column for the *Washington Post* in 1986. "Women, for example, have more career opportunities today, but a number of them are choosing to stay home with their children, at least during the early years, or are working part-time, although this will have a negative impact on their careers. These women and men are the ones who commit most of their lives to the noblest of undertakings: raising children who, resting on the shoulders of the previous generation, will see farther and reach higher than we could." Congress and the administration, Bauer said, should resist schemes that would weaken American business and thus the economy and the family.

"Conservatives don't want to make policy changes that recognize today's richly diverse family; rather they want to perpetuate a nostalgic vision of the family based on male authority and female economic dependence," Schroeder responded in a counterpoint column. "Like the opponents of female suffrage a hundred years ago, who believed that a woman's vote would not only cancel out her husband's vote, but that it would destroy marriages and bring the family down in ruins, conservatives today believe that legislating programs such as child care, parental leave, work sharing, and pay equity would be similarly apocalyptic . . .

"We can no longer afford to hold on to the antiquated notion—no matter how appealing—of two separate worlds. Work and family have become inextricably woven together. Women, especially mothers, are the fastest growing segment in the work force. They work in greater numbers than ever before. And their numbers are going to increase because young couples have discovered for themselves that to maintain the standard of living their parents enjoyed on one income, they now need two."

Schroeder worked tirelessly for her family leave bill in speeches around the country. After a joint appearance in 1988 at the University of Arkansas in Little Rock, Schroeder and Brazelton were honored at a reception hosted by Arkansas first lady Hillary Rodham Clinton at the governor's mansion. By 1990, support for family and medical leave had reached a critical mass in Congress. The bill passed the House on May 10, 1990, by a healthy 287 to 187. The companion bill passed the Senate by a voice vote, essentially without opposition. When President Bush said he would veto "any kind of maternity-leave bill," Schroeder accused him of "coming out against motherhood." Bush vetoed the bill in June, saying he favored family leave, but it should be negotiated between workers and employers rather than mandated by government.

"We keep hearing this notion that people will negotiate [these benefits] with their employer before they go to work," Schroeder told the *Washington Post*. "Well, maybe that works if you're a quarterback. But the average person needs the job. So the idea that you're going to be able to negotiate twelve weeks leave without pay—bullfeathers. It's just not the real world."

In 1991, Schroeder became the only woman in the House to chair a committee, the Select Committee on Children, Youth, and Families. Select committees were at the very bottom of the committee pecking order since they had neither the power to approve legislation nor the ability to attract campaign cash. However, select committees did provide a public platform and extra staff and resources that could be used to draw attention to issues. Schroeder used the select committee in this way to help shape a Democratic family agenda involving child care, family leave, tax breaks, and other proposals that eventually became a critical piece of Bill Clinton's presidential campaign. As the 1992 election drew closer, the family leave bill in particular took on greater political importance. Both parties were trying to claim championship of "family values." The gender gap between the two parties had become a gender canyon. Democratic congressional leaders saw the family leave bill as a sure winner. If it passed and Bush signed it, Democrats would have a major accomplishment to tout to voters. If Bush vetoed the bill as he was promising to do, Democrats could use the issue to undermine the GOP's family values claims.

Democrats held off final passage of the bill until the very end of the One Hundred Second Congress. On September 16, 1992, congressional leaders signed and sent the family and medical leave bill to the White House. With less than two months before election day, both sides were trying to put their own public relations spin on the issue. The same day the family leave bill arrived on his desk, Bush announced his own family leave plan, which would grant employers a $1,200 tax credit per year for each employee they allowed to take a medical or family leave. Bush's "entire solution for every problem is, 'Take two tax credits and vote for me in November.'" Schroeder said, dismissing the plan. A week later, Bush quietly vetoed the family leave bill for the second time. Two days later, the Senate voted 68 to 31 to override the veto—the first time in Bush's three-and-a-half-year term that Senate Democrats had been able to muster the necessary two-thirds majority for an override.

It was then up to the House. On September 30, the House tried and failed to override the veto, falling twenty-seven votes short. "This is social engineering at the expense of job creation," Republican Rep. Tom DeLay of Texas told the House. "We can't legislate family values in this country." After the vote, Schroeder told reporters: "This issue frames this campaign. Yes, it is about who's really for families. I think the president's proposal is nothing but asbestos underwear to cover his backside at the last minute in the middle of an election campaign."

The Clinton-Gore campaign team was already pounding the issue. "It is impossible for President Bush to talk about family values and veto the family leave act," vice presidential nominee Al Gore told audiences. "Those who voted with the Bush-Quayle position chose to say, 'Read our lip-service to family values.'" By election day, family leave was as much a "family value" as mom and apple pie.

In January 1993, the new Clinton administration urged congressional leaders to put passage of family leave on a fast track. Still, some family advocates wondered whether so much had been given away over the years that the legislation no longer had meaning. "I didn't know if I could support twelve weeks unpaid leave. I considered it such a nothing," Dr. Edward F. Zigler, director of Yale's child development center, told the *Hartford Courant.*

As in the past, most Republicans decried the family leave bill as an undue burden on business and a potential fount of lawsuits. "This is a steep, slippery slope of a mandate," GOP Rep. Jan Meyers of Kansas warned during debate in the House. "In this litigious society, our courts will find their dockets overflowing with lawsuits." The House passed the bill by a vote of 265 to 163, with 224 Democrats, 40 Republicans, and 1 independent voting in favor and 29 Democrats and 134 Republicans opposed.

The bill was almost derailed at the last minute in the Senate when Republicans vowed to filibuster the measure unless they were allowed to add a provision opposing gays and lesbians from serving in the military. Republicans were allowed to offer their amendment, but it was defeated in favor of a compromise that put off a decision on the volatile gay rights issue for six months.

President Clinton signed the family leave bill on February 5, only sixteen days after taking office. "I am proud that the first bill I sign as president truly puts people first," Clinton said, echoing his campaign theme. "It took eight years and two vetoes to make this legislation the law of the land." The Rose Garden ceremony in which Clinton signed the bill was a carefully scripted publicity event attended by 150 pro-family activists. Also present were George and Vicki Yandle, a Georgia couple who had both lost their jobs while caring for their daughter, who had cancer. The only members of Congress sharing the limelight on stage with Clinton and Vice President Gore were men: Senators Ted Kennedy, Chris Dodd, and George Mitchell, and Representatives Bill Ford, Bill Clay, Pat Williams, and Tom Foley, the House and Senate leaders and committee chairmen with jurisdiction over the measure.

Schroeder and Roukema were seated in the second row of the audience, behind Hillary Clinton, Tipper Gore, and Marian Wright Edelman of the Children's Defense Fund. Protocol had dictated who was on stage, but Schroeder couldn't help but feel resentful as she recalled the days when she had to struggle to interest committee chairmen and top congressional leaders in the issue. "Often, you see women start the issue, educate on the issue, fight for the issue," Schroeder complained, "and then when it becomes fashionable, men push us aside, and they get away with it."

By 2001, some 35 million people had used the law to take unpaid leave because of a serious illness or to care for a new baby or sick family member. The dire forecasts of crushing financial costs and widespread business failures had not materialized. Neither had the law been expanded, to Schroeder's great disappointment. The Clinton administration "had a commission on it. We went all around the country. We didn't find one business that closed because of family leave. . . . Hearings all around the country and anybody could come in and scream and yell. Nothing happened," Schroeder said.

"We wanted at least a study on what it would cost (for workers' salaries to continue to be paid while on leave). Why can't we expand it beyond twelve weeks? Why can't we expand it to smaller employers?"

Some members of Congress and a number of states have discussed expanding the law to cover more people and to grant partial pay. If extended to businesses with twenty-five or more employees, more than 70 percent of workers would be covered. Another proposal would use state unemployment compensation funds to pay workers a minimum salary while on leave. However, both ideas are strongly opposed by business lobbies, which are easily capable of spending tens of millions of dollars on political donations and advertising campaigns to fend off new labor benefits. Thus, the prospects for expanding the current law remain poor.

"Other countries tend to think of these as family issues," Schroeder said, "but we still tend to think of them as special benefits for women."

When Pat Schroeder arrived at the Capitol on the morning of October 8, 1991, she had no idea that before the end of the day she would help change American political history. She began the day at a rally on a three-sided patch of grass on the east front of the Capitol known as "the House triangle," where she spoke to women seeking greater funding for breast cancer research. As Schroeder chatted with the breast cancer activists, she realized that like herself many of the women were disturbed by news that had broken over the weekend: An obscure Oklahoma State University law professor named Anita Hill had privately told the Senate Judiciary Committee that Clarence Thomas—then a nominee for the U.S. Supreme Court and later confirmed—had sexually harassed her while she had worked for him at the Department of Education and later at the Equal Employment Opportunity Commission, the very government agency that was supposed to protect women from harassment on the job.

Hill had accused the judge of making lewd suggestions to her, boasting of the size of his penis, and describing pornographic movies he had seen, including one in particular starring "Long Dong Silver." However, senators had not deemed Hill's complaint significant enough to call her to testify during Thomas's confirmation hearing. Even though her charges had now become public, Senate leaders still planned to go forward with a vote to confirm Thomas before the end of the day. To Schroeder, it appeared as if the sexual harassment charges were being dismissed out of hand in a rush to award a lifetime appointment to a man who would then be in a position to pass judgment on a vast range of issues critical to women.

By the time she had walked back to her congressional office in the Rayburn building, Schroeder had decided to do something: She would gather as many congresswomen as she could and march over to the Senate, where they would make their case for a delay in the confirmation vote so that Hill's story could be aired. Her press secretary, Andrea Camp, began calling the offices of other congresswomen to explain the plan, telling them to meet Schroeder on the House floor. Camp also called the House gallery where the television and radio reporters who cover Congress have their work cubicles. Camp not only wanted to alert reporters to the march, she was also looking for advice on how to get media coverage. The women staffers who ran the gallery suggested the congresswomen march to the Senate outside in the crisp autumn sunshine rather than through the crowded, dimly lit halls of the Capitol. It would make better "visuals."

Meanwhile, several Democratic congresswomen incensed about the Thomas nomination had already drifted over to the House floor. Schroeder soon joined them. At the start of each day's business in the House, there is a period set aside for "one-minutes" —brief speeches in which lawmakers can raise any issue they choose. Clearly the issue of the day for the women was Thomas. Democrat Barbara Kennelly of Connecticut was the first woman to speak. "The compelling case for the nominee to the Supreme Court was not legal expertise and it was not race. It was character, that out of the crucible of life experience, a man emerges with a vision and a viewpoint that cannot be duplicated on the Supreme Court," she told the House. "That case now has been challenged by charges that the nominee used indecent words to sexually harass a woman. These are serious charges and they deserve a serious hearing."

Next was Rep. Louise Slaughter of New York, and then Schroeder. "A woman has come forward and made very serious allegations and there is an attempt to brush them under the rug," she said. "I hope justice prevails. I hope we can take time to listen to everyone and weigh their words."

Meanwhile, knowing there were more Democratic congresswomen waiting their turn, Republicans on the floor were trying to figure out how to stem the rhetorical attack on Bush's nominee. GOP Rep. Dana Rohrabacher of California stepped up to the microphone: "The last minute personal attack on Judge Thomas is another example of the rotten gutter level politics which is now the standard operating procedure for liberals in America . . . Liberals are making Joe McCarthy look like a nice guy . . . Have you no sense of decency? Confirm Judge Thomas."

When Democrat Rosa DeLauro of Connecticut stepped into the well of the House to say much the same thing as the previous women speakers, Republicans used a parliamentary maneuver to cut her off. Further angered by the effort to gag DeLauro, Schroeder and Barbara Boxer of California grabbed five other Democratic congresswomen and headed out the House door of the Capitol, down the marble steps, across the east plaza, and up the steps to the Senate. Cameras captured every stride. On the television news that night and on the front pages of newspapers the next morning was the image of Schroeder and Boxer leading a band of angry congresswomen to confront male senators with their demands that Hill be heard.

Some women have since called those photographs "the Iwo Jima" of the women's rights movement. "It is the visual of that time," Andrea Camp said in an interview. "If you look at that issue, that picture will come up again and again in history books because it made the statement that this was a small group of women in this huge institution" trying to stand up for a woman's right to be heard.

Having arrived in the Senate, the women went straight to a meeting room where they had been told Senate Democrats were closeted at that very moment discussing what to do about Thomas. The women knocked on the mahogany double doors. An aide cracked a door open. The congresswomen asked to come in to discuss an important issue. The answer that came back was "No." Baffled and somewhat chagrined, the congresswomen knocked again. Again the door opened a crack. "You can't come in," said a senior staffer. "For goodness sakes," exploded one of the congresswomen, "we're members of Congress. Please ask." Again the staffer came back and told them no.

In a quandary, the women huddled together trying to figure out what to do next. They decided to go for a compromise. Can we meet with [senate majority leader George] Mitchell now? they asked. No, you can meet with him later, came the answer. Frustrated, and knowing that there would be no point in talking after a decision had been made, the women decided to play their trump card. "You go tell George that half the Washington press corps is fifty feet away," Schroeder recalls telling the Senate aide in her memoir *24 Years of House Work . . . and the Place Is Still a Mess.*

In Boxer's 1994 memoir, *Strangers in the Senate,* she recalls that she was the one who told the aide: "There are about 100 cameras out there and they all took our picture going up the Senate steps. They know what we came over about and they'll want to know what happened." It's possible they both spoke to the aide. Either way, suddenly Mitchell was willing to meet with them privately in an anteroom down the hall.

Mitchell was furious when he entered the room where the women were waiting, according to Camp, who was with the congresswomen in the meeting. A formidable figure even when in the best of moods, Mitchell lashed out at the congresswomen. "What are you doing here? What's your point? Are you trying to embarrass me?" he roared. From Mitchell's viewpoint, the women were out of line. He was a leader of their own party, and he was no supporter of Thomas or the president who nominated him. It was his job, however, to run the Senate and count votes. If the women wanted to delay a confirmation vote, then they ought to help him drum up the support to accomplish that by lobbying the Democratic senators who had already come out in support of Thomas and not by creating a media spectacle.

Schroeder and Boxer did not back down, according to Camp. Instead, speaking for the group, they calmly told Mitchell that they had come over from the House because they wanted him and other senators to know how serious an issue sexual harassment is and how important it was to women that Hill be heard. At that time, there were ninety-eight men and only two women in the Senate—Democrat Barbara Mikulski of Maryland and Republican Nancy Kassebaum of Kansas.

Later that day, Mitchell gave Senate Minority Leader Robert Dole a list of ten Democrats who had previously come out in support of Thomas's nomination but were now willing to switch their vote unless Hill was allowed to testify. Fearing he did not have the votes to confirm Thomas, Dole agreed to further hearings. It's possible Mitchell would have succeeded in delaying the confirmation vote even if the congresswomen had not marched over to see him. On the other hand, their visit clearly illustrated the strong emotions the sexual harassment issue triggered in so many women. "We convinced him to intervene with Sen. Joe Biden, the chairman of the Senate Judiciary Committee," Schroeder wrote in her book. Clearly, the perception in the media was that the congresswomen had won the day. "A fistful of angry women lawmakers stopped cold the confirmation of Clarence Thomas," was how the *Los Angeles Times* reported the episode.

In the televised hearings that followed, Hill proved to be a crisp, composed, and articulate witness. Thomas, a conservative and a strict constructionist, vehemently denied all the charges, calling the hearings "a high-tech lynching." Accused and accuser were both black, both graduates of Yale Law School, and one of them was lying. It became a case of "he said, she said." With no conclusive proof one way or the other, the Senate confirmed Thomas.

However, the hearings had a powerful, unforeseen consequence. While millions of viewers around the world watched the drama, the Republican members of the Judiciary Committee tried to vilify Hill, suggesting at times that she was a liar, a scorned woman, a publicity seeker, mentally unbalanced, or a partisan pawn. Women, and many men, were outraged by the way Hill was savaged. The video images of the uniformly white, male judiciary committee also dramatized the homogeneity of the Senate more than statistics and polemics ever could. Although polls showed a majority of women, and men, ended up supporting Thomas, Hill's treatment electrified the women's rights movement.

"It was like that scene in *The Wizard of Oz* where they pull away the curtain and we really saw the Senate," Schroeder told the *Los Angeles Times.* "We think that women are doing everything men are doing. But what you saw in the Senate is exactly like every corporate boardroom in America. They all look like the Senate. And you realize how far we have not come."

Sexual harassment and violence against women were very much on the minds of the public that year. In September, the navy's top brass and hundreds of male aviators had gathered for their annual "Tailhook" convention, a name that would ultimately become synonymous with sexual harassment and debauchery. Pollsters reported that although 80 percent of women said they had been sexually harassed in the workplace, only 25 percent had reported it. Few lawsuits were filed because most women felt they would not be taken seriously or would experience retaliation.

The shock waves from the Thomas-Hill hearings were felt at the polls the following year as unprecedented numbers of women ran for election to Congress. Donations poured into political action committees like Emily's List in support of women candidates. In what became known as "The Year of the Woman," 106 women ran for the House and 11 women ran for the Senate out of thirty-five seats up for election. More than a third of them won. The number of women in Congress swelled from twenty-nine to forty-eight in the House and from two to six in the Senate. Later, after winning a special election, Kay Bailey Hutchison would bring the number of women in the Senate to seven. Never before had women increased their numbers in Congress—House and Senate combined—by more than five in an election.

"In 1992, women went from 5 percent to 10 percent," Schroeder later told Radcliffe students. "When the new class was getting sworn in, one of the old bulls came over and said, 'This place looks like a damned shopping center thanks to people like you.'"

In 1988, Harvard Medical School released a highly touted, government-funded study that concluded an aspirin a day could help prevent heart attacks and strokes. The study, which was front-page news, had examined aspirin and heart attacks in 22,071 male physicians. There was only one problem: Women were not included in the study.

At the same time the aspirin study was making headlines, the staff of the Congressional Caucus on Women's Issues was hearing privately from women doctors and researchers at the National Institutes of Health that women were routinely excluded from medical research. Three years earlier, a government task force had found that a lack of research on women's health had compromised their care. In response, NIH, which funds 40 percent of the nation's medical research, had adopted a policy that women be included in research. If the aspirin study and other studies were any indication, the caucus's staff figured, NIH was breaking its own rules by continuing to leave women out.

Schroeder and Olympia Snowe of Maine, the Republican cochair of the caucus, wanted to do something, but they needed more ammunition. They persuaded Democrat Henry Waxman of California, the chairman of the health subcommittee of the Energy and Commerce Committee, to request the General Accounting Office to investigate the exclusion of women in NIH-funded research. The congresswomen needed Waxman because the GAO investigation had to be requested by a committee chairman and, if they introduced legislation, it would have to go through Waxman's committee.

The GAO's report—released by Schroeder, Snowe, and Waxman in June 1990—was shattering to the prestigious medical research community. In study after study, the GAO found women had simply been ignored. In an important study that showed that heavy coffee intake does not increase the chance of heart attacks or strokes all 45,589 subjects were men. There were no data available on women. The fifteen-year Coronary Primary Prevention Trial, started in 1973, studied the effects of lowering cholesterol in 4,000 men at a cost of $142 million. The Multiple Risk Factor Intervention Trial, aimed at cataloging the things that put heart disease victims at risk, looked at 15,000 men. The study's acronym, appropriately enough, was "MR. FIT."

The male research bias was prevalent even on issues predominantly of concern to women. Some breast cancer studies, for example, had involved only men. Indeed, one of the most important studies of aging ever undertaken involved only men even though women make up more than two-thirds of the elderly and more than 70 percent of the very old—those over age eighty-five.

In 1958, federally sponsored researchers launched what became the Baltimore Longitudinal Study of Aging. When the study began, researchers worked in a single room at the city hospital that had access to only one restroom. This restroom also had to be shared with male patients in an adjacent hospital ward. Rather than ask women subjects to use this restroom during overnight evaluations, the scientists excluded women altogether, according to *Just Like a Woman: How Gender Science Is Redefining What Makes Us Female* by Diane Hales. Schroeder would later describe this reasoning as "the restroom excuse." Over the years, the landmark project grew considerably and so did its budget. The researchers acquired more space and more restrooms, but for 20 years their study included no women.

Although NIH adopted a policy in 1985 of encouraging the inclusion of women, it did not publish rules to implement the policy until 1989, and the GAO found that even then the rules were ineffective. Diseases affecting women such as cervical cancer and osteoporosis were also getting short shrift. Only 13 percent of NIH's roughly $10 billion budget was devoted to women's health issues. Women's health research was also hampered by the lack of a gynecological or obstetrical research branch at NIH. Of 19,000 employees, NIH had only three obstetricians-gynecologists on permanent staff. In other words, the world's greatest medical research organization had largely failed to recognize that half the human race is female. Treatments from cholesterol-reducing drugs to AIDS therapies were being recommended for men and women when the vast majority of research had been conducted only on men. Even when women were included in research, there was often no effort to determine whether they were affected differently from men. This gap of medical information might be endangering millions of women, the GAO concluded.

"It's amazing to me that the number one killer of women in America is heart disease, and yet they don't put women in any of the heart disease tests so we don't know what happens if women take aspirin or drink coffee or eat fish or whatever," Schroeder said at the time. "Even on the breast cancer thing, which we've been working on so hard, they did the breast cancer study on men."

Meanwhile, the federal Food and Drug Administration wasn't including women in its drug studies, either. Men were generally the sole subjects of tests of drugs to treat depression even though the disorder affects twice as many women as men. Other drugs tested almost exclusively on men included appetite suppressants and diet drugs, which are used more widely by women than men. When women were included, the agency often didn't analyze the unique effects drugs had on women.

At first, NIH officials dismissed the GAO's findings. The main reason given by both NIH and the FDA for excluding women in their childbearing years from participating in medical research and safety tests of new drugs was to prevent possible damage to their unborn children and reproductive capacity. Gradually, the exclusion had been extended to women of all ages. As Schroeder pointed out, even the lab rats at NIH were male. But the scientists were also making life easier for themselves. If there were no women in their studies, they did not have to take into account complicated monthly cycles and fluctuating hormones.

Drug companies also said they wanted to prevent lawsuits by pregnant women whose unborn children were damaged during trial participation. However, the reality was just the reverse: lawsuits were far more likely to occur when drugs were administered to a population that had not been systematically studied in clinical research, as was the case in the 1960s with Thalidomide, a sedative widely given to pregnant women to counter the effects of morning sickness. The drug turned out to cause catastrophic birth defects, including abbreviated and flipper-like limbs.

The fact remained that women are not men. Men and women respond differently to some drugs because of differences in body structure, fat, and hormones. About a quarter of the women of childbearing age use birth control pills, which, when mixed with another drug, could produce an unintended effect. Those factors were simply being ignored.

The rationale for excluding women should be viewed in the broader context of discrimination against women in the medical field. In the early 1990s, women represented 36 percent of medical students, according to the American Medical Women's Association, while 98 percent of department chairmen at medical schools and 79 percent of instructors were male. The American Medical Association in its 140-plus years of existence had never had a woman as chief executive officer. A woman doctor earned an average of only sixty-three cents for every dollar her male counterpart received.

NIH was the target of sexual discrimination suits by female researchers and a high-profile case in the news was that of Dr. Frances K. Conley, a neurosurgeon who had resigned from the Stanford Medical School faculty because of sexual bias.

After release of the GAO report, Schroeder, Snowe, and other members of the caucus introduced the Women's Health Equity Act, which required the inclusion of women and minorities in clinical research in proportion to how often they are affected by the disease being studied. The $425 million proposal also called for the creation of an Office of Research on Women's Health at NIH and increases in funding to study breast cancer, ovarian cancer, osteoporosis, contraception, and infertility. Other provisions eventually enacted required Medicare reimbursement for screening mammography while putting in place federal standards to ensure the safety and accuracy of the procedure, and new programs to provide mammograms and pap smears to low-income women and to prevent infertility through early screening and treatment for sexually transmitted diseases.

By the end of a summer of congressional hearings, NIH officials were feeling the heat. Rather than waiting for the legislation to pass, they created a women's health research office on their own and vowed to better enforce the policy on including women in research. The following year, President Bush appointed Dr. Bernadine Healy, a respected research director of an Ohio heart clinic, to be NIH's first female director. In her first appearance before Congress, Healy announced that the Bush administration was launching a $625 million, fourteen-year "Women's Health Initiative" to discover how to prevent breast cancer, osteoporosis, and heart disease in older women. "Up until now," Healy acknowledged, "your doctor's advice on estrogen and what it will do to your health has been as good as the woman's next door."

However, Healy opposed the women's health equity act's requirement for including proportionate numbers of women and minorities in clinical research, saying the imposition of "gender quotas" on research was "scientifically flawed." Key provisions of the health equity act were incorporated in the annual funding bill for NIH. Bush vetoed the bill primarily because it authorized federal funding for research on fetal tissue transplants obtained from abortions to fight Parkinson's disease and Alzheimer's, but he also objected to the women's health research provisions, calling them "unnecessary."

"These are the wonderful little political tricks you see," Schroeder said in an interview. "They think that women aren't quite smart enough to figure this out. 'You won't get the bill, but we'll give you a woman to run it. And then we'll all hide behind her skirt and say, how can we be anti-women? We put a woman in.' She was a very good person, very qualified, wonderful, but I mean, here she is trying to defend something that's almost not defensible."

As with family leave, the change in administrations following the 1992 election removed the last roadblock that was holding back Schroeder and other advocates of women's health research. On June 10, 1993, President Clinton signed a three-year NIH reauthorization bill that included the women's health provisions Bush had vetoed the previous year. The bill gave statutory authority to NIH's office of research on women's health and the policy of including women in clinical trials. It also marked a 450 percent boost in breast cancer research over five years, far outstripping that of any other cancer.

"A lot of us who were politicians who had teaching hospitals in our district absolutely got creamed during this period," Schroeder said, looking back on the fight. "They used to call me down . . . [to ask] about why was I politicizing science and messing up the NIH. The University of Colorado was totally opposed to everything I did. . . . So, when the issue of women's health research did catch on, it was amazing to watch how quickly people flip-flopped. The same University of Colorado was asking me if I could get them more grants for women's health. It was like they totally re-wrote history."

The debate continued long after the bill became law. The GAO released a follow-up study in 2000 that showed that while NIH was then doing a good job of including women in clinical trials, it was doing a poor job of determining why men and women respond differently to the same drug. In 2001, the GAO released another study that showed that eight of the ten drugs the FDA had withdrawn from the market in the previous four years had more dangerous health risks for women than for men.

"This new GAO report calls into question whether the FDA and pharmaceutical industry are following a drug review process that adequately protects women," Waxman said at a press conference releasing the report. "In particular, it raises serious questions as to whether the drug companies are including women in clinical trials in adequate numbers and analyzing the data by sex before putting the drug on the market."

1. Pat, left, at a news conference with Gloria Steinem and Cathy Reynolds, right, a future Denver City Council member, during a Colorado Women's Caucus meeting in 1972.

Mel Schieltz, *Rocky Mountain News,* October 11, 1972.

2.

Pat with Scott, 5, and Jamie, 2, early in her first campaign. Her slogan was "She wins, we win."

Dick Davis, *Rocky Mountain News,* May 1972.

3.

Pat Schroeder enters a polling place with her two children.

Dick Davis, *Rocky Mountain News,* November 7, 1972.

4.   With her family viewing the results of her first electoral race.
Rocky Mountain News staff, November 7, 1972.

5. Pat points to a chart showing the power of corporate giants during a press conference on the economy.

John Gordon, *Rocky Mountain News,* October 1974.

6.
Pat and son Scott.

Mel Schieltz, *Rocky Mountain News,* November 5, 1974.

7. Pat spiked politics briefly in favor of volleyball during a picnic.

Howard Brock, *Rocky Mountain News,* August 15, 1976.

8.
Pat with freshman Rep. Tim Wirth in 1976. He would be elected to the Senate in 1986.

Rocky Mountain News staff, September 17, 1976.

9. Pat quickly learned how to attract attention for her causes.

Rocky Mountain News staff, January 18, 1978.

10. Even riding a scooter in the winter was not too much too ask.

Rocky Mountain News staff, February 13, 1978.

11.   Sen. Gary Hart and Pat at a 1980 airport news conference in Denver.
Rocky Mountain News staff, April 1980.

12. Rep. Pat Schroeder works the phones during the 1984 campaign.

Rocky Mountain News staff, 1984.

13. Pat leans on her husband Jim and cries after announcing she would not seek the presidency.

George Kochaniec Jr., *Rocky Mountain News*, September 28, 1987.

14.
Pat sorts through her itinerary and speeches on the plane to New Hampshire.

Janet Reeves, *Rocky Mountain News,* May 21, 1989.

15.
Pat begins the day early on Saturday with an informal meeting with members of New Hampshire's NOW chapter.

Janet Reeves, *Rocky Mountain News,* May 22, 1989.

16. Alta Collins sits on Pat's lap at the Edna Oliver Child Development Center in Denver.

Janet Reeves, *Rocky Mountain News*, November 1, 1990.

17. Pat answers a call on the "Homework Hotline" at George Washington High School in Denver.

Rocky Mountain News staff, September 19, 1991.

18.
Pat Schroeder
speaking.
*Rocky Mountain
News* staff, June 1991.

19. Pat talks to a passerby at the Capitol Hill People's Fair in Denver.

Rocky Mountain News staff, June 1, 1991.

20. Pat addresses a rally for Bill Clinton at Stapleton Airport in Denver.
Rocky Mountain News staff, November 5, 1992.

21. Pat Schroeder addresses gun control.

Rocky Mountain News staff, July 25, 1993.

22. Wearing an Aunt Sam costume, Pat campaigns on the 16th Street mall in Denver accompanied by supporter Philippa Troxell.

Linda McConnell, *Rocky Mountain News* staff photographer, November 1, 1994.

23. Pat Schroeder

Cyrus McCrimmon, *Rocky Mountain News,* 1995.

24. Pat with her mother, Bernice Scott, at her office.
Rocky Mountain News staff photographer, May 12, 1996.

25. Pat Schroeder in front of the Capitol building in her last year in office.
Ellen Jaskol, *Rocky Mountain News*, 1996.

7

Madam President

The morning of May 3, 1987, dawned to a political earthquake. "Hart Linked to Miami Woman," screamed a headline in the *Miami Herald*. The story was that former Sen. Gary Hart of Colorado, the overwhelming favorite for the Democratic presidential nomination, had spent much of the weekend in his Washington townhouse with an attractive young woman who had flown up from Miami to join him while his wife, Lee, was out of town.

Reporters from all over the world, from the venerable *Times* of London to the scandal-hungry *National Enquirer*, descended on Washington to confront Hart. They followed him on a campaign trek to New Hampshire and across the state in a snaking caravan of rental cars and TV trucks until the senator finally paused to answer questions. But when asked if he had ever committed adultery, Hart took a pass. By then, evasion didn't matter. Details had begun to emerge about Hart's relationship with twenty-nine-year-old party girl Donna Rice and a cruise they had taken earlier in the spring to Bimini aboard a yacht aptly named *The Monkey Business*. Five days after the *Herald* story broke, Hart called a press conference in Denver to announce he was ending his campaign for the presidency.

Until Hart's abrupt departure, the quest for the 1988 Democratic nomination had been a somnolent affair. After two terms of Ronald Reagan, Democrats were desperate to regain the White House. Four years earlier, Hart had used his theme of "new ideas," a shoestring budget, and an army of volunteers to nearly wrest the nomination from former vice president Walter Mondale, who had the almost total support of the party hierarchy. Mondale then lost to Reagan in the greatest electoral landslide in U.S. history, leaving Democrats to wonder what might have happened if they had nominated Hart. By May 1987, the latest poll from Iowa, which holds the critical first-in-the-nation caucus, gave the Colorado senator the support of an overwhelming 65 percent of the state's Democrats. Less than a month later, Hart was history and the race for the Democratic nomination was wide open.

Pat Schroeder had taken an early morning flight to California the day the *Herald* story came out. Her phone was ringing as she checked into her hotel room. It was her husband, Jim, calling to warn her that he was besieged by reporters and others who were trying to track her down. "Don't answer the phone," Jim told his wife. "Turn on the TV. You won't believe what happened!"

The congresswoman was the cochair of Hart's presidential campaign. She had flown to California at the campaign's request to meet with newspaper editorial boards that the candidate was unable to fit into his schedule. Pat and Jim Schroeder had long been friendly with Gary and Lee Hart, although they were not close. Aside from their obvious Colorado and Democratic political connections, the two couples shared similar views on most issues. They lived in the same condominium complex when in Denver. They had occasional dinners together over the years that Schroeder and Hart had been in Congress. Pat had helped Gary in his 1974 and 1980 Senate races and in his 1984 presidential campaign, although her role had been small. Her role as cochair of his latest presidential campaign was a practical one for both of them: His association with her enhanced his credentials with feminists and her association with the Democratic front-runner added to her prestige.

Schroeder had heard rumors that Hart was having affairs, but she had been assured by his staff that it was just gossip. So there was a sense of betrayal when she discovered, along with the rest of the world, that he had had a liaison with Rice and perhaps with other women as well. "I felt we'd all been let down by him," Schroeder wrote in her memoirs. "I felt he used me because having a woman at the head of his campaign might deflect these issues."

Until Hart's withdrawal from the race, Schroeder had always laughed off suggestions that she might run for president someday. "You'd have to be crazy to do something like that," she would say. But her daughter, Jamie, then a seventeen-year-old high school senior, told the *Los Angeles Times* that she had detected a new attitude on her mother's part shortly after Hart dropped out of the race. "We'd be doing the dishes and talking or something like that and she'd say, 'What are you going to do when I'm president, ha ha ha.' I never, ever thought my mother would consider something as crazy as that." Jim Schroeder was all for the idea. He scribbled out a three-page memo for his wife outlining the reasons why she should consider running. Then he left the country on a business trip.

Schroeder has always maintained that she decided to launch her exploratory campaign for the presidency in 1987 because friends and supporters were urging her to look at the race. And she did receive many calls from people telling her she would make a good candidate, especially Democratic activists in Colorado who were left in the lurch by Hart's withdrawal from the race. It is not unusual for prominent members of Congress to be nudged that way sometime in their careers, but in the beginning, there was no formal or obvious public effort to persuade her to run. There were no public figures coming forward to say the nation needed Pat Schroeder. It was Schroeder who initiated private meetings with groups of friends and political supporters to gauge the possibilities.

At one of those meetings, which took place on June 5 in her congressional office in the Rayburn building on Capitol Hill, Schroeder had called together press secretary Andrea Camp; her chief of staff, Dan Buck, and the media director for the National Organization for Women Legal Defense Fund, Kathy Bonk. Camp and Bonk, along with Pam Solo, the former nun and anti-nuclear activist who had run Schroeder's House campaigns, would form the nucleus of the exploratory presidential campaign. Although Buck had no official role in the campaign because he continued to oversee Schroeder's congressional duties, he naturally served as advisor and sounding board.

Schroeder's personal office within her larger office in the Rayburn House office building was a warm, informal space with large windows, high ceilings, lots of leafy plants, and many small, personal touches. There was an overstuffed leather couch and a cocktail table flanked by leather chairs. Her desk was at the far end of the room in front of the windows. On the wall behind the couch was a colorful quilt with jungle animals. Family photographs were sprinkled here and there. A poster of Eleanor Roosevelt was on one wall. On another was a poster of a bear riding a bicycle.

At the meeting, which Bonk recounted in an article she wrote for the *Los Angeles Times* later that year, Schroeder sat in the middle of the small group, taking copious notes on a yellow legal pad in her lap as they tried to assess what would be required to launch a credible bid for the Democratic presidential nomination and whether she should indeed take that momentous step. On paper, Schroeder's credentials looked very good. She was forty-six and a Harvard-trained lawyer. She was the senior woman in Congress. She had served in the House longer than Rep. Richard Gephardt of Missouri, one of the leading contenders for the nomination now that Hart had withdrawn. She had campaigned all over the country for Democratic candidates. She was a senior member of the House Armed Service Committee with expertise in military issues. She was a national figure with a base of support among some of the party's important constituencies, such as feminists, environmentalists, and the peace movement.

There were also obvious drawbacks. With a year and a half until election day, it was already late to get into the race. Democratic activists in key states had for the most part already committed themselves to other candidates. It was unclear whether she could raise the money necessary to launch a credible campaign. Just trying to find their way through the Byzantine rules and regulations that had to be met to place her name on primary ballots in each state would be a major, maybe even insurmountable, hurdle. Perhaps most important of all, there was the question of whether the nation was ready for a woman presidential candidate. It had been fifteen years since a woman had made a bid for a major party presidential nomination, and that effort, by Democratic congresswoman Shirley Chisholm of New York, was seen as largely symbolic.

"I know I don't want to run as a symbol. No suicide missions," Bonk recalled Schroeder's telling the group. "I'm not out for a forum. I've got a perfectly good one in Congress. I really don't want to be perceived as being only a women's candidate." Nor did she want to run for vice president. "It's not worth it to me to lose the seniority [in Congress]," Schroeder said. "If I do this, if I really run, it has got to be to win." Yet, from the start, Schroeder probably underestimated the difficulties inherent in launching a presidential campaign. "Somehow in our excitement we never discussed what would later become some of the toughest problems of the Schroeder organization: the difficulty of raising money and the complex technical rules that determine how to get convention delegates on ballots so late in the campaign season," Bonk wrote. As Buck recalled it, the issue of money was raised at the meeting, but was not a major item.

But Schroeder also had something to prove. In 1984, Mondale and the powers-that-be in the Democratic party had passed her over in favor of New York congresswoman Geraldine Ferraro, who was tapped to become the first female running mate on a major party presidential ticket. Mondale's very public search for the right woman for the ticket—a blatant attempt to appeal to the "women's vote" and to make the party appear more progressive—had led to intense speculation in the news media about which woman had the most to offer, which woman had the right stuff. Even in 1984 the field of potential women candidates was very small because there were still relatively few women in high public office. Schroeder was easily the best-known woman in Congress. And, if not universally beloved, she was held in great esteem by the party's liberal base. She had always worked well with labor, blacks, and Hispanics. She was young, attractive, and articulate, a mother of two children. She represented a "safe" Democratic district that the party could hold if she gave up the seat. She had more seniority than Ferraro. Jim Schroeder had even sent Mondale a memo promoting his wife for the job. And yet, there is no indication that Schroeder was ever near the top of Mondale's list. The two women most seriously considered for the job were Ferraro and Dianne Feinstein, who was then the mayor of San Francisco.

When the search first began, Schroeder acknowledged to the press that she was interested. Later, after it became apparent that Mondale was not interested in her, Schroeder would insist that she never wanted the job. When asked by reporters if she had talked to the Mondale campaign—and everyone was asking—she would blow off the role of veep as unworthy of her. "I wouldn't like to be vice president if it's a helpmate-type role," she would say. "In that case, I would much rather be attorney general. You're running your own office and not just a cheerleader doing funerals." Indeed, Schroeder took such pains to make it appear that she was turning down Mondale, as if he were an unwanted suitor, that the denials took on a Shakespearean "thou dost protest too much" quality.

In fact, it was Mondale and the party hierarchy who didn't want Schroeder. She was too controversial. She was too mouthy. You never knew what she was going to say. She had that wacky, offbeat humor that sometimes made her look flaky. In a presidential race, just a single misstep can become political suicide. But most of all, Schroeder wasn't a team player. She marched to her own drummer, and Democratic leaders could never be absolutely sure they could count on her if things got tough. The one quality presidents have consistently valued in their vice presidents is loyalty. "Pat was always issues first instead of party first," Bonk said. "I think they were looking for someone who was party first, someone whose priorities were the party above their belief system and above the issues."

So, Schroeder wasn't being completely disingenuous when she would tell people that she didn't have the personality for the number two job. There is also no reason to believe that she bore Ferraro any ill will and every reason to believe that she was well pleased in an intellectual sense to have had a woman on the ticket. But Schroeder also would have been less than human if she hadn't felt some regret, hadn't been a bit insulted and maybe even a bit bitter, at being passed over. From the moment Ferraro was chosen, she became the national personification of the drive for women's rights, the icon and oracle for anything to do with what women wanted, women needed, or women deserved from their elected officeholders. In short, Ferraro became, for a time, the number one woman in politics, while Schroeder was obliged to take a back seat.

In the end, Ferraro probably would have been better off had Mondale picked someone else. From the moment she was selected, Mondale's campaign was bogged down in controversy over the finances of Ferraro's husband, real estate investor John A. Zaccaro, who initially refused to make the couple's tax returns public. When Mondale lost the race, Ferraro was out of a job. Despite several attempts over the years, she has never returned to public office. By the time the 1988 campaign rolled around, there was a widely held view among political operatives in both parties that Mondale had badly miscalculated when he bowed to pressure from feminists and agreed to put a woman on the ticket. The consensus was that it made him appear to be "pandering to special interests."

At the conclusion of the June 5 meeting in Schroeder's office, it was clear that the congresswoman was leaning toward running. Bonk, Camp, and Buck were all given assignments. Then, Schroeder got up to leave; she had a plane to catch to Denver. What happened next is unclear. According to Bonk, as Schroeder was heading for the door she just happened to get a call from an Associated Press reporter on an unrelated story involving the presidential race. Somehow in the conversation Schroeder told the reporter that she might become a candidate herself.

"People have asked me to look at it seriously, and I feel I have to look at it seriously," Schroeder said. AP immediately sent a story out to newsrooms all over the world that the Colorado congresswoman was giving serious consideration to becoming a candidate for the presidency. CNN, which was airing a congressional hearing live that day on the Reagan administration's secret arms-for-hostages trading that became known as the "Iran-Contra" scandal, scrolled the news about Schroeder across the bottom of the television screen. The phones in the congresswoman's Washington and Denver congressional offices began ringing nonstop. By the time Schroeder landed at Stapleton International Airport in Denver there was a crowd of reporters and cameramen waiting for her. She was all over the evening news that night and the front pages of newspapers the next morning. In Bangkok, Jim Schroeder found out about his wife's plans when he read about them in the *International Herald Tribune.*

The initial reaction among many political insiders was to assume that Schroeder wasn't serious about winning the nomination, but that she was secretly angling for vice president. In an attempt to squelch any speculation, Schroeder took to flatly telling anyone who asked that she would not be available as a vice presidential candidate, even if drafted. "I don't do fund-raisers, funerals, and cheerleading," was her standard reply, a reprise of her explanation in 1984 for why she wasn't interested in becoming Mondale's running mate.

The next few weeks were spent making hundreds of phone calls to test support for Schroeder. A campaign committee called "Schroeder 1988?" was formed. "Don't forget the question mark," Camp would tell reporters, emphasizing that this was truly an exploratory campaign and that Schroeder had not made up her mind to run. From the start, Schroeder knew that money was critical and would be difficult to raise. "That's very serious, that's very sobering," she told the *New York Times*. "You can have the best ideas in the world and they don't get out unless you have the money to get them out."

Schroeder's biggest hope for quick cash was Hollywood, so not surprisingly one of her first official campaign trips after establishing her exploratory committee was to Los Angeles. Gary David Goldberg, executive producer of the popular 1980s TV series *Family Ties,* had symbolically lent his name as finance chairman to her campaign. On July 9, Hollywood glitterati gathered at the spectacular, art-filled Brentwood home of entertainment executive Norman Lear, founder of the liberal People for the American Way, to size up Schroeder. Although Schroeder impressed the gathering with her command of the issues and some checks were collected, the unofficial consensus was that she was "unelectable" and, therefore, that the big donations would be made elsewhere, according to Bonk.

The race for the Democratic nomination had grown extremely crowded by mid-July, with no front-runner. The declared candidates were Sen. Paul Simon of Illinois, Sen. Joe Biden of Delaware, Sen. Al Gore of Tennessee, Rep. Richard Gephardt of Missouri, Massachusetts Gov. Michael Dukakis, former Arizona Gov. Bruce Babbitt, and Rev. Jesse Jackson. With Schroeder's quasi-entry into the race, pundits had taken to calling the Democratic field "Snow White and the Seven Dwarfs."

With so many candidates and no front-runner, the race quickly became a series of cattle calls—events at which most or all of the candidates would show up and try to appear to have more support, more momentum, or more money than the rest. The first cattle call at which Schroeder joined the other candidates was a meeting of the chairs of the state Democratic parties in Cleveland on July 17. While the other candidates traveled with an entourage, Schroeder showed up with one aide, Camp, who fretted that she wouldn't be able to keep up or would make some sort of political faux pas. "What should I do first?" Camp asked Bonk. "Is there anything special I should know?"

Follow your gut, Bonk told her. "If we stopped to think about the enormity of what we're doing," Bonk said, "we'd go nuts." As it turned out, Camp needn't have worried. While the staffs of the other candidates were turning themselves inside out in search of the media spotlight, reporters were following Schroeder everywhere.

The following day, Schroeder received a tumultuous show of support from 2,000 delegates to the National Organization for Women's annual convention in Philadelphia. "Run, Pat, run!" the delegates chanted as they stomped and clapped, repeatedly interrupting her thirty-minute talk in the ballroom of the Wyndham Franklin Plaza Hotel. "If I were president, we wouldn't have a Bork—we'd have a Barbara Jordan," Schroeder told them. "Maybe women would be safer if we had a few more battered women's shelters and fewer missiles," was another applause line. None of the male candidates attended the convention. Volunteers gathered donations from delegates on the floor of the convention hall. Afterward, a NOW vice president carrying a large bag tracked down Solo and Bonk in the lobby. Inside the bag were $25,000 in cash and $325,000 in pledges. "This is too large for the hotel safe, and I don't want to be responsible," she told them.

Stunned, they went up to Bonk's hotel room and stared at the money for awhile. Suddenly Solo and Bonk realized they would have the resources to hire some staff, although they could only afford young, unseasoned campaigners who were willing to work for a meager salary of between $800 and $1,700 a month. Schroeder's staff was also heartened by a test direct-mail solicitation to 25,000 names on a national donor list that drew contributions from 4 percent of the people on the list, which direct-mail consultants told them was a high rate of response. At the same time, people who wanted to work, paid or unpaid, besieged the campaign. There was no time to screen applicants. When one potential state coordinator who had come highly recommended turned out to have been accused of attempting to rape a worker in another campaign, the coterie around Schroeder was thoroughly shaken.

On the campaign trail, Ronald Reagan was Schroeder's chief target, and she used her famous wit for all it was worth. Reagan's foreign policy "comes from the glands, not the brains," he "roars like Rambo and acts like Bambi," she would tell audiences. His economic policy, she said, is reminiscent of Imelda Marcos's favorite saying: "If the shoe fits, charge it."

"I'm not going to be the Tinkerbell of this campaign, bring out the magic poofle dust and everything's OK," Schroeder repeatedly told reporters. "I will run if we're ready to have a rendezvous with reality." That "rendezvous with reality," which became Schroeder's campaign theme, was a reference to Reagan's saccharine 1984 reelection theme, "It's morning in America," and his feel-good rhetoric.

"Mr. President, it's morning in America," Schroeder would say. "We've gotten up, we've had a cup of coffee. Let's have a little rendezvous with reality because we're looking at the Twenty-first Century . . . The threshold. We've got a whole lot of problems that we have not solved and we had better get on with it. We cannot mess around."

Her chief issues on the campaign trail were family issues: medical leave for parents of newborn and adopted children, better child care and child support enforcement, and tax policies that helped parents. "We have a tax code that encourages people much more to raise thoroughbred horses than children," Schroeder would tell audiences.

To the delight of liberals and the chagrin of conservatives, Schroeder's campaign made much of the fact that the congresswoman was ranked as more fiscally conservative than Republican Congressman Jack Kemp of New York, the guru of supply-side economics and the darling of economic conservatives, on a scorecard of members of Congress kept by the penny-pinching National Taxpayers' Union. How could this be? Easy. Schroeder may have favored greater spending on social welfare programs, but she voted against every pork-laden defense budget and questionable weapons system that came down the pike. On balance, she had voted to cut more dollars than Kemp. She also had a 95 percent rating from the liberal Americans for Democratic Action.

Like many candidates, Schroeder was frustrated by the media coverage. She received more of it than most candidates, but it wasn't always the kind of coverage she wanted. Instead of exploring her ideas or positions, much of the coverage of her race focused on the fact that she was a woman, especially the TV coverage. "There were seven candidates, and the TV would always show Jesse Jackson with African Americans, and they would always show me with women. So how you work out that ghettoization was a real issue," Schroeder told the *Los Angeles Times.*

Voters were also a problem. "You would give a speech on some kind of policy, and people would want to ask about why you were wearing earrings, why you weren't wearing earrings, why do you dye your hair, why don't you dye your hair, why do you wear green? You'd say, 'Can we talk about the speech?'" Schroeder said.

Schroeder's wardrobe featured a lot of ruffles, floppy collars, polka dots, and clothes with kitschy themes—not unattractive or in poor taste, but not exactly presidential, either. After the campaign, Schroeder responded to the fashion criticism heaped on her by consulting an image adviser who directed her toward a simpler, more elegant wardrobe with occasional splashes of bold color. Her bangs were cut to look wispier and she added earrings. Ferraro reported much the same problem when she was a vice presidential candidate. "Like Pat Schroeder, I, too, tired of questions about my hair and clothes when I was on the campaign trail," Ferraro said in a letter to the *New York Times.* When she left office in January 1996, Schroeder said the one subject she had received more mail on during nearly a quarter-century in public office was her clothes and her hair.

Money had become all-important by late summer, and Schroeder and her staff were asked about it at every turn. They finally started telling people that she had set a goal of raising $2 million by the end of September, which became the drop-dead date for a decision on whether to formally get into the race. "If there's dough, I go," Schroeder would tell audiences again and again.

Throughout her quasi-campaign, Schroeder generated large crowds. A fund raiser at the University Club in Minneapolis in August organized by Minnesota secretary of state Joan Growe was expected to draw 250 people, but 1,200 showed up. Only a fraction of the people could fit in the room set aside for the event. Schroeder gave her speech to the crowd in the main room and then gave three more speeches in three more rooms to the overflow crowd. She and her staffed lugged her microphone and podium with her from room to room.

Unlike at the NOW convention, all the male candidates joined Schroeder at a convention of the more mainstream National Women's Political Caucus (NWPC) in Portland, Oregon, in August. Schroeder was warmly received by the caucus delegates who, like their sisters at NOW, cheered her with shouts of "Run, Pat, run!" But the caucus delegates were less militant in their feminism than their NOW counterparts and more interested in practical politics. Many members of the caucus interviewed by the media said they would stick with the Democratic candidates they had already pledged to support rather than switch to Schroeder. "I wish her well," Ellen Globokar, a campaign organizer from Washington State, told *Newsweek*, "but no one is going to back somebody just because she's a woman."

Four years earlier, Mondale and other Democratic candidates had tried to appeal to delegates at the NWPC's convention based on their support for "women's issues" like abortion and the Equal Rights Amendment. But the male candidates at the women's political caucus in 1987 were wary of appearing to be pandering, and they adopted a different strategy: Show your respect by treating the women's caucus the same way you would any other important audience. Their effort to talk about everything but that which might be construed as "feminist" was so pronounced that one woman in the audience rose to speak on behalf of Schroeder, declaring: "She's the only candidate who will talk to us and use the word we haven't heard in three days. Pat Schroeder supports choice."

In late August, Schroeder took two weeks off from the campaign and went away with Jim, Scott, and Jamie on a Mediterranean cruise. It was the first time they had had any real time to spend together in months and there were a lot of family considerations they needed to discuss. Would Scott Schroeder, then a twenty-one-year-old senior in his last semester at Georgetown University, drop out to work for his mother's campaign? Would Jim Schroeder have to take a leave of absence from his law firm? It was Jamie's last year in high school. How would she be affected?

Schroeder had raised only $850,000 of her stated goal of $2 million, although it was enough to qualify for federal matching funds if she became a formal candidate. Publicly, Schroeder's advisers were insisting that money would not be a problem if she decided to run. But privately it was a concern. She and her staff were heartened when entertainment billionaire Marvin Davis endorsed her and promised to help with fund-raising. The campaign set October 29 for a fund-raising reception at Davis's Denver home—a month after Schroeder's scheduled announcement. Pundits read the date as a sign she had decided to run.

In a September 1987 *Time* magazine poll, Schroeder led the other Democratic candidates on matters of who would best manage the economy, which candidate people would be "proud" to have as president, and whom they would trust. Yet the same poll found that only 9 percent of respondents named Schroeder their "first choice," compared with 26 percent who cited Jackson and 11 percent who chose Dukakis. A poll sponsored by the National Women's Political Caucus showed that while resistance to a woman president had dropped dramatically, roughly 30 percent of the population still felt that a woman, any woman, would be a "worse" president than a man. The consensus among the political professionals was that Schroeder didn't stand a chance at the nomination, that she was a symbolic candidate at best.

"Can Pat Schroeder be more than the 'women's candidate'?" was the headline in *Business Week* the week leading up to her all-important announcement. Schroeder "could make a difference when she jumps into the race," wrote *Business Week* reporters Douglas Harbrecht and Richard Fly. "The mere fact of her candidacy will mark another key step in women's political aspirations." Schroeder herself was questioning out loud whether she could ever be just a woman candidate rather than the women's candidate. She complained that people kept asking her why she was "running as a woman." Her response: "Do I have a choice?"

"The issue is whether America is ready to accept me as a qualified presidential candidate who is a woman," she would tell audiences. "If my name were Patrick and you look at the qualifications they are certainly equal or better." And yet, Schroeder would play to that very gender difference, asking audiences if the nation was "man enough to elect a woman." The novelty of being a woman running for president also brought Schroeder the kind of media attention that the other candidates struggling to separate themselves from the pack could only envy and perhaps even resent. That her name was not Patrick was a fact that no one was likely to forget, least of all Democratic power brokers hungry for a return to power. "After eight years in the Reagan wilderness, Democrats . . . are looking for a winner," Harbrecht and Fly concluded. "And many feel that while their hearts may be with Schroeder, their votes will probably go elsewhere."

There were other doubts as well. Schroeder acknowledged to the *Washington Post*'s Marjorie Williams that as much as anything else the dreary prospect of "being a presidential candidate like all the other guys I see out there" was causing her to hesitate. It was clear that many of the quirky, offbeat qualities that made up her special political persona would have to change to accommodate a national campaign.

Schroeder frequently complained that the grueling nature of life on the road had turned her body into a "chemical waste dump." Her energy was being fueled by an overload of caffeine from the coffee she drank all day and calories from the ice cream sundaes she craved. She refused to employ any hired-gun political consultants, preferring to rely on a coterie of trusted friends, staffers, and people from liberal cause groups. "I keep asking, can somebody give me a model of a nontraditional way to run a campaign?" Schroeder said.

"Schroeder was a free spirit in an uptight business, a people politician accustomed to saying whatever she pleased and sweeping up afterward," *Newsweek*'s election team wrote in their book recounting the campaign, *The Quest for the Presidency: The 1988 Campaign.* "Presidential politics seemed to her to forbid that; you couldn't even put happy faces at the bottoms of your letters anymore. It was all too stylized, too confined by polls, and photo ops. She had wanted it to be like a congressional race, up close and personal, and it wasn't; it was a scam, she thought, with the candidates and the voters as its common victims."

Jim Schroeder, who had been his wife's sounding board throughout the endeavor, thought she should take the final step. "He had been hustling all the legal expertise and political acumen he could to try to convince me to run," Schroeder recalled in her 1989 memoir, *Champion of the Great American Family.* "He would pace around our kitchen floor, smoking his pipe, playing out various scenarios, and making a Schroeder presidency sound not only possible, but plausible . . . Jim's advocacy of my running was not limited to the kitchen. We debated in the car, in airplanes, over the phone, and at parties. And it was not limited to me. Jim would debate the question with friends, columnists, and my staff. People were stunned by his enthusiasm and confidence. They had expected him to be against the idea."

The week before Schroeder's announcement, Biden quit the race after acknowledging he had been disciplined for plagiarism at law school, had embellished his academic record on the campaign trail, and had borrowed, without crediting, the words of other politicians in his speeches. Coming only four months after the Gary Hart fiasco, the Biden episode served to underscore the personal toll that life in the white-hot spotlight of a presidential campaign can exact and the fragility of political power and the public's favor.

"It is one more down note. I think we all get tarnished by that type of news," Schroeder told reporters. But feminists saw opportunity for Schroeder in the Hart and Biden debacles. "All this [talk] of morality and integrity really makes people ready to look at a woman," Celinda Lake of the Women's Campaign Fund said. "And not just any woman, but a woman who has served on the House Armed Services Committee and the House Judiciary Committee and has an impressive resume."

As Schroeder's September 28 announcement neared, polls were showing her in the middle of the pack of Democratic candidates. The British bookmaking firm William Hill lowered its odds on Schroeder's becoming the next U.S. president, dropping them from a prohibitive 200 to 1 to a more likely 66 to 1. Schroeder was keeping close counsel, but the signs were there for those who looked that she was leaning against running. The week before her announcement, she passed up an opportunity to participate in a debate in Iowa with the other six Democratic candidates. She did give a speech to a standing-room-only crowd at a National Press Club luncheon in Washington, but she refused to hint at what her decision would be. The determining factor, Schroeder said, would be whether she decided the country would accept a woman as a qualified candidate.

By tradition, the Press Club invites all the major presidential candidates to speak to its members. The speeches are aired on C-SPAN and usually attract a gaggle of Washington reporters, so the candidates are generally glad to have the forum. Among Schroeder's guests at the head table that afternoon was folk singer Judy Collins, who was supporting her campaign. At the conclusion of the question-and-answer session following Schroeder's speech, Collins stepped to the microphone. She had written a song inspired by Schroeder, Collins explained, and she would like to sing it for the luncheon guests. The lights dimmed and Collins proceeded a cappella in her matchless voice to describe her dream of a woman president. By the time Collins finished, many of the veteran feminists in the audience were moved to tears. The applause was thunderous. Collins and Schroeder embraced. Members of the audience hugged each other. Autograph-seekers encircled both Schroeder and Collins. It was surely one of the most unusual appearances by any presidential candidate in the Press Club's long history, but then it was typical in many ways of the kind of candidate Schroeder was and had always been: warm, touchy-feely, spontaneous, untraditional, and genuine.

Two days before her scheduled announcement, Jim Schroeder wrote his wife what he described later to writer Susan Ferraro as a "neutral" memo, listing the pros and cons of formally getting into the race. After sending the memo, Jim Schroeder said he got three phone calls that made him even more convinced that his wife should run. One was from an executive of a Texas oil and gas organization, who told him, "We're ready to go, we need a Westerner, we need somebody like your wife; let me know what we can do." Another was from pollster Lou Harris, who told him, "Your wife is already number three and I can promise that by Iowa . . . New Hampshire, she'll be number two." The third was from Bill Dunfey, a former Democratic chairman of New Hampshire, who told him, "We're ready up here, let me know what you want us to do." To the end, Jim Schroeder remained his wife's most ardent advocate for launching a full-fledged candidacy.

By the time the big day arrived, Schroeder was referring to her much-anticipated announcement as "my own rendezvous with reality." Since early June she had traveled some 75,000 miles crisscrossing the country to test support. Schroeder selected the plaza in front of the Denver Civic Center in the heart of her district for her announcement. It was a perfect Indian summer afternoon—sunshine, blue skies, shirtsleeves weather. Denver newspapers had published the time and location of the announcement that morning, and a large crowd of supporters and onlookers had gathered. There was an arch of yellow balloons over the gathering. Paul Simon's *Graceland* blared from the public address system.

When Schroeder stepped to the podium on that elevated stage, Jim at her side, she looked out on a sea of friendly faces. There were people she knew dating back to her first race for the House fifteen years earlier and some she knew from her first years in Denver as a young attorney. Some dated even further back in her life than that. For the most part, they were people who believed in her and wanted her to be their president. "I could see my parents who had never known me to back down before," Schroeder recalled. Also in attendance were the national and international news media. CNN was airing the announcement live. All over the country, thousands watched to learn the Colorado congresswoman's decision. There was a sense of history in the making.

As she faced the crowd, Schroeder tried to explain the difficulties of making a late start and how grateful she was to those who had supported her. In the end, however, her reasoning seemed to come down to a simple feeling that she wasn't comfortable being a presidential candidate and doing the necessary, but sometimes dehumanizing, things that candidates for the highest office in the land must do. "I learned a lot about America and I learned a lot about Pat Schroeder. That's why I will not be a candidate for president. I could not figure out how to run," she said, but broke off as suddenly the crowd understood her intent and there was a collective gasp of disappointment that drowned out her words. Cries of "no, no, no" rang out. Schroeder tried to go on, but she was overcome with emotion. A trickle of tears gave way to full-throated sobs as her face scrunched up. For nearly a minute she was overcome with emotion, unable to speak. She leaned back against Jim for support and he handed her a handkerchief. Some in the crowd chanted "Run, Pat, run." Jim urged her to "take a minute, take a minute." There was a prolonged pause as a national television audience watched her distress before she collected herself and went on. "I could not figure out how to run and not be separated from those I served," she continued "There must be a way, but I haven't figured it out yet. I could not bear to turn every human contact into a photo opportunity." Immediately afterward, she turned to Jim and buried her face in his shoulder, sobbing. "Suddenly I thought I had let everybody down and they didn't let me down. I felt so crappy," Schroeder explained to *Ms.* magazine five months later.

"You had to be there, as they say," Jim Schroeder told the *Rocky Mountain News.* "You had all these people out there. You had all these people that really liked Pat. She had to tell them, basically, 'Look, I just don't think I can do this.' And there was this groan out there in the crowd. And she let a few tears go down.'"

The next morning, newspapers all across the country ran front-page pictures of her crying. The *Washington Post* ran a picture of Jim wiping tears from her cheek. *USA Today* ran a color picture of Schroeder with her face "so screwed up with emotion she looked like a Cabbage Patch doll," according to one pundit. Schroeder's decision not to seek the presidency was overshadowed by a national discussion that immediately ensued about whether it is permissible for politicians to cry in public and what her tears meant for the future of women in politics. Liberals, especially feminists, were embarrassed. Her opponents cited the incident as a character weakness, an example of an emotionalism that was out of place and perhaps dangerous in someone who wanted to hold the highest office in the world. Some of the strongest criticism came from female pundits. *Washington Post* editorial writer Amy Schwartz said in a column that Schroeder's tears, her refusal to accept the dehumanizing aspects of campaigning for high-level office, and her sometimes cutesy-feminine mannerisms provided "ammunition to those who saw women as sugary little girls rather than serious people to be taken seriously." In short, Schwartz said Schroeder was an embarrassment rather than a role model to a new generation of younger, "post-feminist" women.

"I've always been angry with her for that column on the tears," Schroeder told the *Rocky Mountain News* nearly a decade later. "Nobody said when Muskie cried, 'OK, now a whole generation of men can't be president.'" (In the famous February 1972 incident, Democratic presidential front-runner Edmund Muskie of Maine choked up and appeared to cry while defending his wife from editorials in New Hampshire's right-wing *Manchester Union Leader.* He quit the race not long afterward.)

For years, Schroeder would bring up the crying controversy in various forums, often in a joking manner, as if to dismiss the incident as unimportant to her and significant of nothing. "I tried to get Kleenex to be the corporate sponsor of my campaign, but they didn't buy into it," was her standard quip. If probed further, she would simply maintain that crying was human and natural. She never apologized, but the response to the incident clearly pained her deeply.

For the rest of her congressional career, Schroeder's staff would keep a file of prominent men and women who cried in public. Ronald Reagan cried when he left office, George Bush says he cries at the movies, and so on. Each new example would be added to the file and used as a reason for Buck or Camp to point out to reporters that none of these other public figures was criticized for crying, nor told that they were letting down their gender. Schroeder's bitterness was palpable and those closest to her shared it. "You don't see anybody saying never again can a man be governor of New Hampshire because John Sununu Jr. cried so hard he couldn't even finish his speech when he was saying good-bye. Or never again could a man run for president because I think every single one of them has shed tears in public now," Schroeder told the *Los Angeles Times.* "And then people say, 'We don't want somebody's finger on the button that cries.' Okay, you could debate that. I don't want anybody's finger on the button that doesn't cry. But everybody that I've known whose finger has been on the button has been publicly crying."

More than a decade after her brush with presidential politics, Schroeder continued to assert, "The White House is still America's ultimate clubhouse with a 'No Girls Allowed' sign posted."

8

The Tailhook Tale

The year 1973 had been a milestone for both Schroeder and the U.S. armed services. For Schroeder, it marked her transition from first-time candidate to freshman congresswoman. For the military, it marked the end of the draft and the beginning of the All-Volunteer Force.

It was clear from the start that the All-Volunteer Force would not be able to attract enough male recruits to meet all the nation's needs. Thus, of necessity, the military services would have to open their ranks to more women and integrate them more thoroughly than ever before. They did so reluctantly and with the understanding that women would not become members of combat units. In the army, infantry, artillery, and tank units were off limits. In the air force, piloting fighter jets and other combat aircraft was forbidden. In the navy, combat ships would go to sea without women. Further, the prestigious military service academies—the training grounds for future military leaders—remained exclusively male.

Women have served in the U.S. military in one capacity or another since the Revolutionary War. Some women even dressed as men, concealing their gender as they soldiered. World War I marked the first war in which women served openly in the army, navy, and marine corps, primarily as nurses and clerical workers. The role of women in the military expanded greatly during World War II. Women continued to serve as nurses, office workers, cooks, and bakers, but they also worked as non-combat pilots, auto mechanics, truck drivers, radio operators, and cryptographers, freeing up more men for combat. Despite being barred from official combat positions, women were sometimes exposed to hostile fire. Army nurses in the Philippines, for example, worked through Japanese bombing raids and spent the remainder of the war as prisoners. By the war's end, 400,000 women had served their country in uniform.

The Women's Armed Services Act of 1948 established a permanent place for women in the military. Over 120,000 women served in the military during the Korean War era, but only 650 women actually served in Korea. Over 7,500 women served in Vietnam. In both Korea and Vietnam, women served primarily as nurses, sometimes working in close proximity to front lines and under harsh conditions. Six women were killed under fire while serving in Vietnam.

In the debate over the role of women in the armed services after World War II, military leaders gave several reasons for banning women from combat, including a fear that the public wouldn't stand for women's coming home in body bags or being mistreated as prisoners of war, potentially weakening support for military action. Another argument was that women could not physically meet the demands and training required for combat—that most women simply didn't have the strength of most men. Another fear was that men and women living in close quarters under rough conditions would cause embarrassment, lowering morale. But perhaps most significantly, there was a widely shared belief among the military hierarchy that combat was a uniquely male occupation and that all-male fighting units were necessary to good morale and teamwork. Throw women into the mix, they reasoned, and all kinds of problems could occur. Relationships and jealousies might play havoc with morale. Some men might take unnecessary risks and exercise poor judgment either to protect women or to impress them.

Usually unspoken, but intrinsic to the debate over the role of women in the military and their exclusion from combat, was the innate sexism of a military culture in which women are symbolically denigrated, vilified, humiliated, and used as scapegoats in the promotion of male bonding. Reducing women to sex objects through crude jokes, the prominent display of pornography, and the sexually graphic cadence calls of drill sergeants were an ingrained part of military life. In her 1997 book *Ground Zero: The Gender Wars in the Military,* writer Linda Bird Francke cites the example of a marine platoon graduating from recruit training in 1989 who proudly posed with their drill instructor for a formal photograph holding an enlarged picture of a naked woman and a sign reading, "kill, rape, pillage, burn."

"Many individual men in the different services work well with women and respect both their contributions and authority," Francke wrote. "But individuals don't count in the military. The military culture is driven by a group dynamic centered around male perceptions and sensibilities, male psychology and power, male anxieties and the affirmation of masculinity. Harassment is an inevitable by-product."

Thus, by the mid-1970s, the military services had a "can't live with them, can't live without them" problem. On the one hand, they absolutely needed women to fill out their ranks and could not function without them because of shortfalls in the enlistment of qualified men. Women also scored higher than men on most tests and caused fewer disciplinary problems. As the armed forces moved to a more mechanized and electronic standard of warfare, women performed as well or better than men in many positions requiring technical skills. On the other hand, the services treated women as second-class citizens. Combat exclusion rules barred women from the kinds of jobs that were critical to promotion to the senior ranks. Women were also excluded from the leadership academies where they could get the best training and begin to form the kind of network of personal relationships and contacts that boosts careers. And they worked and often lived in an atmosphere that was frequently hostile to them and sometimes even violent. At a 1980 hearing by the House Armed Services Committee's personnel subcommittee, enlisted women testified to widespread sexual harassment and sexual assault in the army—a problem the army refused at the time to acknowledge. In 1990, ten years after the House hearing, a Defense Department study of 20,000 personnel reported that two out of every three women had experienced some form of sexual harassment in the previous year, with 15 percent citing pressure for sexual favors and 5 percent citing attempted rape.

Throughout her career, Schroeder championed the cause of women in the military, whether that meant opening combat units to women or issuing them maternity uniforms. It was a natural fit given Schroeder's feminism and her position as one of the few women on the Armed Services Committee. Beginning in her first term, Schroeder urged opening the major military academies to women. In 1974, she was one of twelve members of Congress to sue the navy in an attempt to force the U.S. Naval Academy in Annapolis to admit female cadets. In a symbolic gesture the same year, Schroeder submitted the name of a female high school student in Denver to all the major service academies for admission. Under public pressure, the naval academy, the U.S. Military Academy at West Point, N.Y., and the U.S. Air Force Academy in Colorado Springs admitted women for the first time in 1976.

Also in her first term, Schroeder began pushing the Pentagon to allow women to volunteer for combat. "Anybody who wants to fill a combat job and is qualified to do it should be allowed to," Schroeder told the *Air Force Times* in 1977. "No one is making them change the qualifications." Women in the military would never be truly accepted or able to function to their fullest potential so long as they were treated differently from men, Schroeder argued. And the military culture would continue to treat them differently and to value them less so long as they were excluded from combat. She further argued that American women have always served in the military and endured the hardships of war; they just don't get credit for it.

"There's a myth in America that all women sat out all wars on a pedestal somewhere," Schroeder said in a 1985 speech to the House in support of a national memorial to women veterans. "Most people do not know that in the combat zones of the West where I came from, back when we were out trying to win the West, out in those different forts, we had some very interesting laws in the Army at that time. That was there had to be a woman in the fort for every seven and a half men that were there. What was the purpose of these women being in the fort? Well, they were there to do laundry. It was really very interesting that when it came down to whether or not the men had to do laundry or to put a woman in a combat zone, we put women in combat zones, and thank you very much. They were not going to have detergent hands for male soldiers; but nevertheless, these women in those forts suffered right along with everyone else. When the forts were overrun, when different things happened, they, too, were taken prisoner or they, too, were shot or whatever. They were not protected. They were there on the front lines."

Indeed, there have been women "camp followers" for as long as there have been armies, ranging from the wives of high-ranking officers to cooks to prostitutes. In past centuries, the term "laundress" was sometimes an army euphemism for "prostitute."

Schroeder also tried to get the services to make accommodations for the particular needs of women, especially more funds for child care. Until 1970, the military required women who became pregnant to quit the service. Even after the rule was changed, the adjustment to mothers in uniform was a slow process. In 1982, the General Accounting Office issued a report highly critical of military day care, saying only 1 percent of the army child care facilities met minimum standards. Schroeder also pushed unsuccessfully for twenty-four-hour child care. "When the balloon goes up . . . everyone will be scrambling to find somewhere to put their kids," she said. The Pentagon disagreed, telling her there was not enough need to justify the cost of providing twenty-four-hour child care for military personnel.

The effort to open combat jobs to women gained ground in December 1989 when U.S. troops took control of Panama and seized strongman

Manuel Noriega. Women made up only 4 percent of the 18,400-member U.S. invasion force. They were also not part of what the army classified as combat units, but no matter what it was called, the female soldiers in Panama engaged in what looked to the American public very much like combat. Two female pilots who successfully ferried troops aboard Black Hawk helicopters through enemy fire were awarded the coveted Air Medal. Female truck drivers and supply officers also displayed bravery while under mortar fire. The episode that grabbed the public's attention, however, was the experience of 29-year-old army captain Linda Bray, who, while serving as the commander of a military police company of about one hundred soldiers, wound up leading troops in a fire fight with Panamanian defense forces holed up in a K-9 compound. Three Panamanian soldiers were killed and one taken prisoner. The rest escaped into the jungle. After taking control of the compound, Bray discovered it was also a secret barracks for special operations forces. Her troops, including a dozen women who had taken part in the fire fight, seized a large cache of weapons and munitions. After reporter Peter Copeland of Scripps Howard News Service broke the story of the female army officer who led troops into battle, Bray became an instant media celebrity. She was praised by the White House. Her picture was everywhere. The *Detroit News* described her conduct "as worthy of a young Douglas MacArthur or George Patton."

As the leading congressional advocate for women in the military, Schroeder was naturally sought out by the media for her response to Bray's groundbreaking battle. When senior officers at the Pentagon turned on *Good Morning America* or picked up *Time* magazine, there was Schroeder blasting the army's combat exclusion policies. Citing Bray's example, Schroeder introduced legislation to open up all jobs in the army to women, whether combat or not, for a four-year trial. The bill created a media splash, but went nowhere.

Initially, army officials were delighted with the positive publicity Bray had generated, but when they realized that the incident called into question the army's combat exclusion policy, they quickly reversed course. Army officials denied that the fire fight at the K-9 compound qualified as combat and set out to discredit media accounts of the battle, saying the incident had been grossly exaggerated. Conservative commentators ideologically opposed to women in combat piled on.

In her book, Francke documents a campaign of professional harassment by the army against Bray after she gained fame in Panama. Bray's company was worked around the clock. Vacancies went unfilled. She became the target of an internal army investigation into allegations she was responsible for slaughtering dogs at the K-9 compound—a charge later proved false. When the army issued the coveted Combat Infantryman Badge for valor under fire, it was given only to men who served in Panama and not to Bray or any other women. The army's explanation was that the badge could only be awarded to members of the infantry, who were by regulation only male. Schroeder protested, as did five senators who wrote a letter to the secretary of the army. Bray was finally given the army's Commendation Medal, which is traditionally given during peacetime because it has no combat requirement. A little more than a year after Panama, Bray had had enough and she wanted out. In April 1991, she was officially discharged.

By then there had been another war, this time in the Persian Gulf, where 37,000 women were deployed alongside more than 500,000 men beginning in August 1990. Among the 150 U.S. casualties in the Gulf War were 13 women. Two other women were taken prisoner by Iraqi troops during operations Desert Shield and Desert Storm. Among the casualties was Army Maj. Marie Rossi, a helicopter company commander who flew into Iraq ahead of the first wave of the Allied ground offensive. She was killed not long afterward when her Chinook helicopter crashed into a darkened communications tower in bad weather. A Black Hawk helicopter carrying Army Flight Surgeon Rhonda Cornum was shot down while on a search-and-rescue mission. Five of the eight crew members aboard were killed. Cornum and two men who survived were captured. While prisoner, and suffering from serious injuries, Cornum was sexually molested by an Iraqi soldier. Three female army specialists were killed when a Scud missile hit an army reserve barracks in Dhahran, Saudi Arabia, well behind the front lines. They were the first U.S. enlisted women to be killed in action.

The Gulf War shattered a number of preconceptions about women in the military. Clearly women could satisfactorily perform a wide range of jobs traditionally held by men. It was also clear that women could be in danger even if restricted from officially designated combat units. "The Persian Gulf War," Schroeder said, "helped collapse the whole chivalrous notion that women could be kept out of danger in a war. We saw that the theater of operations had no strict combat zone, that Scud missiles were not gender-specific—they could hit both sexes and unfortunately did."

The war also called into question the belief that the American public would be unable to accept female casualties or female prisoners of war. The public seemed to respond to the capture and deaths of female soldiers in the same spirit that they responded to the capture and deaths of male soldiers.

The presumption that men and women working in close quarters under rough conditions would cause embarrassment and lower morale was also deflated. A study by the General Accounting Office found that health and hygiene problems for troops in the Gulf were minor for both men and women and had no negative effects on their ability to perform their mission.

On the other hand, the media was full of hardship stories of mothers and fathers who left behind children when they were deployed to the Gulf. At the height of Operation Desert Storm, 16,377 single parents and 1,231 military couples with children were deployed to the Gulf and Saudi Arabia, leaving their children in the care of relatives, friends, neighbors, or whomever they could find. The Gulf War touched off a national debate over the role of women in the military. Opponents of women in combat argued that motherhood and combat don't mix, citing the disruption of families that the war caused. Some opponents accused female soldiers and sailors of deliberately getting pregnant to avoid deployment or so they could get shipped home. The widely reported charges were later called into question by two GAO reports, but that didn't deter critics.

"Sending moms into battle isn't the 'way of life' for any Americans except the radical feminists who are over military and child-bearing age or haven't any daughters," opined conservative columnist Phyllis Schlafly.

Schroeder and other feminists, who saw the overall performance of women in the Gulf War as a resounding success, were taken aback by the criticism. "I've always felt the women in the military got a really bum deal," she told *Ms.* magazine. They "get attacked by the Phyllis Schlaflys of the world and the guys in the military who don't want them. No one pats them on the head and says, 'Good job!' Instead they say, 'Should you really be here? Don't you feel bad that you're not home with your family?'"

When the first news stories appeared about men caring for their families while their wives deployed to the Gulf, Schroeder said she was elated. "My original hope was, 'Wow! When this is over we're going to have a whole new group of people screaming for better child care, for family medical leave, all the stuff we've been trying to get in this country,'" she said. "But then it started to turn. We got this surly thing about America's going to feel much worse if a woman's a POW than if it's a man, and America should never send mothers; it's O.K. to send fathers."

Nevertheless, Schroeder caught opponents of women in combat completely off guard in May 1991 when she succeeded in writing a provision into the annual defense authorization bill to allow women pilots to volunteer to fly combat missions for the first time. Schroeder had initially planned for the provision to apply only to female air force pilots, believing that was the best she could get. But in a surprise move, Congresswoman Beverly Byron of Maryland, the conservative chairman of the military personnel subcommittee, threw her support behind the proposal and urged it be expanded to include women pilots in the navy and the marines. Schroeder was delighted. "We're not talking about lowering standards," she said. "If women can qualify . . . it would be silly to deny ourselves half the brainpower of this country just because they have the wrong chromosome."

Although the legal barriers to women's flying combat missions had been removed by Schroeder's provision, it was up to the Pentagon to decide whether to actually open combat slots to women. It wasn't until April 1993 that Defense Secretary Les Aspin lifted the ban on women's flying combat aircraft and female pilots began fighter training.

In the midst of this national debate over the role of women in the military, the Tailhook Association held its thirty-fifth annual convention at the Las Vegas Hilton Hotel from September 5 to 9, 1991, precipitating what has been described as the navy's greatest crisis since Pearl Harbor. The resulting scandal would sink the careers of fourteen admirals, the chief of naval operations, and the secretary of the navy. It would also focus national attention on the question of whether the military culture of the navy should be held to the same standards of behavior and treatment of women as civilian society, or whether the armed services were intrinsically different, deserving to be judged only by their own standards.

Schroeder was not a principal actor in the Tailhook scandal, but she played an important supporting role, helping to raise the public profile of the scandal by applying pressure on the navy for a more thorough investigation when its first investigation fell short and by demanding that the officers who participated in the most flagrant examples of sexual abuse at the convention be identified and held accountable. Throughout the scandal, Schroeder insisted that what must change was the way women were treated by the warrior culture of the navy. She called it "culture cracking." As a result of her high profile, Schroeder was widely vilified by navy officers and their civilian supporters. They blamed her for the navy's problems rather than the navy culture or their own conduct.

The three-day Tailhook convention had been the most important annual gathering of navy and marine aviators since the 1960s. The word "tailhook" derives from the hook that catches jets as they land on the decks of aircraft carriers, preventing them from continuing to hurtle forward. The association that sponsored the convention was technically private, but its offices were housed at Miramar Naval Air Station in San Diego, California, home of the prestigious "Top Gun" school for fighter pilots, and the navy provided free transportation to Tailhook conventions, which were attended not only by aviators, but by the highest ranking officers in the navy and marines.

During the day, active-duty and retired officers would lead seminars and give speeches to the convention. Defense contractors ingratiated themselves with booths and hospitality suites. The evenings, however, were notorious for debauchery and drunkenness. Squadrons would rent hospitality suites on the third floor of the Hilton, where they would try to outdo each other with raunchy and sophomoric behavior. Aviators wearing baseball caps with fake penises or walking around with their genitals exposed—they called it "ball-walking"—were typical. Strippers, prostitutes, and public sex were also standard. The revelry had a strong misogynist streak to it: T-shirts with slogans like "Women Are Property" and "He-Man Woman Hater Club" and buttons with a red line through the word *women* were commonplace.

The nature of the Tailhook conventions was condoned and even encouraged at the highest levels of the navy. In his book *Fall from Glory: The Men Who Sank the Navy*, author Gregory L. Vistica describes an incident from the 1986 Tailhook convention in which then Secretary of the Navy John Lehman lay on his back on the floor of one of the Hilton's hospitality suites, a rolled-up dollar bill clenched in his teeth and a naked stripper standing over him. To the cheers of about one hundred officers, the stripper gyrated downward until she was able to snatch the dollar bill from Lehman's mouth with her vagina. Tales of lewd sex acts and drunken pranks at Tailhook were legendary throughout the navy.

The 1991 convention took place at a time when naval leaders were warning that the service needed to polish its public image in order to sell Congress and top Defense Department officials on the need for new aircraft and weapons systems. There was a consensus that the air force had done a better job than the navy in generating positive publicity during the Persian Gulf war, and that the navy needed to be more open with the media.

"We're our own worst enemy when it comes to handling the press. All you ever heard from us is that we didn't like the press," Vice Adm. Richard M. Dunleavy, assistant chief of naval operations for air warfare, said in a speech to 1991 Tailhook attendees reported by *Aviation Week & Space Technology*. "But we're going to change that. We have to work very, very closely with the press, because they have direct contact with the American people, who obviously are our leaders. We have to learn how to interact with the press. We have to stop stiff-arming them. Bring them aboard and educate them." Ironically, Dunleavy would become one of the casualties of the scandal.

The Tailhook scandal unfolded slowly, taking more than a year to reach its crescendo. The first the public heard about it was in a front-page story in the *San Diego Union-Tribune* on October 29, nearly seven weeks after the convention. The story was based primarily on a letter the Tailhook Association president, navy capt. Rick Ludwig, had sent out to every aviation squadron commander praising the convention, but also expressing "distress" that five women, including a female officer, had complained that they were sexually assaulted in the hallway outside the hotel's third-floor suites by a gauntlet of aviators. The women said they were hoisted off the ground and passed from one man to the next as dozens of pilots grabbed at their breasts and genitals and tore their clothing. One underage girl, who was severely intoxicated, was stripped of her clothes by the gauntlet and dumped unconscious in a corner at the end of the hall, where she remained until hotel security found her.

The day the story broke, Sen. John McCain of Arizona, a former navy pilot shot down over Vietnam and the son and grandson of admirals, denounced the aviators' conduct in a speech to the Senate. "There is no time in the history of this country that something like this is more inappropriate," McCain said, an apparent reference to the Clarence Thomas–Anita Hill hearings in the Senate that month. "We cannot allow it. It is unconscionable. And we in the military, who pride ourselves on the equal opportunity that is extended to everyone in the military, should be ashamed and embarrassed . . .

"The first question I have for the secretary of the Navy," McCain said, "is if this has been known for over a month, why has action not been initiated until such time as this became known in the media?" McCain also said he had met with Defense Secretary Dick Cheney about the matter. Schroeder was also prominently quoted in the media as demanding an investigation of the incident. Within weeks, the navy had severed its ties with the Tailhook Association and had booted the group out of its Miramar offices. Rear Adm. Jack Snyder, one of the navy's rising stars and a former Tailhook president, became the first officer fired over the incident. His aide, Lt. Paula Coughlin, had complained to him that she was "nearly gang-raped" at the convention by the gauntlet, but Snyder initially dismissed her complaint, telling her she shouldn't have been in a hallway full of drunken aviators. Snyder later formally reported Coughlin's complaint to superiors, but by then it was too late.

The story in the *Union-Tribune* was just the tip of the iceberg. For months, all that was publicly known was that a handful of unnamed women said they had been assaulted by the gauntlet. In April 1992, eight months after the convention, the navy released the results of its internal investigation. At least twenty-six women had been assaulted, including thirteen female officers, but after 1,500 interviews with navy and marine aviators who uniformly stonewalled and tried to cover up for their fellow officers, no one was likely to be charged with any wrongdoing.

The following month, under pressure from Schroeder and other members of Congress, the navy released another voluminous report containing the transcripts of its investigation interviews. It concluded that Tailhook was a taxpayer-supported sex-and-alcohol binge where women were molested and abused with the tacit approval of top navy brass. Navy investigators wrote: "There is still little understanding of the nature, severity, and number of assaults which occurred . . . A common thread running through the overwhelming number of interviews regarding the Tailhook convention was, 'What's the big deal?'" The report was an eye-opener, as writer Katherine Boo explained in the *Washington Monthly*:

Deep in the 2,200 pages of Naval Investigative Service transcripts about the infamous Tailhook weekend, a moment of humanity interrupts a catalog of outrage and indifference. A man sees a distraught woman flee onto a hotel balcony, her clothes stretched and torn and three naval aviators fast behind her. As the men laugh and taunt, the Samaritan intervenes. Ordering the offenders to leave her alone, he ferries her out of the melee and into safety. Unfortunately, our hero isn't a serviceman. He's a bartender. And that woozy night, it seemed as if you had to live outside military culture to recognize that attacking women isn't just boys being boys.

In their defense, the aviators responded that the overwhelming majority of the women on the third floor that evening were willing and even eager participants in the debauchery. Some went laughingly through the gauntlet two and three times. However, that was not true of all of the women. Two women who filed complaints with the Las Vegas police, for example, were simply guests in the hotel with no connection to the navy. They said they were lured by a pilot to the third floor, where they were molested by the gauntlet after stepping out of the elevator. When two airline stewardesses staying at the hotel began warning women guests to stay away from the third floor, they were chewed out by a pilot who was upset that they were spoiling the fun.

None of the names of the women assaulted was reported until June, when Coughlin went public, giving interviews to the *Washington Post* and *ABC News.* "I went down a hallway where every man in that hallway got a shot at me, made sure that I did not pass untouched," she told ABC. The harder she fought, Coughlin said, the more viciously she was manhandled. When she tried to escape through a doorway, two pilots deliberately blocked her way.

Meanwhile, it turned out that not only was navy secretary Lawrence Garrett at the Tailhook convention, but interviews placed him on a hotel patio near the third floor corridor in which the women were abused. Garrett had said he didn't know anything had gone on until three weeks after the convention. A key interview that placed Garrett near the gauntlet had been mysteriously deleted from the report when the navy released it to the press. "I don't know of a parent in America that would buy that story from their child," Schroeder told ABC. "So I would hope the taxpayer doesn't buy that story from their secretary of the Navy."

Also at the convention was Adm. Frank Kelso, the chief of naval operations, and as many as forty active-duty admirals and about an equal number of retired admirals, none of whom made any serious effort to control the event after it got out of hand. Garrett resigned two days after Coughlin went public, saying he accepted full responsibility for the handling of the incident. The Senate Defense Committee froze promotions for nearly 6,000 navy and marine corps officers until they could each be cleared of any wrongdoing at Tailhook. Schroeder appealed unsuccessfully to the Justice Department to become involved in the investigation. "Secretary Garrett's resignation does not close the book on this case," Schroeder told National Public Radio. "We want this book totally gone through. I think it's very important to find out how many other types of associations are there like the Tailhook Association in all the different services. I think it's time for the military, through Secretary Cheney and through everyone else, to say: This is the end. There will be no more of this."

Soon after Garrett's resignation, the House approved a defense budget that cut 10,000 navy jobs. Schroeder applauded the punitive job cuts during "this difficult period we've been going through with the military and whether or not our servicewomen are going to be considered equal or not."

At the same time the House was cutting navy jobs, aviators at Miramar were hosting the base's annual Tomcat Follies, which was renowned for its sexually explicit humor. Despite warnings to tone down that year's show because of fallout from Tailhook, two of the skits included crude sexual references to Schroeder. One of the skits had a sign with words about Schroeder and oral copulation in conjunction with a nursery rhyme, "Hickory-dickory-dock, Patsy Schroeder . . ." There was also a poster of Schroeder with the legend "Beer is Better than Schroeder because Beer Never has a Headache."

Coming in the midst of the Tailhook investigation, the off-color skits made national headlines. Five officers were disciplined or stripped of command, prompting a torrent of hate mail and hostile phone calls to Schroeder's office. Some of the officers involved in the follies complained that they should not have been disciplined because they were simply exercising their free speech in criticizing Schroeder. Three of the officers were later reinstated. Kelso went to Schroeder's office to personally apologize for the incident. At one point, nearly the entire navy was ordered to shut down for a whole day of training seminars and lectures on avoiding sexual harassment.

The following month, Schroeder's office received an anonymous fax from Camp LeJeune, a marine corps base in North Carolina. It consisted of lurid photos of women, along with a suggestion that Schroeder perform a particular sex act for the sender. Jamie Schroeder was in her mother's office at the time and was stunned. "I remember that day so well," she told John Brinkley of the *Rocky Mountain News.* "It was so crude. It was pretty devastating." Her mother, however, "was laughing about it, and saying, 'These guys are such yo-yos. Look what they sent me,'" Jamie said.

"That was one of the most difficult periods of time" for Schroeder's family, Scott Schroeder told Brinkley. "But, she said, 'Look, it kind of comes with the territory. This is sort of the dark side of being a public figure.'" Paula Coughlin's mother, Rena Coughlin, wrote to Schroeder to thank her for her "most visible support of the cause of women in the military. . . . I do hope you can bring to justice the Navy aviators who inflicted this wrong on my daughter."

Schroeder later went to Miramar, where she explained her reasons for pressing the Tailhook investigation in private meetings with sixteen officers and enlisted sailors. Schroeder said she asked for the meetings to end the hostility by navy pilots toward her and other women. She described the meetings as "very intense." None of the officers involved in the follies was at the meetings. Six months later there was another spate of news stories, this time about navy reserve pilots in San Diego wearing softball team T-shirts emblazoned with references to Schroeder's "screwing" the navy.

"The thing that tickled me so much was their thinking that I was the reason that Tailhook could no longer be allowed as the kind of outrage it was," Schroeder told PBS's *Frontline* in 1996. "I mean, their view was, Tailhook has now got to be catered by Mrs. Smith and her cookies and we're going to have it—what were they saying? We're going to have it in Salt Lake City, and can only have milk, and all this. They're thinking that I was the only one, and that everybody in the House and Senate and the administration was running because of me. No. They just couldn't deal with the fact that society had changed so much."

Under pressure from Schroeder and other members of Congress who were demanding hearings, the navy turned its investigation over to its inspector general in June 1992, effectively removing the investigation from the influence of the navy secretary and top admirals. However, the navy dragged out the release of the inspector general's final report for months. Schroeder responded by leading fifteen congresswomen in signing a letter to Defense Secretary Les Aspin, who succeeded Cheney after the change in administrations in early 1993, stating that "delaying the release of the final report sends a message to the nation that sexual assault and harassment of women are not sufficiently important to warrant immediate discipline."

The inspector general's final report, released in April 1993, concluded that eighty-three women and seven men were assaulted during the convention. The men who said they were groped by women appeared mainly to be officers angered by the investigation and out to even the score. The inspector general, who had earlier reported that senior navy officials had manipulated the previous investigation to avoid negative publicity and to protect colleagues, identified 140 navy and marine officers who had engaged in misconduct at Tailhook, including twenty-three who were cited for indecent assault. The report also cited thirty-four admirals and a marine general who had attended the convention and, under the navy's ironclad principle of command responsibility, shared in the blame.

In the end, no one was convicted of sexual assault or any other crime in connection with Tailhook. Six junior officers who took part in the gauntlet or other alleged sexual misconduct were charged with crimes. One was acquitted and the charges against the rest were dismissed. About fifty officers received administrative penalties, which in some cases eliminated their chances for promotion. Navy Secretary John Dalton ordered one retired admiral reduced in rank, censured two others for failing to prevent

Tailhook incidents, and ordered nonpunitive administrative actions against thirty other admirals.

The military judge who handled the Tailhook cases, Capt. William Vest Jr., placed the blame for the incident squarely on Kelso, who as chief of naval operations was the most senior officer in the navy and the most senior official at the convention excluding Garrett. Vest also charged that Kelso had lied about his knowledge of misconduct at the convention. Schroeder angrily called upon Defense Secretary Aspin to act, saying no one had been held accountable for the incident.

On February 7, 1994, Coughlin, who had been shunned by fellow officers since going public nineteen months earlier, resigned from the navy. In the end, she was the only junior officer who was out of a job as the result of Tailhook. A week later, Kelso announced he would retire two months ahead of schedule. "When you finally look at where we are after three years in this very sad saga, where we are is it's the women who are quitting," Schroeder said. "Paula Coughlin quitting, giving up, saying they're still harassing her to no end for even talking about this. And the Navy saying, 'Well, it's over, we're done,' and really no one has been penalized for this at all."

Two months later, in a reprise of her trek during the Thomas-Hill hearings, Schroeder led nine congresswomen in a march across the Capitol to the Senate to try to keep Kelso from retiring with full honors. Admirals automatically retire at two stars unless the Senate votes to allow the officer to retire at an additional star or two, which is usually approved as a matter of course. One difference between two and four stars was a considerable amount of retirement pay. Schroeder and the other congresswomen stood in the back of the Senate as Sen. Barbara Mikulski of Maryland led the effort to deny Kelso the extra stars, arguing that since he was in charge of the navy and at the convention, he should bear responsibility for Tailhook. After an emotional six-and-a-half-hour debate, the Senate voted 54 to 43 to permit Kelso to retire with four stars. All seven women senators voted against awarding the extra stars. Yet, as author Jean Zimmerman noted in her book *Tailspin: Women at War in the Wake of Tailhook*, Kelso was "an odd straw dog for the she-bears of the Senate to tear apart" since he had ushered the navy into a new era of including women in combat duty and was generally viewed as an advocate for women in the military.

The fallout from Tailhook and the larger debate over the role of women in the military did not fade away with Kelso's retirement. Resentment in the navy continued to fester, especially after several admirals were fired or penalized for matters unrelated to Tailhook but involving either sexual misconduct by men under their command or the fair treatment of women in the navy. Much of the bile was directed toward Schroeder. In a 1995 made-for-TV movie about the Tailhook scandal, there is a bar scene in which disgruntled navy officers sipping draft beers and nibbling peanuts at an officers' club suddenly start hissing, booing, and flinging their plastic cups at a television screen. On the screen is a mock newscast with Schroeder commenting on the scandal.

There were dramatic moments in real life during the Tailhook years, too. After one interview with *Good Morning America,* Schroeder said she was accosted in the news studio by a cameraman who had served in the navy. He managed to take a swing at her, but missed, before he was pulled away by other network employees. "I was advocating that [women in the military] should be allowed to do whatever they are qualified to do. To me, this was not a radical statement," Schroeder said. "When I got done, the cameraman . . . just comes out from behind the camera and goes at it. It took five people to pull him off. He went crazy. ABC was appalled."

On another occasion, Schroeder and her husband were having dinner in a restaurant in Annapolis when a navy fighter pilot who had been drinking at the bar with several other men came over to their table, belligerently accusing her of making pilots look like sexual deviants. She tried to explain that Tailhook was "about criminal assaults," but that only infuriated the pilot more. "Look, you haven't proven rape, so what are you talking about?" he shouted at her. Finally, the bartender asked the men to leave.

Peter Pfabe, a naval academy graduate and former F-14 pilot, spoke for many retired and active-duty officers when he editorialized in *Investors Business Daily* in 1996 that "the antics of rowdy aviators at a private convention on their free time pale in comparison with the immensity of running the most powerful seagoing force in the world . . . The Tailhook witch hunts are a far greater injustice than anything that took place there. After numerous investigations, not a single court martial conviction resulted from Tailhook. No matter. Schroeder won. Careers were ruined. And the Navy's top brass stood by and watched—cowered."

The theme of betrayal by the navy's top leaders was echoed by former navy secretary James Webb on April 25, 1996, at the Naval Institute's 122nd annual meeting in Annapolis. Webb had succeeded Lehman as navy secretary, but later resigned on principle over the issue of fleet reductions. A

Naval Academy graduate and former marine who had served in Vietnam, Webb was well known for his fervent opposition to women in combat.

"Many whose very duty it was to defend the hallowed traditions and the unique culture of their profession declined to do so when their voices were most urgently needed," Webb told the prestigious gathering. "Some are guilty of the ultimate disloyalty: to save or advance their careers, they abandoned the very ideals of their profession in order to curry favor with politicians.

"The aftermath of Tailhook was never about inappropriate conduct so much as it was about the lack of wisdom among the Navy's top leadership. Tailhook should have been a three- or maybe a five-day story. Those who were to blame for outrageous conduct should have been disciplined, and those who were not to blame should have been vigorously defended, along with the culture and the mores of the naval service. Instead, we are now at four years and counting, and its casualty list reads like a Who's Who of naval aviation."

Webb received a standing ovation, and copies of his speech were widely circulated in the naval community. Although Webb never mentioned him by name, it was clear that one of the navy leaders he was referring to was Adm. Jeremy Boorda, a "mustang" who had risen from the enlisted ranks rather than coming out of the hallowed Annapolis training ground. Boorda, who had replaced Kelso as chief of naval operations, had pledged to put women on every ship in the navy.

Exactly three weeks after Webb's speech, Boorda shot and killed himself at his home in Washington. He had recently learned that reporters from *Newsweek* magazine wanted to question him about medals he had worn but may not have been awarded. Schroeder had opposed Boorda's rise to chief of naval operations, arguing that he hadn't made a sincere effort to fight sexual harassment.

In a column published in the *Wall Street Journal* five days later under the headline "The Navy's Enemies," former navy secretary Lehman blamed the admiral's suicide on three villains: the media, the Clinton administration (which he said was staffed by former war protestors), and Pat Schroeder. "What should have been at most a week's story," Lehman wrote, "instead ignited a firestorm that has been consuming the Navy ever since." Lehman pointed to the case of Adm. Stan Arthur, a combat-tested officer who had ruled that a female helicopter pilot failed to meet standards. "For that he was cashiered, because everybody was afraid—afraid of Pat Schroeder and her McCarthyite slurs, afraid of the White House commissars, afraid of the media." On TV talk shows and in other forums, Lehman continued to blame the navy's problems on Schroeder and other critics who he said wanted to impose a standard of political correctness on the military that undermined morale. "This is not a touchy-feely bureaucracy here. It has to have a macho, tough, warrior culture, and that's what's being eroded," he told CNN.

Schroeder responded in a speech on the House floor. Recalling Lehman's active participation in Tailhook debauchery, she said: "That is the standard Mr. Lehman set for the Navy on his watch. He blames Boorda's suicide on 'the Navy's enemies.' Guess who the Navy's enemies are? Anyone, myself included, who tried to clean up the Tailhook scandal."

Schroeder had her admirers as well. "Almost single handedly she forced the Navy to lift the blanket of official acquiescence off the Tailhook sex scandal," wrote *Newsday* columnist Marie Cocco.

As Schroeder was wrapping up her congressional career, she found herself tackling an issue depressingly similar to Tailhook: charges of sexual harassment, assault, and rape of female soldiers at the army's Aberdeen Proving Ground in Maryland. Yet the Aberdeen case was more disturbing than Tailhook in many ways because it involved drill sergeants in boot camp, who have tremendous power over recruits, pressuring vulnerable young women to have sex.

"Tailhook was a professional convention that naval aviators went to that got more out of control every year," Schroeder told the *Los Angeles Times.* "It was wrong that the whole command went there and saw it and didn't pay any attention." However, Schroeder said, the key difference between the drill sergeants at Aberdeen and the naval officers at Tailhook was that at Tailhook the officers were sexually harassing fellow officers— women who understood their rights and were not as easily intimidated as raw recruits. "They were not eighteen-year-olds, and they were able to finally bring the system to its knees," Schroeder said.

Ironically, in September 1992, four years before the scandal at Aberdeen broke, Schroeder had requested in a letter to then-defense secretary Dick Cheney that the Pentagon create a special civilian office to investigate charges that the military for years had covered up rapes and sexual assaults. Schroeder said she was responding to an "overwhelming" number of calls to congressional offices from women in the military claiming their rape or assault charges had been brushed aside. Her request was not approved.

In January 2000, the navy announced it was restoring ties with the Tailhook Association after being assured that the group will not permit another of its conventions to degenerate into debauchery and abusive treatment of women. To regain official recognition, the association pledged to support the navy's drive to recruit and promote women in carrier aviation.

One of the indirect effects of Tailhook was that in 1993 Congress repealed the law barring women from serving on navy combat ships. The following year, the Defense Department lifted the so-called "risk rule," opening most jobs, including some combat jobs, to women. Women are still excluded from front-line ground combat duty, such as serving in the infantry, field artillery, or tanks, or as special operations commandos. They are also barred from submarines.

Today, women represent about 15 percent of the nation's 1.4 million-person military. About 91 percent of the army's jobs and 99 percent of the air force's jobs are open to women, although the navy and marines continue to have more restrictions. However, even though most jobs are technically open to women, the more elite positions are overwhelmingly filled by men. In 2002, the air force had just 16 female bomber pilots out of a total of 759 and just 43 female fighter pilots out of 3,500. On the USS *Theodore Roosevelt*, deployed to the Arabian Sea for the war in Afghanistan, the overall crew of 5,600 included about 700 women, but only two female combat pilots.

The military "is a lot more progressive than when I came in," Schroeder told the *Rocky Mountain News*. "It's still behind society a bit, and of course it's constantly changing."

9

Pat vs. Newt

In political terms, the 1994 election was an earthquake for Democrats who had controlled the House without interruption for four decades. They had acquired a sense of permanence that seemed impregnable. Now, Schroeder and other Democrats saw dozens of their colleagues washed away overnight by the GOP tsunami. Even Speaker Tom Foley of Washington lost his seat to a conservative Republican newcomer. Their power to control the legislative agenda, committee chairmanships earned over decades of service, authority over the House's multibillion-dollar budget, and patronage involving hundreds of jobs was gone overnight. Their public policy goals and legislative proposals had become thin hopes.

To Republicans, it felt like the Berlin Wall of domestic politics had come tumbling down. Their rejoicing was euphoric, and there was broad, heartfelt gratitude toward the Moses who had led them to their first majority in the House after forty years in the political wilderness, Newton Leroy Gingrich of Georgia.

Millions of Americans who watched the opening of the historic One Hundred Fourth Congress on television on January 4, 1995, saw a strained Richard Gephardt of Missouri, the leader of House Democrats, hand a ceremonial gavel to Gingrich and say, "With resignation but resolve, I hereby end forty years of Democratic rule in this House." As Gingrich assumed the Speaker's chair, the first Republican to sit in that chair with a gavel in his hand since 1954, an exuberant GOP congressman shouted, "It's a whole Newt world!"

Pat Schroeder first encountered Newt Gingrich in 1978, when the then obscure Georgia history professor was making his third try for the House after two unsuccessful races. His previous races had been against an entrenched incumbent, but this time the incumbent had retired and the seat was up for grabs. Schroeder had traveled to suburban Atlanta to campaign for the Democrat in the race, Virginia Shapard, a reform-minded state senator and mother of two. At that time, Georgia had never elected a woman to Congress.

Shapard "had a reputation for being savvy, classy and able to get things done in a political body that did not welcome her," Schroeder wrote in her memoir *24 Years of House Work . . . and the Place Is Still a Mess.* "I went to stump for her because the idea of electing such a terrific woman to Congress would be a huge boost. In the South, political women had trouble breaking through."

The tone of the Gingrich-Shapard race was harsh and ugly. Gingrich employed a two-pronged political strategy: paint Shapard as far to the left as possible and assert his moral leadership. He accused Shapard of coddling welfare cheaters in league with Julian Bond, the black civil rights activist. He sought to make Shapard's gender an issue and implied that she put her ambition ahead of her husband and children. When Shapard said her family planned to remain in Georgia and she would commute home on the weekends, Gingrich responded by promising to bring his wife and children to Washington with him.

"Newt will take his family to Washington and keep them together; Virginia will go to Washington and leave her husband and children in the care of a nanny," Gingrich's ads in rural newspapers said. It was a less than subtle appeal to those voters who thought that a wife and mother belonged at home with her family and not in the House. Gingrich's attacks were reminiscent of Schroeder's first campaign for the House six years earlier when she was repeatedly quizzed about how she intended to handle the role of congresswoman and mother at the same time, and she felt great empathy with Shapard.

"I didn't meet him, but I had seen some of the literature that was being handed out and it was really vicious stuff," Schroeder said in an interview. "It was about how she was running for Congress to get away from her husband and kids, how she was this awful wife and mother. I thought, 'Wow, what kind of person would say that? That's just so despicable.'"

Gingrich wound up defeating Shapard, but when he went to Washington he left his wife and two daughters behind in Georgia. A little over a year later, he filed for divorce from his wife of nearly twenty years. He brought the separation papers to the hospital where she was recovering from cancer surgery and asked her to sign them. When the divorce became final in 1982, he promptly married a Washington lobbyist.

Gingrich did not remain an anonymous freshman for long. It had been his goal in life from an early age to become a political boss. While still in his first term, Gingrich would lecture colleagues and conservative activists on his plan to make himself Speaker of the House by wresting control from the Democrats, using a crayon on a board in his office to illustrate his points. That strategy included relentlessly attacking both the public policy agenda and the personal character of congressional Democrats, and sometimes his own party leaders if Gingrich thought they were too accommodating toward the Democrats. In 1990, when George Bush reached a deal with congressional Democrats on the budget, Gingrich opposed the compromise because it included a tax increase. He succeeded in putting together a large enough coalition of anti-tax Republicans and Democrats that he was able to kill the deal, delivering a major embarrassment to his party's president.

Like Schroeder, Gingrich skillfully used the media and employed a biting rhetorical style. Unlike the Colorado congresswoman, Gingrich's rhetoric was not softened by humor. It was more like a knee in the groin. He once referred to the succession of Democratic House Speakers Tip O'Neill, Jim Wright, and Tom Foley as "a trio of muggers." Democratic party leaders in Georgia were "pleasant people who behind the scenes are thugs." The Democrat-led Iran-Contra hearings were a "left-wing lynch mob." The federal government was always the "liberal welfare state." Al Gore's book on environmental decline, *Earth in the Balance*, was "nutty left-wing goo-goo stuff." Experts at universities and think tanks who disagreed with him were the "intellectual elite" or the "counterculture elite." Democrats who wanted to negotiate with the Sandinista-led government of Nicaragua were "procommunist." Washington was "an imperial capital that wallows in the American people's tax money" and Congress was a "sick institution."

"The Democrats in the [Capitol] building get up every morning knowing that to survive they need do only two things: They lie regularly and they cheat," Gingrich told the *Washington Times* in 1989. Bill Clinton, he said, was "the enemy of normal Americans." Asked once by *Atlanta Journal* columnist Martha Ezzard about criticism of her rhetorical style, Schroeder said: "It's the same style Newt Gingrich uses. I think we look pretty classy by comparison."

It wasn't long after his victory over Shapard that Gingrich came to Schroeder's attention in a more direct way. During a trip to Colorado to attend a GOP event, Gingrich held a press conference in Denver to criticize Schroeder for a letter she had written on a defense matter, according to Dan Buck, who was Schroeder's top aide for more than twenty years. Schroeder wasn't in Denver at the time and the press conference drew relatively little notice, but calling a press conference to attack another member in their district was considered pretty aggressive in the House at the time.

"I remember it because it hit me that this guy was a little screwy, but ambitious and we began paying attention to him and warning the institutional Democrats that they should be paying more attention to what he was doing," Buck said.

It was about that time that Buck began keeping a file on Gingrich—news clippings, bits of information from the *Congressional Record*, and other background. Over the years, Buck would frequently share his file with opposition researchers from Democratic campaign committees and with the press. In 1985, Buck printed a compilation of things Gingrich had said or had been said about him titled, *Talking Heads: A Newt Gingrich Chrestomathy*. (A "chrestomathy" is a selection or anthology. A lover of words, Buck came across chrestomathy in an H.L. Mencken essay.)

Gingrich "touts himself as the politician with the requisite integrity, vision, courage, and principle to lead the Republican party," says the chrestomathy's introduction. "A look at his public record, however, leads one to conclude that he is all sail and no keel. His dinghy, the Conservative Opportunity Society—which has been more accurately called the Conservative Opportunist Society—goes wherever the winds of confrontation and demagoguery take it. . . . His attacks on his congressional colleagues are frequently personal and disruptive. During House debates he does not shy from impugning the integrity, honesty, and patriotism of his colleagues."

Those are unusually strong words for one House member to use about another. Buck may have written the tract, but it was released by Schroeder's office and there is no reason to think that it didn't carry her blessing and reflect her view of Gingrich as well. In 1989, Buck followed up with an updated compilation titled *Skinhead Politics: A Newt Gingrich Sampler*.

When Buck first started keeping tabs on Gingrich, hardly anyone except perhaps Gingrich himself believed he would ever be more than a loud irritant catcalling from the bleachers. But to Buck and Schroeder, Gingrich was a dangerous extremist who was not to be taken lightly. Consumer advocate Ralph Nader was another person who began keeping a file on Gingrich about that time. "There were a few people back then who thought that Gingrich was an especially destructive force in American politics. That club of people was small, but they were paying attention," said Gary Ruskin, director of Nader's Congressional Accountability Project, a congressional watchdog group.

There were other Schroeder-Gingrich encounters over the years. In the mid-1980s, Schroeder's staff looked into the military records of about a dozen of the House's most passionate defenders of the Reagan administration's defense buildup. It turned out that many of them were of draft age during the Vietnam War, including Gingrich, and but they had not served. Schroeder pointed this fact out to the press, prompting a spate of stories about "hawks without wings."

"Gingrich was the famous one because he petitioned to get a hardship deferment during Vietnam. Dick Cheney was another one," Buck said. Gingrich requested and received a deferment because he had a wife and children at the time he was draft-eligible. Cheney, a former congressman from Wyoming, was married and his wife was pregnant at the time he requested a deferment.

One of the ways Gingrich was able to boost his visibility and carry his message beyond the Washington beltway was through lengthy, after-hours speeches on the floor of the House while the fixed cameras of the Capitol Hill cable channel, C-SPAN, recorded them. He was perhaps the first House member to recognize the partisan, political potential of the cable channel. What C-SPAN viewers couldn't see was that Gingrich was giving his impassioned speeches to an empty chamber. The situation exasperated Schroeder, who felt that Democrats were giving Gingrich a free platform from which to sling arrows their way. She brought the matter to the attention of House Speaker Tip O'Neill, who agreed. O'Neill then embarrassed the Georgia Republican by directing that the cameras intermittently pan the chamber so that viewers could see he had no audience.

Still, many Democrats—and some Republicans as well—were caught off guard in early 1989 when Gingrich moved in one swift stroke from backbencher to the number two GOP leader in the House. The opening for the post of GOP whip was created when President Bush tapped Cheney, who had been the whip, to be secretary of defense. Gingrich was able to win election to the leadership post by drawing on sentiment among rank-and-file Republicans that the party needed more aggressive leadership. It was a sentiment Gingrich had helped create and tirelessly cultivated. Rep. Bob Michel of Illinois—a Republican from the old school who preferred a civil exchange of differences with his Democratic colleagues on the House floor, and then to settle those differences over a game of golf on the weekend—remained as GOP leader, but the real power rested with Gingrich and everyone knew it.

It wasn't long before Gingrich's more aggressive style bore fruit. Even before his election as GOP whip, Gingrich had pressed ethics complaints against House Speaker Jim Wright of Texas, including allegations that Wright had accepted about $145,000 worth of gifts from a Texas real estate developer who was in a position to benefit directly from legislation over which Wright had influence. Another was that Wright had labor unions buy large quantities of a book he had written as an indirect way to enrich himself through royalties. On June 30, 1989, after a critical report from a special counsel, Wright resigned from office, warning in a speech to the House against the "mindless cannibalism" of partisan attacks on personal character—the first Speaker ever to resign from the House in disgrace.

According to Schroeder, despite Gingrich's central role in bringing down Wright, Democratic leaders Tom Foley and Dick Gephardt cut a deal with him in 1990, agreeing not to work against the Georgia Republican in his reelection campaign. In exchange, Gingrich agreed to support a congressional pay raise that rank-and-file Democrats (and Republicans) wanted. The deal stunned and angered Schroeder, who said she "disobeyed orders from on high" and went to Georgia anyway to campaign for lawyer Dave Worley, Gingrich's Democratic campaign opponent. Statistically, the race ended in a fifty-fifty tie. Gingrich was reelected by 974 votes. Democrats had missed their best shot at defeating the Republican leader who would eventually wrest control of the House away from them.

Schroeder was heartsick. "I'll always be sorry that I didn't publicly expose the stupidity of the Democratic leadership for protecting him, foolishly believing that they could exact some sort of quid pro quo," she wrote.

The Wright scandal was followed three years later by the House bank scandal. The "bank" consisted primarily of checking accounts for House members. Their paychecks were automatically deposited into their accounts and then members could write checks on the accounts. However, unlike checking accounts in the rest of the world, there was no penalty or interest applied for overdrawing an account. Realizing this, House members fell into the habit over the years of overdrawing their accounts, knowing that the House would make their checks good. They were receiving, in effect, interest-free loans.

After the news media seized on the bank issue, Gingrich strove for partisan advantage, saying Democrats controlled the House and were therefore responsible. In truth, both Democratic and Republican House members had taken advantage of the hidden perquisite, and there had been a bipartisan tolerance of the situation by both party leaderships for many years. Under the direction of Gingrich, a team of younger conservatives in the House, most of them in their first or second terms, worked to keep public attention on the bank scandal with frequent attacks on Democratic leaders and demands for disclosure of the names of House members who had overdrawn their accounts. Eventually, a list of members totaling about a third of the House was released along with the number of checks each lawmaker had written for which there had been insufficient funds. The amounts of the overdrafts were never made public. Both Gingrich and Schroeder had overdrawn a small number of checks, but some lawmakers had overdrawn their accounts hundreds of times. Immediately the rubber checks became a campaign issue. The National Republican Campaign Committee launched a TV and radio ad campaign titled "Bounce the Democrats." The campaign's logo was the face of a defeated-looking donkey on a red rubber ball.

The bank scandal helped set the stage for the historic Republican sweep in the 1994 election. It was certainly not the only reason for the GOP takeover. President Clinton's rough sledding with Congress his first two years was another factor. And the incumbent president's party generally loses ground in midterm elections. But perhaps the most important factor was a general public perception that Congress, which was controlled by Democrats, was corrupt and out of touch with average Americans, that Democrats in Congress had permitted and encouraged government to become too big, and that Republicans would shrink it down to size. It was a perception that had been fostered by Gingrich from the moment he first crossed the threshold of the Capitol sixteen years earlier.

In the wake of the 1994 election, Democrats long accustomed to the perquisites of power found themselves stripped of staff and chairmanships. They were left wondering when hearings would take place and who would testify. Once-generous political action committees now spurned them, in some cases under pressure from Gingrich through his subordinates, particularly GOP whip Tom DeLay of Texas. The GOP's previous financial advantage began to look as if it would become insurmountable. Some political analysts warned that the Democratic party had leaned too far to the left and had become obsolete. Bill Clinton found himself asserting that, as president, he was still "relevant." The party's base in the South had all but vanished. A handful of conservative Democratic House members and two senators defected to the GOP, including the Democrats' chief welfare reform champion, Rep. Nathan Deal of Georgia, whom Democratic leaders had endlessly cultivated in an effort to make moderates and conservatives feel welcome in the party.

The class of seventy-three Republican newcomers in the House were, as a group, ardently antiestablishment and openly disdainful of Washington. They were convinced that government was the problem, not the solution. Their intent was to tear down as quickly as possible many of the programs that Schroeder and other Democrats had spent years building up.

Schroeder had accumulated two decades of seniority only to find she was further away from a full committee chairmanship than ever before. Until the GOP takeover, she had been in line to chair the Post Office and Civil Service Committee. One of the first acts of the new GOP-controlled House was to eliminate that committee and two others—Merchant Marine and Fisheries and the District of Columbia—on the grounds that they were unnecessary and wasteful. As a member of the minority, she no longer chaired a sub-committee and she couldn't even claim the spot of "ranking Democrat" on her two remaining committees, Armed Services and Judiciary, because there was one Democrat more senior than she on each committee. One of the accepted truisms in the House is that staff equals power. Unless you are in the leadership or chair a committee or subcommittee or are the ranking member of a committee, you don't receive any extra staff or operating budget. For Schroeder, this meant she was back where she started when she entered the House twenty-two years earlier with just her regular office staff to rely on.

Another blow fell on the first day of the One Hundred Fourth Congress as Republicans voted to prohibit members from using their office funds or dedicating any of their staff to support legislative service organizations like the Congressional Caucus on Women's Issues or the Congressional Black Caucus or the environmental caucus or the farm caucus or any of the dozens of other groups that focused on special areas of interest. It was a typical Gingrich power ploy. He understood that if Democrats could no longer pool their resources on key issues, their power was diluted. Individually, members could not afford within their office budgets to hire very many staffers with expertise devoted to a single issue. They often got around this problem by pooling their resources through membership dues to special interest caucuses paid from their office budgets. That enabled members of the legislative service organizations to hire experts on women's health or environmental issues or national defense and to share that expertise among themselves. With no more caucuses and Republicans in charge of the staffs of the standing committees, Democrats' access to the expertise and man-power necessary to advance a legislative agenda was greatly diminished.

"The one thing that I will never forgive him [Gingrich] for is what he did to the Congressional Caucus on Women's Issues," Schroeder said. "It was a bipartisan group. It was also men and women. We really got a lot of things done: the Women's Health Equity Act, all of our work on breast cancer, the Family Medical Leave Act, and innumerable others. It was the largest bipartisan group in the House, and Gingrich's very first act was to take away its staff and the ability to really make the committees function. The women on his side of the aisle were basically told they were not to participate. With that he pretty much put an arrow through the caucus as an effective bipartisan group."

The Republican Revolution had increased the number of GOP women in the House and Senate to twenty, while the number of Democratic women in Congress dropped from forty to thirty-five. In the House, seven new Republican women were swept into office. For the most part, they were not traditional politicians who had risen through local or state government. Rather, they sprang from the conservative grass roots—the Eagle Forum, Concerned Women for America, the Christian Coalition, and church groups. Four of them had never held elective office. One of the new women lawmakers, Andrea Seastrand of California, had suggested that California's record number of natural disasters might be a sign of God's wrath against feminism and multicultural education. Barbara Cubin of Wyoming and Helen Chenoweth of Idaho had campaigned against what they described as the federal government's secret war against the West. Chenoweth had spoken darkly of black helicopters and the United Nations. Cubin had proposed wiping every federal regulation off the books and reinstating only those that could be justified. Sue Myrick of North Carolina had proposed opening concentration camps for drug dealers and putting armed military police in the halls of public schools.

These women were determined to cut spending for welfare and other social programs—exactly the reverse of Schroeder's mission when she was first elected twenty-two years earlier. Pointing to a photograph of her grandchildren, newly elected GOP Rep. Linda Smith of Washington told a writer for the *New Republic:* "I'm going to show their picture when we debate the budget. I'm having it blown up right now. I'll tell them that they're taking freedom and opportunities away from my little grand-daughters. Imagine then if Pat Schroeder gets up and starts whining about killing old people and children. It's a lot different when she's fighting with a grandmother."

Clearly these were not the Republican sisters-in-arms that Schroeder was used to working with—Olympia Snowe of Maine, Marge Roukema of New

Jersey, and Connie Morella of Maryland, for example—women who might have a more conservative perspective on economic issues and the role of government, but who were often allies on issues of importance to women and children, from abortion to family leave to child support. Schroeder took to calling the new, conservative GOP congresswomen "femi-Newties," a take-off on hard right radio talk show host Rush Limbaugh's "femi-Nazis" insult to feminists.

Gingrich and other GOP leaders pushed the Republican congress-women out front at press conferences and photo ops. They gave them token leadership positions and titles. Jan Meyers of Kansas became the chair of the Small Business Committee, the first woman to chair a House committee capable of passing legislation since Democrat Leonor Sullivan two decades earlier. It was, however, considered a "B" committee inside the House, not a center of legislative power.

Nancy Johnson of Connecticut was made chair of the ethics committee and was asked to be a good soldier. Serving on the ethics committee is regarded among members of the House as an onerous duty for which one expects to be rewarded by party leaders at the end of the day. Wading into the slimy morass of ethics violations doesn't earn you any points with your constituents. It doesn't bring you any campaign contributions. And it can damage your relations with your colleagues and hurt your public image and your career. (In Johnson's case, it nearly cost her her congressional seat. She survived the 1996 election by a mere 1,587 votes, weakened by a public backlash against Gingrich and charges that she had used her position as ethics committee chair to protect the GOP.)

Gingrich often gloated about the Republican congresswomen, saying that the GOP had more women in their leadership, more women committee chairs, than the Democrats ever had. His inference was that it was Republicans, not Democrats, who were truly diverse and progressive. Just look at Pat Schroeder, Gingrich would frequently say, she's been here nearly twenty-four years and she's never chaired a real committee. Why not? Why have Democrats never given their senior woman a chairmanship?

Schroeder was quick to point out that she had chaired the Select Committee on Children, Youth, and Families, but it was a hollow rejoinder. Inside the House, select committees were not considered a "real" committee and they had been eliminated in 1993 as a cost-cutting measure.

Democrats may have been demoralized after the 1994 election, but they did not fade quietly into the night. Indeed, Republicans and Democrats were already deep in combat before the new Congress settled in, and Schroeder was one of the most active and visible of the partisan warriors. "Nobody knew there would be such an earthquake, and the Democrats needed someone to carry the battle afterward. They needed seasoned people to help them regain their legs," Schroeder told the *Denver Post*'s Adriel Bettelheim.

Democrats held Gingrich personally responsible for the climate of personal attack that now prevailed among the two parties, and there was little sympathy for him. It wasn't long before he presented them with an opportunity for revenge. On November 22, 1994, HarperCollins, a publishing company owned by Rupert Murdoch, announced it had signed a $4.5 million book deal with the incoming Speaker of the House. The multimillion-dollar deal was far more than any member of Congress had ever been paid for a book and more than the book could reasonably be expected to generate in profit. Democrats immediately attacked the deal as a favor from a political special interest and a blatant conflict of interest. Murdoch, who had a strong financial interest in antitrust legislation that Congress would be considering, had met privately with Gingrich in the Capitol before the book deal was announced. Both men insisted that the visit was informal and that no legislation was discussed.

Responding to the storm of criticism, Gingrich announced on December 30 that he had decided to turn down the advance for his book, *To Renew America*, and would accept only a one dollar advance plus royalties. But questions continued to dog him about whether the publishers' payment of the costs to promote the book constituted illegal gifts and travel under House rules. The book deal was the first of many wounds Gingrich's public image would suffer over the next two years. Some of those wounds would be self-inflicted, but Democrats would rub in salt and make them far more painful and debilitating than they might otherwise have been. It was more than simple revenge. Part of the Democrats' political strategy was to make House Republicans synonymous with Gingrich and to portray the GOP leader as a mean-spirited extremist.

The initial ethics complaint against Gingrich that would ultimately lead to his becoming the first Speaker to be formally reprimanded by the House for violating its rules was actually filed five months before the 1994 election by Bob Terrell, a Republican challenging him in his primary race. The House ethics committee rejected the complaint because it was filed too close to the date of the primary.

Former Rep. Ben Jones, Gingrich's Democratic opponent in the general election, refiled the complaint again a short time later, focusing on a college lecture series Gingrich was giving called "Renewing American Civilization." In essence, the lecture series was a thinly veiled vehicle for promoting Gingrich and his political philosophy. He was accused of using tax-exempt foundations—which are supposed to refrain from partisan politics—to pay for dissemination of the lecture series through books, tapes, and a cable television program. Democrats would later complain that an outside counsel was appointed only two weeks after Gingrich filed an ethics complaint against Jim Wright, but it took fifteen months of public pressure before the ethics committee hired an outside counsel, Republican attorney James Cole, to investigate the charges against Gingrich.

After the 1994 election, House Democrats began to involve themselves in the ethics case against Gingrich. In February 1995, Schroeder, Cynthia McKinney of Georgia, and Harry Johnston of Florida filed an additional ethics complaint accusing Gingrich of accepting $150,000 to $200,000 in free cable TV time to air his lecture series. Rep. George Miller of California filed a complaint alleging that Gingrich misused his office by allowing GOPAC consultant Joe Gaylord, a longtime Gingrich confidante, to act in an official capacity in the Speaker's office. Rep. David Bonior of Michigan filed a complaint alleging Gingrich violated House rules by using C-SPAN coverage of House floor proceedings to sell videotapes of his lecture series.

From start to finish, Gingrich maintained that there was no substance to the ethics charges against him and that he was simply being hounded for partisan advantage. "The truth is, our victory in November 1994 not only defeated the liberals electorally, but seemed simply to have unhinged some of them," Gingrich wrote in his 1998 book *Lessons Learned the Hard Way: A Personal Report.* He cited a column in the *New Republic* in which Democrats were urged to beat him "to a pulp." He cited another story in the *Miami Herald* headlined "We'll find Some Dirt on Gingrich, Democrats Promise Party."

"The promise to the party was fulfilled when Congresswoman Pat Schroeder of Colorado, Congressman Harry Johnston of Florida, and Congresswoman Cynthia McKinney of Georgia filed an ethics complaint against me, followed by further filings in the following month by David Bonior of Michigan," Gingrich wrote. "I should perhaps have been more chilled by all this than I was at the time . . . You cannot let yourself become mesmerized by your opponents even if it sometimes cost you dearly to ignore them. Still, there were times when the Democrats so overreached in their pursuit of me that anyone who paid attention would have found their claims absolutely ridiculous."

Schroeder was not the leader of the Democratic attacks on Gingrich, but she was one of a dozen or so key players. The point man was Bonior, a gray-bearded, acerbic former seminarian and the number two Democratic House leader. When Republicans began their drive to pass the various proposals that comprised their "Contract with America," a legislative agenda and public relations tool Gingrich had helped craft during the 1994 election, Bonior, Schroeder, and other Democrats tried to wreck the machinery. They needled the GOP to pass real reform, including a ban on lobbyists' gifts and a cap on royalties that would have precluded Gingrich's original megabuck book deal. "Why should one congressman make more in one day than an average American makes in a lifetime?" Bonior asked.

Gingrich's ethical vulnerabilities became an essential element of the Democrats' message, intertwined with assaults on Republican policies. At times, it was hard to differentiate between the two thrusts. Through news conferences, coordinated one-minute floor speeches, television talk-show appearances, and town hall meetings in their districts, Democrats continually raised questions about the GOP leader's character. "It became part of what we do," a Democratic aide told the *Washington Post.* "On days when Newt said something dumb or did something dumb, the message of the day was pound on Newt."

"Cheap, petty, partisan," Gingrich called the attacks. But he had the House parliamentarian issue a memo that any mention of the ethics complaints against him on the House floor would be considered a personal attack and therefore a violation of House rules. "That sounds like a tantrum. It looks like a tantrum," Schroeder said on the floor. "I think there is a real question about who is being childish in protecting this imperial speakership."

Two weeks after Gingrich became Speaker, Democrats leaked a transcript of a recent Gingrich "Renewing American Civilization" lecture to the press in which the GOP leader offered his views of why women don't belong in combat:

We know [what] personal strength meant in the neolithic: You carried a big club and you had a rock. What does personal strength mean in the age of the laptop? Which, by the way, is a major reason for the rise in the power of women. If upper body strength matters, men win. They are both biologically stronger and they don't get pregnant. Pregnancy is a period of male domination in traditional society. On the other hand, if what matters is the speed by which you can move the laptop, women are at least as fast and in some ways better. So you have a radical revolution based on technological change and you've got to think that through. If you talk about being in combat, what does combat mean? If combat means living in a ditch, females have biological problems staying in a ditch for thirty days because they get infections and they don't have upper body strength. I mean, some do, but they're relatively rare.

On the other hand, men are basically little piglets. You drop them in the ditch, they roll around in it—it doesn't matter, you know. On the other hand, if combat means being on an Aegis class cruiser managing the computer controls for twelve ships and their rockets, a female may again be dramatically better than a male who gets very, very frustrated sitting in a chair all the time because males are biologically driven to go out and hunt giraffes.

In a flash, Schroeder was on the House floor to skewer Gingrich: "For a person who wears his history Ph.D. like an FBI badge he should be embarrassed by his statement on women and combat."

"I am standing here defending my husband, my son, my uncle, my father," Schroeder continued. "I mean, I have seen them in ditches, but they do not roll around like little piggies. . . . I have been working in a male culture for a very long time and I have not met the first one who wants to go out and hunt a giraffe."

With the public already suspicious of Gingrich, his frequent off-the-cuff remarks were leaving him strikingly vulnerable to personal attack. He was the Democrats' symbol for all that was excessive about the Republican Revolution. Democrats would describe the Republican agenda as Gingrich's agenda and Republican lawmakers as Gingrich's troops carrying out his agenda. Democrats' charges that the GOP majority was controlled by Gingrich had the ring of truth much of the time because Gingrich did, in fact, exercise unusual power as Speaker and he was very open about it.

Schroeder enthusiastically lent her voice to Democratic efforts to depict Republican budget-cutting proposals as helping the rich while trying to undermine Social Security and Medicare. In some ways, Schroeder and other Democrats found the guerrilla warfare oddly liberating. No longer did they have to sweat the details of legislation and coalition building. Democratic congressmen, wearing ties with smiling children in crayon colors from the Save the Children Federation, attacked GOP cuts in the school lunch program, accusing Republicans of taking food out of the mouths of poor children. They staged school lunch events with examples of the meals in their home districts, drawing local television coverage. Democratic leaders hired a talk radio producer to help book Democrats on popular talk shows.

It was a role and an atmosphere best suited to masters of the partisan dig and the quick comeback, like Schroeder and Barney Frank of Massachusetts, who soon were viewed with new appreciation by their Democratic colleagues. Schroeder accused GOP members of "goose-stepping" their way through their Contract with America. "She was taking her guerrilla war approach to the Republican leadership and was more appreciated by some of her Democratic colleagues and was doing some things they weren't comfortable doing like ethics complaints and such," Dan Buck said.

Lacking the votes to push her agenda forward, Schroeder became more selective, introducing amendments designed to force Republicans to take positions on uncomfortable issues. Less than two months into the One Hundred Fourth Congress, she offered an amendment to a crime bill that would have set aside money to protect abortion clinics threatened by violence. While that measure was squelched, it forced moderate Republicans to hastily craft a compromise that enhanced security but was silent on abortion.

On the Judiciary Committee, Schroeder joined Frank and John Conyers of Michigan in opposing a startling number of Republican-proposed constitutional amendments related to flag desecration, tax limitation, school prayer, the federal budget, and term limits for members of Congress. Republicans "run on the theory that the Constitution is a rough draft and that they really have got to get it all rewritten in these two years, that the last 200 years means nothing. They have got the best ideas, and it must be changed," Schroeder said. The House approved balanced budget and flag desecration amendments, but amendments regarding school prayer, tax limitation, and term limits failed.

Schroeder and other Democrats were quick to portray Gingrich's failure to pass the term limits amendment, a high-profile element of the Contract with America, as an example of conservative hypocrisy and a sign that the GOP leader was beginning to lose control of his troops. Gingrich, Schroeder noted, was able to marshal the votes to cut funding for public broadcasting and social welfare programs, but not proposals that would require a sacrifice by lawmakers.

"The Speaker has made his side vote lock-step for all these Draconian things that were in the contract," Schroeder said. "You know, you cut school lunches, you can do anything to little kids, pull the feathers out of Big Bird, zero out the summer jobs program, you can do all these heartless things, but when it comes to affecting you, a member of Congress, oops, a lot of guys take a pass and go south on them."

Still, Democrats could only look on from the sidelines as Republicans repealed labor protection and workplace safety laws, while passing new tax breaks for business and "legal reform" legislation aimed at making it more difficult for consumers injured by business and industry to seek recompense in court. As House Republicans gathered on the Capitol steps to celebrate their first one hundred days in power, Schroeder and several aides climbed into the high reaches of the building's dome, opened a window, and hung out a 15-foot red banner reading, "Sold."

"The new guys came in and said, 'We're going to change everything, we're going to get the [business] lobbyists out of the lobby,'" Schroeder told the *Rocky Mountain News*. "What they forgot to tell you was that they were going to bring them into their office and let them write the legislation."

Abortion was another battlefront as Schroeder and pro-choice lawmakers fought not only a myriad of proposals that would erode abortion rights, but GOP efforts to undermine federal support for family planning at home and abroad. In debate on the House floor, family planning opponents began redefining the pill and other forms of contraception as "abortifacients"—something that induces abortion. Rep. Chris Smith, a New Jersey Republican and leading opponent of abortion, called oral contraceptives "baby pesticides."

In a speech to the National Press Club, Schroeder warned that not only were a majority of the lawmakers in the House now opposed to abortion, but many of them also opposed federal funding of family planning programs and the distribution of most forms of contraception. "What they [Republicans] want to call family planning is what we call in Colorado the rhythm system—they call it natural family planning—and we call everybody in Colorado that uses it 'parents,'" Schroeder said.

Rather than contraception, the Republican solution to out-of-wedlock births was chastity. Working with the Heritage Foundation, a prominent conservative think tank, Republicans proposed funding "abstinence education," a catch-phrase for federally funded grants to community programs designed to convince teenagers and adults that only monogamous sexual relations between married men and women were acceptable. Written into the legislation was the requirement that grant recipients stress that sexual relations outside marriage were potentially harmful, both psychologically and physically.

"One of the new [Republican] freshmen came to see me early on. I couldn't figure out why, because we were so different, and he said to me, 'I've come to talk to you about chastity.' And I said, 'Don't you think it's a little late for me?' and he said, 'No.' And, you know, you kind of go, 'Whoa, what have we got here?'" Schroeder told the press club. The GOP freshman apparently was under the misimpression she might vote in favor of funds for abstinence education.

Eventually, Republicans would win $250 million over five years for "abstinence education" grants. Picking up on the idea, Texas Gov. George W. Bush made doubling funding for abstinence education a part of his successful presidential campaign platform in 2000.

In May 1995, the Christian Coalition unveiled its "Contract with the American Family," a list of legislative proposals, including antiabortion and antipornography measures, the elimination of some federal programs, and a school prayer constitutional amendment. Gingrich had kept the abortion issue off the House floor during the first one hundred days of the new Congress as the GOP pushed through a legislative agenda that focused primarily on economic issues. But social conservatives were not to be denied. The summer of 1995 saw a broad and concerted drive to reverse abortion rights. There were so many abortion-related votes that the National Abortion Rights Action League had trouble keeping its running tally up to date. Abortion opponents called 1995 the "summer of life." Abortion rights activists said it was a campaign to "demonize women."

Schroeder was in the forefront of the fight. She opposed a proposal to prohibit military abortions overseas and lost. She fought an amendment to a foreign aid bill that would prohibit the United States from giving money to international family planning agencies that also perform abortions and lost. Another GOP measure would have ensured that no medical accreditation board could mandate that medical residency programs teach or pay for instruction in abortion techniques. She fought a "partial birth" abortion ban that would outlaw many mid- and late-term abortions. It passed the House, but narrowly failed in the Senate to get enough votes to override a presidential veto. The partial birth abortion ban was "intrusive government at its very, very worst," and "but one part of a concerted, multi-step effort to effectively deprive women of access to abortion," Schroeder said.

Republicans also passed a prohibition on health insurance for federal employees paying for abortions, even in cases of rape or incest. Funding for the twenty-five-year-old federal family planning program known as "Title 10" was eliminated. Schroeder withdrew legislation she had planned to offer on health programs for women in the military, acknowledging it had no chance of passing.

The addition of Republican congresswomen strongly opposed to abortion gave the debate a new woman versus woman quality that had not been present in previous congresses. "We're back to the fighting-cat syndrome," Schroeder said. "That makes everything difficult."

The Religious Right was ecstatic. "I feel like I've died and gone to heaven," the Rev. Louis P. Sheldon, a Presbyterian minister in Anaheim, California, and chairman of the Traditional Values Coalition, told the *Baltimore Sun.* "This is our finest hour in the last half-century."

On July 21, an outraged Schroeder gave an after-hours speech to the House on what she called, "the worst of times for America's women."

"I feel like Paul Revere riding through saying the British are coming. Only we are saying the fundamentalists have won. You know, we are in real trouble here," Schroeder said. "It is truly amazing that as we are saying get government out of regulation, get government out of all these areas, we are moving right into the classroom, into the doctor's office, into people's bedrooms, into all of these different areas."

In August, Gingrich visited the Tattered Cover bookstore in Denver to promote his new book and found 200 protesters waiting for him with "No Newt is Good Newt" signs. Schroeder's Denver district director, Kip Cheroutes, said he organized the protest on his own time. His boss was delighted.

"I have no problem with Pat being maniacally negative," said an irritated Gingrich. "It's fascinating that instead of having her own book, ideas and solutions, the best she can do is encourage people to make noise. It tells you what has happened to the reactionary left."

At one point, Gingrich tried to keep Schroeder off a congressional delegation traveling to Stockholm, Sweden, for an international meeting of parliamentarians, until House Judiciary Chairman Henry Hyde of Illinois intervened on her behalf. "When that happened to me the first time [with Hebert], I had to pay my own way," Schroeder said. "This time Newt realized if I went to the press with it, he'd lose." Gingrich backed down and Schroeder joined the delegation.

By the fall of 1995, political support for Gingrich's political agenda had begun to weaken. Clinton had initially been largely overshadowed by Gingrich and his Republican troops as they pushed through their Contract with America, but as the thirteen annual spending bills that keep the government running began arriving on his deck laden with conservative initiatives, the vetoes started rolling.

In the ensuing standoff between congressional Republicans and Clinton, the American public endured the two longest partial government shutdowns in the nation's history. It was not long after the first shutdown that Gingrich made one of his most costly errors. In a breakfast interview with several dozen reporters, Gingrich complained about being forced to sit in the back of Air Force One with Senate Republican leader Bob Dole on a return trip from Israeli Prime Minister Yitzhak Rabin's funeral while Clinton huddled with his staff up front. If Clinton had been friendlier on the trip and put his time to better use, the GOP leader suggested, Republicans would have been more accommodating with the White House on the budget and the shutdown of federal agencies might have been avoided.

Word of the House Speaker's gaffe spread like wildfire. The headlines across the country the next morning were that Gingrich had shut down the federal government because Clinton made him sit in the back of the plane. The *New York Daily News* devoted its entire front page to a drawing of a bawling, tantrum-filled Gingrich in diapers, stamping his feet and waving a baby bottle. The headline: "CRY BABY." New York Democrat Charles Schumer brought a blowup of the front page to the House floor in the midst of a fresh round of anti-Gingrich speeches. Standing in the well of the House in full view of C-SPAN cameras, Schroeder brandished a mock Oscar, which she said was Gingrich's Academy Award for "best performance by a child actor."

"Now that this country has paid dearly for his temper tantrum and paid dearly for his shutting down the whole country because of his little peeve, could we get a performance that's a little more statesmanlike?" Schroeder asked.

A short time later, the White House released photos of a smiling Clinton, Gingrich, and other officials gathered around a table aboard Air Force One on the same trip in which Gingrich said he'd been ignored by the president. The episode proved pivotal in turning public opinion in the budget standoff against congressional Republicans and in favor of Clinton.

At the same time, Schroeder herself was smarting from attacks by a new, aggressively conservative brand of media, particularly talk radio hosts like Rush Limbaugh and Janet Parshall, who frequently invoked her name as a synonym for liberal excess. Iran-Contra figure turned radio talk show host Oliver North put her on his list of the "twenty-five most dangerous politicians in America." To be a liberal and a feminist was no longer merely misguided, but downright dirty and dangerous.

"Now you can fire hose people with your ideology twenty-four hours a day and never let the other side on. Listen to the Rush Limbaugh Show—they don't air callers who disagree with him. It's made to sound like all of America agrees with this idiot. Those of us who would like to answer can't because now there is no FCC requirement for balance," Schroeder complained to *Ms.* magazine.

Yet Schroeder was still willing to stand up publicly and defend both liberalism and feminism. "Women are now living much longer, they can vote, which they couldn't have done a hundred years ago, they can participate in all sorts of things. I think we're going to decide that really wasn't such a bad thing," she told the press. "And so what's so wrong with being a progressive or a liberal? I don't know what any of those labels mean, but obviously talk radio has been fire-hosing people with, 'That's a liberal! That's a liberal!' My gosh, you know, get out of the room—you may catch it! But I just hope that when we put it in a bigger context it will not be such a snarl word."

In December, the ethics committee agreed to hire an outside counsel to assist in a "preliminary inquiry" into the charges dealing with the college course. The committee also found Gingrich guilty of three offenses involving other issues, but they recommended no punishment. A week later, Bonior, Schroeder, and three other Democrats filed a new complaint against Gingrich based on recently acquired documents made public by the Federal Election Commission. After six weeks of deliberations, the ethics committee rejected the complaint. Bonior, Schroeder, and three other Democrats then refiled the complaint with 8,000 pages of supporting documents. On February 1, the committee finally accepted the complaint, but turned back the documents.

Meanwhile, Schroeder waded into two other ethics controversies, one involving Gingrich and the other involving GOP Rep. Bud Shuster of Pennsylvania, the powerful chairman of the transportation committee. In the first instance, Schroeder had discovered that the Pentagon had secretly assigned six army and marine colonels to work in the Speaker's office on political strategies for pushing the GOP agenda through Congress. There were no corresponding officers working for Democrats and it appeared to be a case of politicization of the military.

Gingrich had long had a fascination with the military and would some-times quote Chinese military philosopher Sun Tzu. He had ordered his staff to study books by Heinz Guderian, the German general who invented the Blitzkrieg, and Miyamoto Musashi, a samurai warrior, in the hope of deriving political lessons from the art of war. Gingrich had specifically requested that the officers assigned to him have backgrounds in "operations and doctrine," that is, military strategy.

Schroeder gave speeches about the officers assigned to Gingrich and wrote letters to top defense officials, but drew little response. When she filed a request for information about the officers under the Freedom of Information Act, the Defense Department sent her back a report with every word on every page blacked out. (Typically, federal agencies are only supposed to censor information that is classified secret or of a personal nature.) No other modern Speaker—and possibly no other Speaker ever—had been assigned active-duty military officers for use as staff. "What was important about it was that it was a separation of powers issue and an issue of keeping our military from being politicized and the disas-ter that happens to any country that has a politicized military," said Gary Ruskin of the Congressional Accountability Project.

Schroeder was not the only lawmaker concerned about the situation. Several other House Democrats and GOP Sen. Charles Grassley of Iowa also complained. It would take two years, but eventually the Defense Department's inspector general concluded that military personnel should not have been assigned to such overtly partisan organizations as the House Republican Conference Committee. And a separate Defense Department audit report concluded the army had absorbed $15,000 in improper expenses for Gingrich and other GOP lawmakers and their staffs to receive training in battlefield tactics at army bases.

In Shuster's case, the Justice Department had been reviewing poten-tially illegal gratuities the congressman had received from Ann Eppard, who was Shuster's top aide for twenty years before leaving his staff to become a transportation lobbyist. Shuster lived at Eppard's townhouse when in Washington and they maintained a close personal and political relationship even though she was lobbying his committee. Shuster's reelec-tion campaign was paying Eppard $3,000 per month in consulting fees while raising tens of thousands of dollars from her clients. Those same clients, according to complaints from congressional watchdog groups, received favorable treatment from the transportation committee, which oversaw billions of dollars in federal transportation projects.

Despite the seriousness of the situation, no member of the House was willing to file an ethics complaint against Shuster. To do so could put transportation projects in their own congressional districts at risk. Congressional watchdog groups like Common Cause and the Congressional Accountability Project were eager to file a complaint against Shuster, but House rules forbade anyone outside the House from filing a complaint unless they could first get letters from three House members stating that the members had refused to file a complaint. Getting these "letters of refusal" was nearly as difficult as convincing a House member to directly file a complaint themselves. Finally, in the waning days of the One Hundred Fourth Congress, Ruskin obtained three letters of refusal, including one from Schroeder, enabling a formal complaint against Shuster to be lodged with the ethics committee.

"Given how powerful Congressman Shuster was at the time," it took "guts" for Schroeder to provide one of the letters, Ruskin said. "The prospect of some type of retribution had to be on her mind and rightly so. I can tell you that it took us six months of begging and pleading and bowing and scraping in order to get even just the three letters of refusal that allowed us to file on the Shuster case."

More than four years later, the ethics committee finally concluded that Shuster had engaged in a pattern of official misconduct. In testament to Shuster's power, the finding was greeted with virtual silence by House members of both parties. Even Schroeder and former Democratic Rep. Pat Williams of Montana, who also provided a refusal letter, no longer wanted to talk about the case when contacted by *Roll Call*, a twice-weekly newspaper that covers the internal workings of Congress.

As the ethics case against Gingrich dragged on, Schroeder urged the ethics committee to release a report by the special counsel, which she charged the Speaker was trying to delay until after the 1996 election. She cited Gingrich's demands during the Wright case that a special counsel's report be made public. "What is good for the goose is good for the Gingrich," Schroeder said. "The Republicans cannot have it both ways. They have to play this game by the rules they established in the Wright case, and they should release the report." The ethics committee, Schroeder told the National Press Club, is "really is looking like the Newt Gingrich Protection Association."

By December, both parties were eager to conclude the ethics case against Gingrich in an attempt to clear the poisonous atmosphere of the past two years. Democrats and Republicans on the committee cut what appeared to be a political deal. In exchange for bringing the case to a close, Gingrich was required to concede only that "in my name and over my signature, inaccurate, incomplete and unreliable statements were given to the [ethics] committee." In addition, he agreed to a committee statement that he had failed to "seek and follow" legal advice that would have told him he was improperly using tax-exempt organizations to further political aims. Gingrich acknowledged he had brought discredit to the House. The committee recommended he be reprimanded by the House and fined $300,000. Gingrich borrowed the money to pay the fine from former Senate Republican leader Bob Dole of Kansas.

"I was not careful enough partly because I underestimated the fight I was in," Gingrich wrote later in his book *Lessons Learned the Hard Way*. "Certain Democrats had targeted me and I had handed them the means."

On January 6, 1997, Gingrich was narrowly reelected Speaker of the House. Fifteen days later, he became the first Speaker to be formally reprimanded by the House for ethical misconduct. However, the culmination of the Democrats' ethics battle with Gingrich unfolded without Schroeder. She had opposed Gingrich and his conservative agenda with every means available to her, but the fight had taken a toll. Weary and disheartened, Schroeder had made a pivotal decision more than a year earlier that would remove her from the front lines of partisan warfare and put her life on a new course.

10

A Legend Bows Out

After a year of introspection and taking stock, Pat Schroeder was leaning strongly toward ending her twenty-four-year political career and moving on to something new when she boarded a ship with her family for a Thanksgiving cruise in November 1995. The three-day cruise aboard the *Fantasy* from Port Canaveral, Florida, to the Bahamas was an opportunity to sound out her husband, Jim, and her two grown children, Scott and Jamie.

Her children urged her to make the change, to teach or speak out on issues. If she found she missed politics, she could run for some other office, they told her. But, according to an account by Guy Kelly of the *Rocky Mountain News*, Jim urged her to stick it out. "You're nuts. It's great fun," he told her. Besides, he added, what was at stake was bigger than Pat Schroeder—she was an important part of Congress, a leader. His argument was underscored by the other passengers on the ship, some of whom recognized Schroeder and urged her to keep fighting for the principles of the Democratic party despite the Republican domination of Congress.

But Schroeder had been living up to that responsibility for more than two decades. Now, her heart was no longer in it. At the end of the three days, Schroeder had made up her mind. One of the most prominent members of the House, a political legend, the doyen of the liberal establishment, had decided to call it quits.

On the morning of November 29, 1995, Schroeder gathered her staff in her Washington office and told them of her decision to retire the following year at the end of the One Hundred Fourth Congress. Many of them had been with her for nearly twenty years, a lifetime on Capitol Hill. Schroeder then went to Democratic party headquarters a few blocks from the Capitol, where she taped a brief video of her announcement for Denver television stations. Returning to her office, she gave an interview to two Denver newspaper reporters. Afterward, her staff called a general press conference in the television studio of the House radio and television gallery on the third floor of the Capitol.

Standing at a podium with flags draped on either side, Schroeder told reporters she was determined to depart on her own terms. "I always said I wasn't going to be here for life, and life was ticking by," she said. "I'm fifty-five years old. I wanted to go out at the top of my game. As of this year, I got into the national women's history museum, Ollie North is terrified of me and I'm on his twenty-five most dangerous [politicians'] list . . . That means if I'm not going to be a lifer, this is the time I probably have to go. But it's very hard. It's been a great place and a lot of fun."

Schroeder's office was immediately flooded with calls from well-wishers, the media, and cranks. Rep. David Skaggs, the only other Democrat in the Colorado delegation, sent over a bouquet of red and yellow flowers. Rep. Carolyn Maloney, a New York Democrat, decided not to bother with the phone, but went straight to Schroeder's office.

"I'm upset," Maloney told Lloyd Grove of the *Washington Post* as they both waited in the office's reception area to see Schroeder. "It's a tremendous loss to the women in Congress, not to be selfish about it. She's got very big shoes and nobody can step into them. She was the coach, the leader, the strategist. . . . She was, by far, the greatest feminist of my time!"

As Schroeder prepared to retire from Congress, she was the senior woman in the House, having served longer than any of the current female House members. When she arrived in 1973, she was one of only fourteen women members. There were no women senators. When she announced her retirement, there were fifty-six women in the House and nine in the Senate. Five years later, there would be thirteen women in the Senate and sixty in the House.

"We have some very, very prestigious and capable women, and they'd bloody well better show up in leadership positions," Schroeder said as she was leaving office. "I think the Democratic party, who has come to power on the gender gap—let's face it, it's a gender canyon, I think, of late—is going to have a lot of answering to do." (Since the early 1980s, the term "gender gap" has been used to refer to the edge Democratic candidates in close races generally hold over their GOP opponents among women voters. Conversely, Republican candidates tend to hold an advantage over their Democratic opponents among male voters.)

Schroeder denied that she was disappointed never to have chaired a major committee. "I came to be an ideas person and to try and change the place," she told the *Washington Post.* "I never wanted to have a little mountain and be some power broker standing on top." (Five years later, there was still not a single major committee in the House that was chaired by a woman, although two Republican congresswomen chaired minor committees in the One Hundred Fourth Congress. In 2001, Republican leaders passed over two moderate GOP congresswomen for chairmanships—Marge Roukema of New Jersey on the banking committee and Sue Kelly of New York on the small business committee—in favor of conservative men with less seniority.)

At her press conference, Schroeder also denied that the Democrats' minority status in the House had affected her decision. "I was in the minority when we were in the majority," Schroeder said. "I was very frustrating even to the Democratic leadership. Western Democrats are a little different, and I was hard to paper-train." But expounding on her reasons for retiring in an interview with Charles Lewis of the Center for Public Integrity, a government watchdog group, it was clear that a role limited primarily to being Newt Gingrich's nemesis had begun to wear thin:

"In all honesty, I had a lot of fun the last two years because you didn't have to do any work. You just got up every morning and read the paper. It was hysterical. I mean, they [Republicans] gave me so much to work with . . . [But] at the end of the day you never had anything in the out box that was really productive . . . I got a little bit depressed that more Democrats weren't joining in trying to rebuild the party. There was just kind of a sense of mourning. And there were a few folks that were taking the floor every day and trying to reclaim some ideological ground, but there were a lot that were just kind of mourning the loss and couldn't get on with it and that kind of made me sad. . . . It was clear to me [Democrats weren't] going to win the House back and I didn't want to forever just be out there as this spear carrier. I enjoyed doing it. It was a lot of fun. But I still like to have something in the out box."

The fight had clearly wearied Schroeder. "The whole Gingrich thing did sort of take a lot out of her," her aide, Kip Cheroutes, said. "She did say things like, 'I spent all this time climbing the seniority ladder and power platforms and now it's all kind of wiped away and I find myself again as sort of a backbencher bomb-thrower. I'm getting a little too old for this.' But then she would say that she didn't see any of her Democratic colleagues taking them on so she felt an obligation to get up there and do this stuff."

Another factor, Schroeder said, was her age and her long tenure. "One of the things I sensed about Congress is that it's easy to stay too long. I always wanted to go out at the top and not have to have somebody tap me on the shoulder and say, 'Um, there's something we need to talk about.'"

Of her legislative accomplishments, Schroeder said: "I carried an awful lot of things for which there was no big power groups on the outside, no big lobbying group, and still [I] was able to get them moved into law." She compared her advocacy of family medical leave and pension sharing for divorced spouses to cable television deregulation legislation in the 1980s, which her former Colorado colleague, Democrat Tim Wirth, was noted for pushing through the House. "If you say, 'You did cable deregulation,' yeah right, but you had all the telephone companies and the cable companies, you know, you had a thousand other teammates pushing on the outside and stuffing people's campaigns full of money." In other words, she managed to push legislation through—family medical leave, for example—over the fierce opposition of moneyed special interests.

In June 1996, six months before she was due to leave office, Schroeder's Democratic colleagues held a roast in her honor. "Pat, we will miss you. Not quite the same way as the Republicans will miss you, but we will miss you nonetheless," said crusty Rep. John Dingell of Michigan, the longest serving Democrat in the House. "We'll miss the smiley faces in your signature, the bunny suits, your hard work and commitment, and your flair for language. Without you we never would have known whether the president was Teflon or Velcro, or which hawks were really chickens in disguise. . . . For two decades you've been fighting the good fight, on behalf of women, kids, and all the others looking for nothing more than a fair shake. You've done it with good humor and great grace. You've made a serious business a lot of fun, and for that we will always thank you—and love you."

Republicans, right-wing radio talk show hosts, abortion opponents, and other critics were delighted to see Schroeder retire. "I wish her well in her retirement. It's a wish I've had for 24 years now," Newt Gingrich's press secretary, Tony Blankley, said dryly.

No one questioned Schroeder's ability to win reelection easily had that been her choice, but her decision to retire freed her from the necessity of making twice-monthly trips back to Denver and of planning yet another political campaign for the House. In December 1995, police at Denver International Airport towed away her ramshackle Dodge Colt. The car had been sitting unattended in an airport parking lot for so long that police thought it had been abandoned. By the time Schroeder retrieved it, there were mice living inside. It took some weeks after her announcement before Schroeder was able to fly back to Denver, but when she stepped off the plane at the airport she was surprised to find that her Denver district office staff had gathered at the gate to greet her, including an aide dressed in a bunny suit. "We thought she needed some spirit-lifting," said Kip Cheroutes, her district staff director. "That did the trick. She loved that."

Her greatest achievement, Schroeder said, was keeping her family intact and "coming out of here standing up . . . I don't have an indictment, and I don't have the FBI investigating me. I have a husband who's still married to me, I have two children who are normal and have jobs, thank God, and even my dog is still alive, and he's fifteen."

Her son, Scott, is a graduate of Georgetown University and works in the financial services industry in New York. Daughter Jamie is a graduate of Princeton University and has done graduate work at Cambridge University in England. She is married and lives in Montana. Her family "was her huge priority," Scott told the *Rocky Mountain News* in 1996. "I can't really point to a time when I can say I was 'neglected.' I never had that feeling."

"The thing that has impressed me most is, I know my family comes first, no matter what," said daughter Jamie. "I think that that's the secret to my brother and I not having drug and alcohol problems and not having been in jail five times."

Schroeder's retirement decision coincided with a growing need to spend more time caring for her elderly parents. Her father was ailing with lung cancer and her mother with Alzheimer's disease. The couple moved to Celebration, Florida, in 1997, where Pat's brother, Michael, lived. Pat would fly down to visit them on weekends. It was a difficult period. Her parents, who were in their mid-eighties, didn't want to move to Florida, which they thought of as "God's waiting room." Schroeder described those visits in an interview with Jane Gross of the *New York Times* as a "Salvador Dali painting." She would pay bills, buy groceries, and try to persuade her father that he was too old to drive. Sometimes Jamie would fill in if her mother was traveling on business. Lee Scott died on July 15, 1999. Bernice Scott died a year and one month later.

Schroeder had always been close to her parents. If her parents didn't like what one of the Denver newspapers was saying about their daughter, they would cancel their subscription and subscribe to the competing paper. If the competing newspaper wrote something they didn't like, they would switch back to the other paper. One of Schroeder's favorite memories of her mother was from the year a man who was supposed to play Santa Claus didn't show up at a Christmas party at the congresswoman's Denver district office. Bernice Scott stepped into the breach and donned the Santa suit. Later, she sent out pictures to friends with the note: "The things one does for one's children."

"I am not retiring in the sense of I'm going to take up needlepoint or something," Schroeder told the National Press Club in a farewell speech in 1996. "I'm going outside to make even more noise than I made inside." Of course, that was not possible. As with any other retired House member, once Schroeder left Congress she had lost her podium. She has remained active in public life and is still invited to appear on television talk shows, but not nearly to the same degree as when she was in Congress.

Schroeder was fifty-six when she left office, still young enough, she said, for a second career. Immediately after her last term in Congress ended in January 1997, she taught a graduate-level course titled "The Politics of Poverty" at Princeton University's Woodrow Wilson School of Public and International Affairs in New Jersey for a semester while Jim continued to live in Washington. "I couldn't stand the commute," Schroeder said.

Even outside of Congress, Schroeder continued to stir controversy. On February 25, 1997, less than two months after leaving office, Schroeder was named the new president and chief executive officer of the Association of American Publishers (AAP). In the world of Washington lobbying, which is a large part of what the publishers' association is about, the position of president of AAP is a very choice plum. In 2000, Schroeder's salary at AAP was $370,000. That's in addition to the $75,000-a-year pension she's eligible for after twenty-four years in the House.

Schroeder's new role as president of AAP is not surprising. During her last two years in the House, she was the senior Democrat on the courts and intellectual property subcommittee of the Judiciary Committee, which deals with copyright issues, and she had shown sympathy for the publishing and music industries as they grappled with conflicts created by technological change.

In taking the job, Schroeder knew she was wading into a raging debate over intellectual property protection in the digital age. Just as the Internet had created turmoil in the movie and music industries, it was also roiling the waters of the book publishing industry. All three industries share a common concern: the loss of control and profits as technology changes the rules of business. "Just because technology makes it so much easier to copy creative works, many people have forgotten it is not any easier to create them!" Schroeder said as she joined AAP. "We have lots of work to do to protect intellectual property and I'm ready to do it!"

During her first year at AAP, Schroeder was able to help pass a significant bill to guard intellectual property rights over the Internet, the No Electronic Theft or "NET" bill. It was signed by President Clinton on December 18, 1997. The bill grew out of recommendations made in a national information infrastructure "white paper" produced by an interagency task force during the Clinton administration. The recommendations were heavily supported by the entertainment, publishing, and software industries, although librarians and educators were somewhat wary. The NET legislation was a change to the federal copyright statute. Its most controversial element provided for the first time for criminal prosecution for copyright violations. An individual who "willfully" infringes copyrighted material worth at least $1,000 over any 180-day period could be subject to criminal prosecution, fines, or jail time, even if the individual does not profit from the violation.

The criminal prosecution provision was a significant change. In the past, it was often assumed that copyright violators would not be taken to court unless the plaintiff had a good expectation of collecting monetary damages. But with criminal prosecution, it is up to the government to decide whether to pursue a case. Legal costs and potential recovery become secondary to the principle of deterrence.

However, passing legislation simply provided the publishing industry with a new tool to combat electronic piracy. By no means did it solve the problem. Despite the collapse of much of dot.com retailing, the publishing industry still sees the Internet as the wave of the future for selling books, either in digital form or for home delivery. Publishers see e-books—books you can read using handheld devices—as a major untapped source of revenue. But having watched the music industry's vulnerability to Napster, where millions of ordinary Internet users were able to circumvent copyright laws and download music for free, publishers are wary of pirates and hackers who believe all information online should be free. In 2000, Forrester Research forecast a loss of $1.5 billion for publishers to electronic piracy over four years.

Consequently, the industry has focused on trying to figure how to charge customers for digital books and periodicals per use, and how to prevent people from copying books and periodicals they have purchased and from passing them along to people who haven't paid for them. With the e-book market still in its infancy, publishers have been anxious to set standards and ground rules now for how retailers will interact with customers online in the future. "We knew that if we didn't move out there, someone else might and they might begin giving our stuff away," Schroeder said at a January 2000 press conference where she outlined publishers' plans to protect copyrighted digital material.

Enter the nation's librarians, who see their mission as providing as much information as possible to as many people as possible at no charge. "As long as the commercial marketplace has established a metered, encrypted system for access, the ability of libraries to serve a public mission—which allows for no fee access to published and unpublished works—may be diminished," attorney Arnold Lutzker warned in a legal analysis for librarians and educators.

Thus, one of Congress's legendary liberals found herself locked in a battle with, of all groups, librarians. Research librarians in particular fear that publishers will limit their access to expensive research journals online and restrict their ability to share their subscriptions to those journals with other libraries as has been the practice with printed copies. They also believe that library users should be able to duplicate limited amounts of information for educational purposes. Historically, that has been the practice under the "fair use" provision of the copyright law. But the digital world is a whole new arena, and "fair use" appears to have shrunk to almost nothing, librarians contend. Indeed, Schroeder has acknowledged that publishers fear that giving libraries access to expensive research materials online undermines publishers' ability to sell customers the same material. As a result, publishers are looking for ways to charge library patrons.

"Politically, it's the toughest issue," Schroeder told *Washington Post* reporter Linton Weeks. "Libraries have a wonderful image." In the same interview, she went on to say that the publishers "have a very serious issue with librarians . . . Markets are limited. One library buys one of their [members of the publishers' association's] journals, and they give it to other libraries. [And] they'll give it to others . . . These people [publishers, writers, and others involved in making books] aren't rich. They have mortgages."

A brewing backlash among librarians against Schroeder and the publishers association burst forth after the *Post* story, which has become known in the library world as "the infamous Schroeder interview."

"Looting the library. . . . Pat Schroeder and the publishing industry are trying to paint libraries as organized pirates. For shame," was the headline of one commentary in *Technology Review*. Nowhere was tension more evident than online. University of Michigan librarian Grant Burns, who pens an online library column for *Newpages.com* under the name "Uncle Frank," laid out the librarian viewpoint:

In Schroeder's view of the publishing world, librarians are busy giving away the farm that poor publishers work so hard to tend. The
main problem with Schroeder's observations is that they are all
wrong. Libraries do not pass around free copies of periodicals to
one another. In the tight guidelines that determine interlibrary
lending procedures, what goes from one library to another (and
ultimately to a specific library user who has requested it) is a copy
of a periodical article. Under the strict copyright compliance rules
that American libraries follow, only a very limited number of articles from a specific periodical may be freely passed along in this
manner over a specified period. Libraries exceeding the allowed
quantity must pay for the privilege.

Thanks to interlibrary lending, a car mechanic from a northern
Wisconsin village can go to his little public library and request a copy
of an article from a medical journal owned by only a few major
research libraries in the Midwest. An informed public is the first line
of defense against tyranny. The same dynamic that allows these individuals to pursue their unique informational needs at little or no personal cost is the one that helps create a climate of freedom for
publishers, that helps make it possible for American publishers to
flourish. The situation that we have serves everyone involved. Pat
Schroeder hates it, evidently, because too often people can read or see
something without ponying up some dough for the privilege.

There is also a healthy balance between pay-as-you-go reading
and everything-free-for-all at all times. If Schroeder and the AAP
have their way, the balance will be gone, and we'll be living in a
world that no one concerned about the principles of either political freedom or publishing in a democratic society wants to see.

Librarians also point out that U.S. libraries already spend $2 billion a
year on licenses for electronic publications.

Despite the volatility of the issue, Schroeder seemed shocked when she
found herself the target of open hostility as she participated in a panel on
digital copyright protection and piracy at the Text One Zero digital book
publishing conference in Brooklyn in May 2001, according to an account
of the event in *Publishers' Weekly*. Other panelists included several critics of
the Digital Millennium Copyright Act, which prohibits removing encryp-
tion protection from digital content. Schroeder even drew hisses from the
audience when she noted that the publishers association supported both

the digital copyright act and tighter "digital rights management," the practice of defining, protecting, and enforcing the rights of owners and producers of electronic content.

Panelists hectored Schroeder about the digital copyright act, calling it "flawed" and "unconstitutional," but she refused to give ground. "Publishers, not pirates" will decide what business model to use, she said over shouts from the audience. "How else do you protect intellectual property? Publishers are the stewards of authors' rights."

⁂

In the spring of 1998, after she had been retired from Congress for more than a year, Schroeder joined about a dozen reporters over lunch to discuss her new book, *24 Years of House Work . . . and the Place Is Still a Mess,* a memoir of her years in Congress. The discussion soon turned to presidential politics and a question was asked of Schroeder: "Are there any women out there that you see as possible candidates for president in 2000?"

With barely a pause, Schroeder fired off the names of a half-dozen women governors and members of Congress, all Democrats. The reporters seated around the U-shaped table dutifully scribbled down the names even though they knew none of the women Schroeder had mentioned were considered credible contenders. Another journalist spoke up. "What about Republicans? Aren't there any Republican women who would make credible candidates for president? What about Liddy Dole? What about [Rep.] Jennifer Dunn?"

Schroeder paused for a longer moment, refolding the napkin in her lap as she thought about her answer. "I know them both, and I like them, but I didn't take all the barbs for 24 years . . . to elect a woman who says, 'I'm not just a woman,'" she said carefully. "I don't want a Queen Bee type. I want someone who is in there trying to move all women forward. They were a little late coming to help. I would really prefer women who are proud of being women."

What is a "Queen Bee type?" the reporters wanted to know, catching a whiff of controversy. Well, Margaret Thatcher, the former British prime minister and Tory leader, would be one example, Schroeder said. "What I don't want," she said with emphasis, "is a woman who forms a government without any other women in it." There was a light, amused murmur as the reporters scribbled some more.

It was blunt talk, but the remarks also went to the heart of Schroeder's political career. By the time she left the House, Schroeder had become the preeminent supporter of women's rights in Congress, even when advancing those rights wasn't always popular, even though other women didn't always thank her. Indeed, one of the key accomplishments of her career was simply proving that women could have a voice in Congress, that a lone woman or a group of women working together could be a force to be reckoned with even on such traditionally male terrain as national defense.

"When I came, the concept of women being in the debate was a shock. Women weren't supposed to be on the committee, women weren't supposed to be in the debate, they [male colleagues] didn't want any part of it," Schroeder said in an interview. "The one thing that I really wanted to do was show that women could get into the debate, that women had legs to stand on . . . I think we did that."

Still, there is much Schroeder would have liked to have accomplished that remains undone. Defense spending continues to be wasteful and to consume far too much of the budget, she said. Family medical leave, she said, should have been expanded to include paid leave and to cover more women. Women still made up only 13.8 percent of the House, a far cry from parity.

"I'm stunned at how slow women's progress has been," Schroeder said not long after leaving office. "We'd hoped that the work and family issues would be much more resolved. We're still making women feel guilty about everything. They're guilty if they stay home because they're supposed to be working. They're guilty if they work because they should be home taking care of the family. We really should have buried a lot of that. I find it sad that women haven't used their political power a lot more to just say, 'Stop this! We're not going to have full-time jobs twenty-four hours a day!' We've got to have some kind of support."

During a visit to Utah in 2000, Schroeder told reporters: "If you would have told me then that after nearly thirty years there would only be fifty-seven women in the House, I wouldn't have believed you. I thought we'd be much further along. The rest of America—sports, business—is moving much faster. Obviously, we are not where I want us to be. It's been evolutionary rather than revolutionary."

Progress on the presidential level has moved with similarly glacial speed. "We are not there yet" when it comes to electing a woman president, Schroeder told a conference on marriage at the University of Tennessee. She noted that a poll taken in 1999 showed a very high percentage of respondents said they would vote for a woman president. However, when asked if they thought their friends and neighbors would do the same, the percentage dropped to around 45 percent. Women, Schroeder said, simply don't fit the image of a president in the minds of much of the public despite a small but growing number of women leaders around the world. "When people vote for president, what they're really voting for is 'president, commander in chief and leader of the free world,'" she said.

One of her greatest disappointments, Schroeder said, is that many younger women just starting their careers no longer believe that women's rights are in need of protection. "I am astounded that women just think that their justice is preordained and they don't have to do anything and that anybody who talks about equal rights is some high-strung hysterical female and they're not part of the group," Schroeder said bitterly.

On the other hand, there is a presumption of equality among girls and young women today that contrasts starkly to the attitudes Schroeder grew up with in the 1950s. "I see little girls and I say to them, 'Are you thinking about being president?' and they'll say, 'Yeah!' Now, no one said that to me when I was growing up. I mean, that was just the furthest thing from my mind," Schroeder reflected. "So out there somewhere there is a young American woman that has that idea in her mind, and I think that she will come forward and do it. I think what we want to do is make sure that she is a power in herself, that she is not viewed as a token or not viewed as a voice for someone else, and that I hope we can come to terms with."

While much had changed since Schroeder had entered Congress in 1973, much had also remained the same. Schroeder's successor in Colorado's First Congressional District is Democrat Diana DeGette, an attorney, former state legislator, and mother of two daughters. Her husband, attorney Lino Lipinsky, has had to adjust to the role of House spouse much the way Jim Schroeder had to adjust to having a congresswoman for a wife twenty-five years earlier.

"While male congressional spouses are rare enough, only a handful have small children. The typical female member of Congress deferred her political career until her children had grown. While young men with children are viewed as rising political stars, few women with school-age children are considered viable candidates," Lipinski wrote in the *Denver Post* more than four years after Schroeder left office.

"Two years ago, we spouses were invited to tape public-service television spots. In Jim's era, the spouses focused on breast cancer awareness. Jim dutifully recorded commercials on the subject until someone suggested that constituents might conclude he had an unseemly fixation on this portion of female anatomy," Lipinsky wrote. "I assumed that times had changed by 1999. I looked forward to doing my small part to advance literacy, which the spouses had selected as one of their gender-neutral causes. Until I received my instructions. I was told to appear for the taping dressed in red and with my usual make-up. I await the day when no one assumes that all congressional spouses wear foundation and blush. And I don't think the Colorado judiciary would approve if I appeared in court wearing a red dress."

DeGette's and Lipinsky's children were two and six years old when she was elected to the House, the same ages as the Schroeders' children. Unlike Schroeder, who was unique for her time, DeGette is one of a small but growing number of women serving in Congress who have young children. And yet, the controversy over whether mothers of young children can or should serve is still very much alive. In 1998, when former congresswoman Blanche Lincoln—the mother of twin toddlers—decided to run for the Senate from Arkansas, conservative columnist Mona Charen asked the same question that was asked of Schroeder twenty-six years earlier: Can she be both a good mother and a good representative? Charen clearly believed the answer was no.

"It's not impossible for a mother of twins to work—some," Charen wrote. "But running for and serving as a United States senator is not a job one would call 'family-friendly' . . . What will our senator/mother do on the weekend? Will she schlep two babies, a double stroller, two diaper bags, two favorite stuffed animals and a portacrib back and forth to Arkansas?" Charen predicted that if elected—which Lincoln was—she would likely be forced to submit her twin sons to a "substantial degree of child neglect."

In Massachusetts, Republican Gov. Jane Swift and her husband, Chuck Hunt, seemed to have completely reversed the traditional model of the political family. She had the high-powered political career; he quit his job to stay home with the kids. Yet even with a house husband, when a pregnant-with-twins Swift stepped into the governor's office in April 2001 she was the focus of a frenzied public debate over whether she could both mother and govern. The couple already had a toddler at home.

Similarly, four decades after Congress passed the Equal Pay Act, women and men still do not earn equal dollars for equal work, although the wage gap has narrowed. In 1962, when the act was signed into law, a white woman working full time year-round earned an average of fifty-nine cents to a white man's dollar, according the U.S. Department of Labor. In 1996, women's earnings peaked at seventy-four cents, dropping to seventy-three cents in 1998 and seventy-two cents in 1999. The wage gap for African American and Hispanic women is even greater.

However, many other indices of social progress have changed markedly, and more are continuing to evolve. For example, most law schools have come 180 degrees from their former reluctance to accept women. In 1960, just two years before Schroeder entered Harvard Law, women accounted for only 4 percent of first-year law students nationwide. In 2000, women accounted for 49.4 percent of first-year law students nationwide and made up 46 percent of the entering class at Harvard Law. Women are projected to soon outnumber male law students. On the other hand, women are a long way from parity in the judiciary, on law school faculties, or in law firm partnerships. Of 655 federal district judges in 2001, only 136 were women, according to the Alliance for Justice, a nonprofit advocacy group. Women also account for only about 20 percent of law school full professors.

Still, the trend has profound implications for society because law degrees have traditionally been used as credentials for launching careers in business and politics, careers that can eventually become springboards into positions of power. Now, they may function similarly for women.

Women also continue to break new ground in politics. During Schroeder's twenty-four years in the House, not a single woman held a top-tier leadership post in either party. In October 2001, Congresswoman Nancy Pelosi of California was elected the number two Democratic leader in the House, defeating a male colleague, Congressman Steny Hoyer of Maryland, in a 108 to 95 vote of her Democratic colleagues.

A year later, after disappointing results for Democrats in the 2002 election, Rep. Richard Gephardt of Missouri announced he would step aside as his party's top leader in the House. Within days Pelosi had lined up the support necessary to elect her to the post of minority leader, another first.

In January 2001, Schroeder was in the Senate chamber—a privilege allowed former members of Congress—when Hillary Rodham Clinton, the newly elected senator from New York, took the oath of office, breaking more new ground for women. The ceremony took place just days before the end of Bill Clinton's second term in the White House. "It was so funny seeing the president of the United States follow his wife behind like the tail of a kite," Schroeder said. "It tells you these role models are changing so radically that it makes it a very interesting time to be alive."

Note on Sources:

Key resources in researching this book were Pat Schroeder's two published memoirs, *24 Years of House Work . . . and the Place Is Still a Mess* (Kansas City: Andrews McMeel Publishing, 1998), and *Champion of the Great American Family* (New York: Random House, 1989). I also interviewed Schroeder and submitted follow-up questions, which she graciously answered.

Several of Schroeder's former aides also were willing to share their recollections with me, including her administrative assistant, Dan Buck; district director, Louis X. "Kip" Cheroutes; her first administrative assistant, Michael Cheroutes; press secretary, Andrea Camp, and retired navy Capt. Jim Bush, a defense aide. Several Colorado journalists who covered Schroeder over the years were also helpful, including Leonard "Buzz" Larsen and Ann Schmidt, both of the *Denver Post,* and Charlie Roos of the *Rocky Mountain News.* Other interviews included Dee Dukehart, a campaign aide in the 1972 race; Kathy Bonk, a campaign aide in the 1987 presidential exploratory campaign, and Gary Ruskin of the Ralph Nader–founded watchdog groups CongressWatch and Commercial Alert, who worked with Schroeder's staff on issues related to congressional ethics.

When Schroeder retired from office in January 1997, her staff estimated that the congresswoman had given 10,000 media interviews over the course of her twenty-four years in public life. That may actually be an underestimate. There is a rich body of contemporary news reporting on issues and events in which Schroeder was involved and on the congresswoman herself. This book has drawn on hundreds of those news accounts for information, background, and quotes.

Among the most informative newspaper and magazine articles about Schroeder are: Rhea Becker, "Pat Schroeder Recounts Tales of Congressional Strum und Drang," *Harvard University Gazette,* April 23, 1998; Adriel Bettelheim, "Audacious Schroeder Lashes GOP; Lawmaker Leads the Charge While Others Seek Cover," *Denver Post,* June 19, 1995; "Schroeder Bows

Out; House Career to End at 24 Years," *Denver Post*, November 30, 1995; Kathy Bonk, "The Campaign That Never Was," *Los Angeles Times*, November 15, 1987; John Brinkley, "Schroeder to Step Down," *Rocky Mountain News*, November 30, 1995; "Schroeder Looks Back on 12 Terms," *Rocky Mountain News*, November 30, 1995; "Pat Answers: Highs and Lows of Congress Never Got Schroeder Down," *Rocky Mountain News*, December 8, 1996; "A Brave Woman Leaves Her Mark; Pat Schroeder Exits Congress," *Scripps Howard News Service*, December 31, 1996; Fred Brown and Robert Kowalski, "Schroeder Kept Fighting Spirit," *Denver Post*, September 30, 1995; Marian Christy, "Conversations; Schroeder—Without Tears," *Boston Globe*, February 26, 1989; Marie Cocco, "No Ship Is Named for Pat Schroeder," *Plain Dealer (Cleveland)*, December 11, 1995; Diane Duston, "Longest-Serving Woman Leaving Congress," *Palm Beach Post*, November 30, 1995; and Martha Ezzard, "Gutsy Schroeder Has Made Her Mark," *Atlanta Journal and Constitution*, December 10, 1995.

Also, Susan Ferraro, "The Prime of Pat Schroeder," *New York Times Magazine*, July 1, 1990; Phil Gailey, "Schroeder Considers Running for President," *New York Times*, June 6, 1987; Michelle Green and David Chandler, "Pat Schroeder's Ambition To Be First Lady in the Oval Office Nears the Moment of Truth," *People*, September 7, 1987; Jane Gross, "Out of the House, but Still Focused on Family," *New York Times*, April 19, 1999; Lloyd Grove, "Laying Down Her Quip; For Rep. Pat Schroeder, A Hard-Hitting Decision," *Washington Post*, December 1, 1995; Douglas Harbrecht and Richard Fly, "Can Pat Schroeder Be More Than the 'Women's Candidate'?" *Business Week*, October 5, 1987; Melissa Healy, "Patricia Schroeder, Fighting for 24 Years to Expand Women's Role in Government," *Los Angeles Times*, December 1, 1996; Karen Hosler, "Schroeder Announces Retirement from Office; House Liberal Leaves after 24-year Fight for Women's Rights," *Baltimore Sun*, December 1, 1996; Karen Elliott House, "That's No Pretty Young Thing . . . That's Congresswoman Pat Schroeder," *Family Circle*, July 1975; Tamar Jacoby, Howard Fineman, Sue Hutchison, and Michael Reese, "Women: A New Politics," *Newsweek*, September 7, 1987; Tamara Jones, "'I Won't Be Tinkerbell of Campaign'; Schroeder Seeks Answers in A Question-Mark Effort," *Los Angeles Times*, August 30, 1987; Guy Kelly, "How Pat Decided to Call it Quits," *Rocky Mountain News*, December 3, 1995.

And further, Diane Mason, "Pat Schroeder: A Presidential Bid?" *St. Petersburg Times*, July 6, 1987; Rudy Maxa, "The Very Happy Signature of Rep. Pat Schroeder," *Washington Post Magazine*, September 26, 1982; Winzola McLendon, "This Woman's Place is in the House," *McCall's*, January 1980; Jane O'Reilly and Gloria Jacobs, "Watch Pat Run," *Ms.*, February 1988; T.R.

Reid, "Schroeder, Talking Tough; Message for '88 Tested on Whirlwind Tour," *Washington Post,* August 4, 1987, and "Schroeder Rules Out '88 Bid, Citing Time, Political Process," *Washington Post,* September 29, 1987; Charles Roos, "Pat Will Be Remembered for a Lot More Than Quips," *Rocky Mountain News,* December 8, 1995; Roger Simon, "Schroeder's Tears Make Women Cry," *Chicago Tribune,* October 5, 1987; Paul Taylor, "Schroeder Pitches Families' Plight; New Chair of Panel on Children Vows It Will Be Seen and Heard," *Washington Post,* March 12, 1991; Judith Viorst, "Congresswoman Pat Schroeder: The Woman Who Has a Bear by the Tail," *Redbook,* November 1973; Linton Weeks, "Pat Schroeder's New Chapter," *Washington Post,* February 7, 2001; Marjorie Williams, "Pat Schroeder & the Agony of Decision," *Washington Post,* September 25, 1987; and David Wood, "Military Sends Schroeder an Unfriendly Parting Shot," *Newhouse News Service,* October 11, 1996.

Useful profiles of Schroeder and other members Congress can be found in *Politics in America* (Washington, D.C.: Congressional Quarterly, editions 1986 to 2000.)

There is also a tremendous body of information available on the history of women in politics and women in Congress. Among the sources used for this book are: Bella Abzug with Mim Kelber, *Gender Gap: Bella Abzug's Guide to Political Power for American Women* (Boston: Houghton Mifflin, 1984); Mildred L. Amer, "Women in the United States Congress: 1917–1999," special report, *Congressional Research Service,* July 28, 1999; Clara Bingham, *Women on the Hill: Challenging the Culture of Congress* (New York: Times Books, 1997); Barbara Boxer, *Strangers in the Senate* (Bethesda, Md.: National Press Books, 1994.); Elinor Burkett, *The Right Women: A Journey through the Heart of Conservative America* (New York: Scribner, 1998); Hope Chamberlin, *A Minority of Members: Women in the U.S. Congress* (New York: Praeger Publishers, 1973); Karen Foerstel and Herbert Foerstel, *Climbing the Hill: Gender Conflict in Congress* (Westport, Conn.: Praeger Publishers, 1996); Marcy Kaptur, *Women of Congress: A 20th Century Odyssey* (Washington, D.C.: Congressional Quarterly, 1996); Hanna Rosin, "Invasion of the Church Ladies," *New Republic,* April 24, 1995; and Harriet Woods, *Stepping Up to Power: The Political Journey of American Women* (Boulder, Colo.: Westview Press, 2000).

Online resources included the Women's Hall of Fame in Rochester, New York, at <http://www.greatwomen.org/>; the Clerk of the U.S. House of Representative's site "Women in Congress" at <http://clerkweb.house.gov/105/womenbio/alpha/alpha.htm>; and Sunshine for Women, *30 of the Most Influential Women of the Millennium: Martha Griffiths,* at <http://www.pinn.net/~sunshine/whm2001/whm_01.html>.

Especially valuable for background on women in the military and the Tailhook scandal are: Linda Bird Francke, *Ground Zero: The Gender Wars in the Military* (New York: Simon & Schuster, 1997); Stephanie Gutmann, *The Kinder, Gentler Military* (New York: Scribner, 2000); Vickie Lewis, *Side-by-Side: A Photographic History of American Women in War* (New York: Steward, Tabori & Chang, 1999); Gregory L. Vistica, *Fall from Glory: The Men Who Sank the U.S. Navy* (New York: Touchstone, 1995); and Jean Zimmerman, *Tailspin: Women at War in the Wake of Tailhook* (New York: Doubleday, 1995). Also, Jim Abrams, "Ex-Navy Secretary Blames Media, White House, Congress for Woes," Associated Press, May 27, 1996; Alicia Brooks, "Rank Misconduct: Angered by the Abuse of Women in the Army, a Congresswoman Says Attitudes Have to Change," *People,* November 25, 1996; David F. Burrelli, "Women in the Armed Forces, Congressional Research Service Issue Brief," *Congressional Research Service,* December 12, 1996; John Corry, "Going Over Boorda; Why Was Everyone So Quick to Dismiss the Part Lost Honor Played in Admiral Boorda's Tragic Death?" *American Spectator,* July 1996; Gregory Gross, "Schroeder Finds New Sensitivity in Navy," *San Diego Union-Tribune,* February 21, 1993; Juliana Gruenwald, "Women in the Military: Mission in Progress," *Congressional Quarterly,* August 16, 1997; Lisa Hoffman: "Women in the Military No Longer Remarkable," *Scripps Howard News Service,* January 10, 2002; John Lehman, "The Navy's Enemies," *Wall Street Journal,* May 21, 1996; Edgar Prina, "Navy Soundings of Deep Denial," *Washington Times,* August 4, 1996; H.G. Reza, "Rep. Schroeder Seeks Peace with the Navy," *Los Angeles Times,* February 21, 1993; Kelly Richmond, "Schroeder Seeks Investigation of Military Rape Coverups," *States News Service,* September 29, 1992; and Gregory Vistica, "Schroeder Hopes Navy Vitriol Has Faded," *San Diego Union-Tribune,* February 20, 1993.

There are many transcripts available of Schroeder's interviews and speeches during the course of her career. The Tailhook chapter also draws on "What Ails the Navy," which includes transcripts of interviews with Tailhook figures recorded as part of the Public Broadcasting System's *Frontline* documentary "The Navy Blues," first aired on October 15, 1996. For more information on Schroeder and Newt Gringrich, see the transcript of Katie Bacon's interview with Schroeder, "A Conversation with Representative Schroeder," online at *Atlantic Unbound,* The Atlantic Monthly Company, September 1996, and the transcript of Peter Boyer's 1998 interview with Schroeder, "Interview, Pat Schroeder," for the Public Broadcasting System's *Frontline* documentary "The Long March of Newt Gingrich." Charles Lewis's July 1997 interview with Schroeder on campaign finance reform and money in politics is available from the Center for Public Integrity, Washington, D.C. The text of speeches Schroeder gave to the National Press Club on June 25, 1991, and September 16, 1996, was obtained from Federal News Service, Washington, D.C. A transcript of the April 22, 1997, broadcast of the radio show "The Real Bottom Line, with guest Pat Schroeder," hosted by Jim Hartz, is available from Trinity Church, Wall Street.

Published articles and opinion columns by Schroeder include "At Least I Didn't Mention My Dog," *Washington Post,* October 4, 1987; "A Government Agenda for Today's Family," *Washington Post,* December 16, 1986; and "A Freshman in the Weapons Club," *The Nation,* November 5, 1973.

For background on the 1988 presidential campaign, including Schroeder's exploratory effort, see Peter Goldman, Tom Mathews, and the *Newsweek* Special Election Team, *The Quest for the Presidency: The 1988 Campaign* (New York: Simon & Schuster/Touchstone, 1989).

Information on Congressman Ronald Dellums is drawn in part from: Ronald V. Dellums and H. Lee Halterman, *Lying Down with the Lions* (Boston: Beacon Press, 2000); John Jacobs, "Dellums's Exquisite Agony," *Sacramento Bee,* March 11, 1993; and Megan Rosenfeld, "A 21-Gun Send-Off; California's Ron Dellums Departs House with Bittersweet Memories and Fond Farewells," *Washington Post,* February 7, 1998.

The quote from Congresswoman Marjorie Holt in chapter 1 is taken from Joni Guhne, "Former Congresswoman Holt Looks Back Fondly Mostly," *Baltimore Sun,* July 23, 1992.

Information on Elizabeth Dole in chapter 2 comes from Bob and Elizabeth Dole, *Unlimited Partners; Our American Story* (New York: Simon & Schuster, 1988). Information on Betty Endicott, Schroeder's college roommate, in chapter 2, is drawn in part from Patricia Brennan, "Betty Endicott; She's Washington's Top Female TV Executive," *Washington Post,* May 31, 1987. Information on Bernice Scott is drawn in part from Kevin Vaughan, "Bernice Lemoin Scott, Mother of Former Rep. Pat Schroeder," *Rocky Mountain News,* August 17, 2000, and "Mother of Former Rep. Pat Schroeder Dies," Associated Press, August 17, 2000. Information on Allard Lowenstein is drawn in part from John Nichols, "Activist Allard Lowenstein Changed Many Lives," *Capital Times,* March 21, 2000. Information on Jim Schroeder's early life is draw in part from Marie Lazzara, "Mr. Schroeder Goes to Washington," *The Elmhurst (Ill.) Press,* January 20, 1999.

Information on Pat and Jim Schroeder's coping with family life in Washington is taken in part from: Deborah Churchman, "Washington's

Flip Side: The Man Behind the Woman; Life as a Congressional Husband," *Christian Science Monitor,* August 20, 1981; Julie Connelly, "How Dual Income Couples Cope," *Fortune,* September 24, 1990; Linda Bird Francke, "A Vote for Two Careers," *Newsweek,* November 24, 1975; Sarah Honig, "Yes, Dear," *Jerusalem Post,* December 28, 1990; Iris Krasnow, "Husbands of High-Power Women; Basking in the Reflected Glory of High-Profile Wives," *United Press International,* December 29, 1985; and Gary Libman, "For Better or Worse, More Men Are Following Their Wives to New Jobs," *Los Angeles Times,* September 11, 1988.

An account of the 1977 pay raise fight in the House can be found in John A. Farrell, *Tip O'Neill and the Democratic Century* (Boston: Little, Brown & Company, 2001). An account of the controversy over Richard Schweiker's *Dossier* magazine cover photo can be found in Christopher Connell, "Schweiker Says Never Again to White Tie Posing," Associated Press, September 16, 1981.

Accounts of the effort to pass pension-sharing legislation can be found in: Judy Mann, "Justice," *Washington Post,* September 8, 1982; "Help Is On the Way for Ex-Spouses of GIs," *Washington Post,* September 25, 1981; and "Foreign Service Wives: What Price 'Service'?" *Washington Post,* July 27, 1979.

Information in chapter 5 on Schroeder's efforts to cut defense spending can be found in part in Colman McCarthy, "In Defense of Cuts," *Washington Post,* August 9, 1981, and "Military Contractors: Their Feast Goes On," *Washington Post,* November 1, 1986.

Background on the nuclear freeze resolution is drawn in part from: Ellen Goodman, "Ronald Reagan in Arms Control, a Tragedy," *The Record (Hackensack, N.J.),* August 7, 1986; Charles Krauthammer, "Another Name for Nuclear Freeze," *Washington Post,* September 5, 1986; Daniel Lazare, "The House Shows Some Guts on Nuclear Test Halt," *The Record,* August 13, 1986; and Tom Wicker, "Tying Reagan's Hands," *New York Times,* August 1, 1986.

The most authoritative source on the effort to pass family medical leave is Ronald D. Elving, *Conflict and Compromise: How Congress Makes the Law* (New York: Simon & Schuster, 1995). Other information on family medical leave can be found in: Nadine Brozan, "Infant-Care Leaves: Panel Urges Policy," *New York Times,* November 28, 1985; Judy Holland, "Lawmakers Look at Expanding Family and Medical Leave," *San Antonio Express-News,* February 4, 2001; and Carol Kleiman, "Bill Seeks Job-Protected Leave to Care for Kids," *Chicago Tribune,* September 23, 1985.

An account of gender bias in medical research can be found in Diane Hales, *Just Like a Woman: How Gender Science Is Redefining What Makes Us Female*

(New York: Bantam Books, 1999). Also useful are: "Most Drugs Withdrawn in Recent Years had Greater Risks for Women," press release from Senator Tom Harkin (February 8, 2001); Mary Beth Caschetta, "The Identity Politics of Biomedical Research—Clinical Trials, Medical Knowledge, and the Female Body," *Sexuality Information and Education Council of the United States Report* (October 1993); "Seminar Highlights: The History and Future of Women's Health," *National Women's Health Information Center* (June 11, 1998); and Anna Roufos, "Women Are DIFFERENT," *Ladies Home Journal,* September 1, 2000.

Information on abortion legislation in the One Hundred Fifth Congress can be found in: Edwin Chen, "Abortion Foes See Major Gains in House," *Los Angeles Times,* June 16, 1995; Karen Hosler, "GOP's Social Agenda Beginning to Bud," *Baltimore Sun,* June 12, 1995; "House Passes Limit on Some Abortions," *Buffalo News,* June 15, 1995; and Kevin Merida, "Antiabortion Measures Debated; House Republicans Push for New Restrictions in Several Areas," *Washington Post,* June 14, 1995.

For background on Newt Gingrich, see Amy D. Bernstein and Peter W. Bernstein, eds., *Quotations from Speaker Newt* (New York: Workman Publishing, 1995); Damon Chappie, "Audit Details Military Training Tab," *Roll Call,* August 13, 1998; "Gingrich Enlists Army, but Top Officials 'Wary,' *Roll Call,* October 3, 1996; Newt Gingrich, *Lessons Learned the Hard Way: A Personal Report* (New York: Harper Collins, 1998); Sandy Grady, "The Newtonian World Similar to Old One," *Philadelphia Daily News,* January 6, 1995; John King, "It's Supposed to be a History Class, but the New Speaker Digresses," Associated Press, January 18, 1995; Kevin Merida, "Speaker Has Faced Determined Attack; Democratic Pressure Grew from '94 Defeat," *Washington Post,* January 6, 1997, and "The Gingrich Case: The Unabridged Ethics Chronology," *Roll Call,* January 20, 1997.

For background on the ethics case involving Bud Shuster, see: Damon Chappie, "Shuster Decision Met with Silence," *Roll Call,* October 12, 2000; and William Roberts, "House GOP Pushes Ethics Clearance for Shuster," *Journal of Commerce,* June 13, 1996.

Information on conflicts between librarians and book publishers is drawn in part from: "AAP, Microsoft Teaming Up to Confront Digital Rights Piracy Issues Book Publishing Report," *Book Publishing,* August 14, 2000; Grant Burns, "Says Schroeder, 'We Have a Serious Issue with Librarians,'" *Uncle Frank's Diary, Number One,* <NewPages.com>; D. C. Denison, "Steal This E-Book (Go Ahead, Try)," *Boston Globe,* February 11, 2001; Charlotte Moore, "Publishers, Sellers Prepare for Pending E-book Boom," *Austin American-Statesman,* July 28, 2000; Tom Pullar-Strecker, "Digital

Documents Also Need a Home in Libraries," *Infotech Weekly*, March 5, 2001; Calvin Reid, "Schroeder Defends Need for Digital Rights Management," *Publishers Weekly*, May 28, 2001; and Michael Rogers and Norman Oder, "Librarians Thrive at a Less-Glitzy, All-Business BookExpo," *Library Journal*, July 1, 2001.

Quotes from Lino Lipinsky in chapter 10 are taken from Lino Lipinsky, "The Denis Thatcher Society," *Denver Post*, May 17, 2001.

Index

Entries in bold indicate there is a photograph. Photographs are on pages 111–28.

Mondale, Walter, 129, 132, 133; and feminists, 134; and NWPC, 139
Morella, Connie, 174
Murdock, Rupert, 175
Musgrave, Marilyn, 38
Muskie, Edmund, 144
MX missile program, 66, 72, 73, 74
Myrick, Sue, 173

Nader, Ralph, 168
National Institutes of Health, 106–110; and Office of Research on Women's Health, 109
National Organization for Women (NOW), 136, 138
National Press Club, 11, 38, 46, 142, 180, 186, 193
National Wildlife Federation, 82
National Women's Party, 87
National Women's Political Caucus (NWPC), 34, 40, 138, 139
Nixon, Richard, 12, 22, 31, 37, 39, 45; and enemies list, 11
No Electronic Theft bill, 194
North, Oliver, 11, 184, 189
nuclear freeze movement, 46, 66, 77
nuclear weapons testing ban, 14, 77–78
Nunn, Sam, 73–74, 76

O'Neill, Thomas P. "Tip", 4–5, 51, 70, 73, 167, 169
opinion polls, 38

Packwood, Robert, 49
Passman, Otto, 52–53
Patman, Wright, 68, 69
Paul, Alice, 93
pay raise issue, 50–52
peace movement, 82, 132
Pelosi, Nancy, 201
Pension Rights Center, 96
pension sharing and ex-wives, 89–92, 191
Pentagon, 6–7, 54, 58, 64, 67, 69, 80, 81, 163; on child care for military personnel, 149; and cost overruns, 73; and military spending, 71; and politicization of the military, 184–85; and testing moratorium, 78; and waste, fraud, and abuse, 73; on women flying combat aircraft, 153
Planned Parenthood, 29
Poage, Bob, 68, 69
posters, 35–36, 131, 158
Post Office and Civil Service Committee, 46, 58
Powell, Colin, 76

pregnancy: Gingrich on, 177–78; as temporary disability, 92; and women in military service, 149, 152
Pregnancy Discrimination Act, 92
Price, Melvin, 69, 73
Price-Anderson Act, 69
Proxmire, William, 67
Public Citizen, 54

racism, 5
Rankin, Jeannette, 11–12
Reagan, Ronald, 59, 60, 71, 77, 79, 136–37, 145; as "Teflon president", 53
Redbook magazine, 8
Regan, Donald, 59
Reno, Janet, 22, 27
Reuss, Patricia, 90
Reynolds, Kathy
Rice, Donna, 129
Rocky Flats nuclear weapons plant, 2
Rocky Mountain Arsenal, 2, 46; conversion to wildlife refuge, 81
Rocky Mountain Planned Parenthood, 29
Roe v. Wade, 12
Rogers, Byron, 30
Rogers, Edith Nourse, 41
Rohrabacher, Dana, 102–103
Roosevelt, Eleanor, 19, 42, 131
Roosevelt, Franklin D., 41
Rossi, Marie, 151
Roukema, Marge, 97, 100, 173, 190
Ruskin, Gary, 50, 168, 185

Schlafly, Phyllis, 152
Schlindler, Allen, 75
school busing, 1, 31, 65
Schroeder, Jamie, 139, 158, 188, 192
Schroeder, Jim, 11, 24, 31, 57, 63, 188; and breast cancer awareness, 199–200; and career, 43–44, 61–62; early life of, 25–26; encourages PS to seek Democratic nomination for President, 130–45; and home restorations, 30
Schroeder, Pat (*photo section*, 111–28): and alternative defense budget, 72; and amendment targeting wasteful defense spending, 71–72; and Armed Services subcommittee chairmanship, 74, 80; arrest at embassy of South Africa, 59; assaulted by ABC cameraman, 161; base of support, 132; campaign issues, 137; chairs Select Committee on Children, Youth, and Families, 98; as champion of military personnel and families, 80; and chapels, 80; children of, 62–63; as co-chair

income, 51; racism in, 5; sexism in, 5; shift in balance of power, 68; and stationery store, 46–47; and tax deduction for living expenses, 52; and Watergate class, 68

Vietnam War, 1, 5, 30, 31, 32, 33, 36, 77; hawks who avoided, 169
Vistica, Gregory L., 154

Waters, Maxine, 54
Watt, James, 58
Waxman, Henry, 106
Ways and Means Committee, 3, 87
Webb, James, 161, 162
Williams, Pat, 100, 186
Winter Olympics (1976), 33–34
Wirth, Tim, 191
women, 84–110; and acceptance by nation as presidential candidates, 198; in Colorado politics, 38; and combat exclusion policy, 147–50, 177–78; in Congress, 3, 11–12, 15, 40–42, 44, 173, 198; and economic injustices, 84; exclusion from medical research, 106–110; and feminist movement, 13; and military academies, 148; in military service, 146–64, 152–53, 181–82; and politics in the South, 166; in Reagan administration, 58; seeking presidency, 39, 132; sexual harassment of, 101–106; slow rate of progress on issues related to, 198; as successors to husbands in Congress, 40–41; and suffrage, 38; in U.S. Senate, 39; violence against, 105; and wage gap, 201
Women's Armed Services Act, 146
Women's Health Equity Act, 109, 173
Women's Legal Defense Fund, 93, 96
women's rights, 1, 9, 13, 53, 88, 199; and Anita Hill, 101–106; and Geraldine Ferraro, 134; PS as preeminent supporter of, 198
Worley, Dave, 170
Wright, Jim, 50, 167, 170, 176

Young, Dick, 33

Zaccaro, John A., 134
Zimmerman, Jean, 160